Economic Development and Consumption Patterns in Asian Countries

Shashika D. Rathnayaka · Saroja Selvanathan · Eliyathamby A. Selvanathan

Economic Development and Consumption Patterns in Asian Countries

Springer

Shashika D. Rathnayaka
The Rowett Institute
University of Aberdeen
Aberdeen, UK

Saroja Selvanathan
Griffith Business School
Griffith Asia Institute, Griffith University
Nathan, QLD, Australia

Eliyathamby A. Selvanathan
Griffith Business School
Griffith Asia Institute, Griffith University
Nathan, QLD, Australia

ISBN 978-981-97-2627-1 ISBN 978-981-97-2628-8 (eBook)
https://doi.org/10.1007/978-981-97-2628-8

This Springer imprint is published by the registered company Springer Nature Singapore Pte Ltd.
The registered company address is: 152 Beach Road, #21-01/04 Gateway East, Singapore 189721, Singapore

Paper in this product is recyclable.

To my parents for instilling the value of education in me,
Mr. Dharmasena Rathnayaka, Mrs. Prema Rathnayaka
and
To my husband for making immense sacrifices to support my academic career,
Mr. Dhanushka Wijesooriya

Shashika D. Rathnayaka

To our parents who have made enormous sacrifices to give us the precious gift of education,
the late Mr. Murugesapillai Pathmanathan
Mrs. Parameswary Pathmanathan
the late Mr. Velupillai Eliyathamby
the late Mrs. Pooranam Eliyathamby

Saroja Selvanathan and Eliyathamby A. Selvanathan

Acknowledgements

We wish to express our sincere gratitude to our mentor Professor Ken Clements of The University of Western Australia for his encouragement and guidance to undertake our research. We gratefully acknowledge the research grants received from the *Griffith Asia Institute* at Griffith University. We also acknowledge the constructive and helpful comments and suggestions of the anonymous reviewers of the book.

We sincerely thank the staff at *Springer* for all the support, especially Ms. Anushangi Weerakoon, Editor for Business, Economics and Law, for her continuous support throughout the publication process and also Mr. Praveen Anand, Production Editor, for his help during the production stages of the book. We wish to thank Ms. Tanya Parker for her excellent research and editorial assistance throughout this book project.

We also thank our family and friends who have always been supportive of our academic endeavours. Last but not least, our heartfelt appreciation is extended to our children, Dr. Arthavan Selvanathan, Dr. Prabha Selvanathan, and Miss Osithma Wijesooriya for their love, care, and understanding.

Technical Notes

This book contains seven chapters. To aid the reader, each chapter has been written in such a way that it is more or less self-contained.

Each chapter contains several sections and subsections. The sections in each chapter are numbered at two levels; the first level refers to the chapter number and second level to the section in each chapter. For example, Sect. 2.3 refers to the third section in Chap. 2.

Equations are indicated by two numbers; the first refers to the section and second to order of the occurrence of the equations within the section. For example, equation (4.2) of Chap. 3 denotes the second equation in Section 4 of that chapter. This equation is referred to, in Chapter 3, as 'equation (4.2)'. If this equation is referred to in another chapter, then we use the terminology 'equation (4.2) of Chap. 3'. Equations in the Appendices are numbered independently.

Tables and figures are indicated by two numbers; the first refers to the chapter and second to the order of the occurrence of tables or figures within that chapter. For example, 'Table 3.2' refers to the second table in Chap. 3, and 'Fig. 3.1' refers to the first figure in Chap. 3.

Abstract

This book analyzes consumption patterns in Asian countries that are at different stages of economic development and highlights the similarities and disparities of consumption patterns across countries using a system-wide framework.

In a departure from previous studies in the literature which mainly present only single-country analysis, this book aims to provide a comprehensive analysis of cross-country consumption patterns considering several Asian countries, using the most recent consumption expenditure data for aggregate commodity groups.

In comparing consumption patterns across countries, the book use unit-free measurements such as budget shares and changes in logarithms of price and quantities, thus avoiding problems associated with exchange rate conversions.

The book also analyses the dynamic behaviour in the consumption patterns of the Asian consumers. The findings of this book will be invaluable to researchers in development economics as well as policymakers in the formulation of fiscal policy or other types of economic control.

Contents

About the Authors

Dr. Shashika D. Rathnayaka is a Research Fellow at the Rowett Institute, University of Aberdeen, United Kingdom. She is also an Applied Economist at the Scottish Environment, Food and Agriculture Research Institution (SEFARI) and a Fellow at the University of Aberdeen's Centre for Research in Energy Economics and Finance (ACREEF). She was educated at Griffth University (Australia), University of Peradeniya (Sri Lanka), and Uva Wellassa University (Sri Lanka). Before joining the University of Aberdeen, she worked as a Senior Lecturer at the Uva Wellassa University (Sri Lanka) and a Teaching Fellow at Griffith University (Australia). She has also taught postgraduate courses at the University of Kelaniya (Sri Lanka). Her research interests include Consumer Demand Analysis, Food and Agricultural Economics, and Econometric Modelling. Shashika has published in leading international refereed journals such as *Agricultural Economics*, *Economic Modelling*, *Applied Economics*, *Empirical Economics*, *Economics Analysis and Policy*, and *Agriculture and Food Security*.

Professor Saroja Selvanathan is Professor of Econometrics at Griffith University, Queensland, Australia, and Co-editor-in-chief of the *Journal of the Asia Pacific Economy*. She has also taught previously at the University of Jaffna (Sri Lanka), Murdoch University (Australia), and The University of Western Australia. She was educated at the University of Jaffna, Murdoch University, and The University of Western Australia. Her research interests include consumer demand, time series analysis, tourism economics, and applied econometrics. She has published five research monographs and over 75 journal articles. Her publications have appeared in internationally refereed journals, such as *Review of Economics and Statistics*, *Energy Economics*, *Resource Economics*, *Economic Modelling*, *Journal of Travel Research*, *Tourism Analysis*, and *Tourism Economics*. She is a co-author of the Australian best-selling textbook, *Business Statistics*, published by Cengage.

Professor Eliyathamby A. Selvanathan is Director of the Economics Policy Analysis Program (EPAP) and Professor of Econometrics at Griffith University, Queensland, Australia. He has also taught previously at the University of Jaffna (Sri

Lanka), Murdoch University (Australia), and The University of Western Australia. He was educated at the University of Jaffna, University of Bucharest (Romania), Murdoch University, and The University of Western Australia. He is one of the authors of the best-selling textbook in Australasia, *Business Statistics*, published by Cengage. His research interests include applied econometrics, tourism economics, consumer demand models, and stochastic index numbers. He has published eight research monographs and well over 100 articles in leading journals such as *Review of Economic Studies*, *Journal of Econometrics*, *Journal of Business and Economic Statistics*, *Review of Economics and Statistics*, *Energy Economics*, *Journal of Travel Research,* and *Tourism Economics*.

Abbreviations

ADF	Augmented Dickey and Fuller
AIDS	Almost Ideal Demand System
CBS	Netherlands Central Bureau of Statistics
CBS/PI	Central Bureau of Statistics/Preference Independence
CBS/SI	Central Bureau of Statistics/Substitution Independence
CEDS	Constant Elasticity Demand System
CGE	Computable General Equilibrium
DAP	Demand Analysis Package
DLDS	Double-Log Demand System
ECM	Error Correction Model
FAO	Food and Agriculture Organization
FBS	Food Balance Sheets
GDP	Gross Domestic Product
GNP	Gross National Product
GST	Goods and Services Tax
ICP	International Comparisons Programme
ISUR	Iterative Seemingly Unrelated Regression
LA	Linear Approximated
LES	Linear Expenditure System
LS	Least Square
OECD	Organisation for Economic Co-operation and Development
PI	Preference Independence
PIGLOG	Price Independent Generalised-log System
PP	Phillips Perron
QES	Quadratic Expenditure System
QUAIDS	Quadratic Almost Ideal Demand System
SUR	Seemingly Unrelated Regression
UK	United Kingdom
USA	United States of America

List of Figures

List of Tables

Chapter 1
Introduction

1.1 Introduction

Over the past three decades, Asia has experienced an economic revolution of unprecedented scale. Once considered the world's economic underdog, Asia is now at the forefront of global economic development. Asia continues to be both the fastest-growing region in the world and the main engine of the global economy, contributing to more than 70% of global economic growth (ADB, 2023; IMF, 2023). This remarkable shift is primarily attributed to a combination of factors such as globalization, technological advancements, political stability, and pro-market policies. Consequently, Asia has experienced a profound overhaul in its economic landscape, with a notable surge in its Gross Domestic Product (GDP). This surge has resulted in the upliftment of millions from poverty and the emergence of a thriving middle class.

Urbanization and industrialization have also played crucial roles in propelling this growth, leading to increased participation in the labour force and the expansion of the manufacturing and service sectors. The rapid economic expansion in Asia has not only altered its economic structure but has also brought about a significant shift in consumption patterns. Rising disposable incomes have prompted individuals and households to redefine their priorities and preferences. Furthermore, globalization has played a dual role in initiating and accelerating this transformation, creating interdependence, interconnectedness, and networking across different parts of the world through satellite and information superhighways. With a substantial increase in both exports and imports, a myriad of global consumer products is now accessible in any domestic market, fostering similarity in consumption patterns across countries.

S. D. Rathnayaka et al., *Economic Development and Consumption Patterns in Asian Countries*, https://doi.org/10.1007/978-981-97-2628-8_1

1.2 Changing Consumption Patterns in the Asian Region: An Overview

The massive influx of people into urban areas has fostered greater demand for convenience and services, influencing consumption patterns towards more processed and prepared foods, as well as online shopping and modern retail. As incomes have risen, so too has the demand for diverse diets, including a preference for more protein-rich and varied food options. This has affected agriculture, food production, and supply chains. The housing sector in many Asian countries has witnessed substantial changes in consumption expenditures. Urbanization and rising incomes have led to increased demand for housing, including modern apartments, condominiums, and smart homes.

There is also a growing interest in sustainable and energy-efficient housing solutions, reflecting a broader awareness of environmental concerns. The middle-class expansion in Asian countries has resulted in higher demand for consumer electronics, including smartphones, laptops, and home appliances. The communication sector has been revolutionized with the rapid adoption of digital technologies. Increased spending on mobile phones, internet services, and data plans is common. The transport sector has witnessed significant changes as well. The automobile sector has seen remarkable growth as more households can afford cars, leading to increased expenditures in this category. Also, greater urbanization has led to increased use of public transportation systems, while higher incomes have boosted car ownership and air travel. Electric and hybrid vehicles are gaining traction, reflecting a growing emphasis on sustainability.

As healthcare awareness and accessibility have improved, there has been a notable increase in consumption expenditure on medical services and pharmaceuticals. Rising healthcare costs, coupled with an ageing population in many Asian countries, have led to greater spending on healthcare and insurance. Education expenditures in Asia have risen substantially, reflecting a growing emphasis on education as a pathway to economic and social advancement. Private tutoring, test preparation, and international education e-learning and online courses have seen increased spending. Economic growth has also fuelled an interest in travel, leading to greater spending on tourism and leisure activities both within and outside the region.

These shifts in consumption patterns are not uniform across all countries in the region and may be influenced by local cultural and economic factors. Understanding these trends is crucial for policymakers, businesses, and industries to adapt and cater to the evolving needs and desires of consumers in this diverse and dynamic region. Increasing consumer demand and changing consumption patterns in the Asian region have led international operators to invest resources, grow their operations in Asia, and capture new opportunities in these growing markets. Asia is becoming home to many large companies and a lucrative proposition for global brands. Communication is one of the fastest-growing categories for consumer spending in Asia. Therefore, the region offers abundant and diverse opportunities in online marketing, online advertising, e-commerce and m-commerce.

Research on consumer demand is an important field of applied economics; economists have been studying the relationship between prices, income and consumption for over a century (see for example Chen, 2001; Clements & Chen, 1996; Clements & Theil, 1996; Clements et al., 2006; Houthakker, 1957; Lluch & Powell, 1975; Rathnayaka et al., 2022; Selvanathan & Selvanathan, 1993, 2003a, 2003b; Selvanathan et al., 2023, 2024). However, empirical studies that investigate cross-country consumption patterns in the Asian region are lacking. Other consumption studies concentrating on Asian countries focus on individual countries, or on food demand to estimate single commodity nutrition-specific demand equations. There are no recently published comprehensive econometric studies available that analyse recent trends in consumption patterns in Asian countries in a system-wide manner that uses recent data. Moreover, the economic prosperity in Asia, the blending of global consumer markets, and the impact of globalization have heightened the importance of scrutinizing consumption patterns in Asian countries from both scientific and economic perspectives. Therefore, there is a pressing academic and policy need for such a study, and this book will make a significant contribution towards filling this gap. This book aims to analyse the consumption patterns of consumers in several Asian countries that are at different stages of economic development and to look at the similarities and disparities of consumption patterns across countries using a system-wide framework.

This book will consider ten Asian countries: Hong Kong,[1] India, Japan, South Korea,[2] Malaysia, the Philippines, Singapore, Sri Lanka, Taiwan,[3] and Thailand. This selection was driven by a deliberate consideration of diverse factors. Within the United Nations classification, Asia comprises 48 countries. However, to ensure precision and relevance in our consumption analysis, we excluded 23 countries, namely Middle Eastern countries (Western Asia, 18 countries) and Central Asian countries (formerly part of the Soviet Union, 5 countries), which are not commonly considered as part of the Asian region. Our focus then turned to a sample of 10 representative countries carefully chosen from the pool of 25 Asian (Eastern, South-Eastern and Southern Asia) countries. The primary objective was to construct a representative sample that spans a wide spectrum of variables, including income levels, religious diversity, cultural distinctions, and geographical representation. This strategic selection allows for a comprehensive understanding of consumption behaviours across Asia, capturing the inherent heterogeneity present in the region. The decision to focus on these 10 countries was further influenced by the availability of reliable and consistent data series, ensuring the robustness and reliability of our empirical analyses. While acknowledging the existence of 48 countries in Asia, our deliberate subset enables us to derive meaningful insights indicative of broader trends in consumption patterns, all while addressing practical considerations related to data availability and comparability.

---

[1] Special administrative region of the People's Republic of China.

[2] Republic of Korea.

[3] Republic of China.

Although Japan and South Korea are Asian countries, they are also members of the Organisation for Economic Co-operation and Development (OECD), suggesting a level of development that rivals those of Western countries. Japan is a highly developed nation in Northeast Asia and the world's third-largest economy; it is renowned as a worldwide exporter in a wide range of industries and serves as a model for numerous other Asian nations (Hubacek et al., 2007). In addition to its economic prowess, Japan plays a pivotal role in influencing and shaping international trade.

South Korea, while still classified as an emerging economy, is a highly developed global player, securing the position of the world's the world's 15th largest economy by GDP. This distinction underscores South Korea's substantial economic contributions and its influence on the global stage. The nation's progress exemplifies the trajectory of many emerging economies aspiring to attain developed status. Singapore, a key hub for Asian business, contributes to what can be described as an essential 'holy trinity' of influential economies in East Asia. Singapore's economic significance extends beyond its modest size, setting the pace for regional economic development. As a vital financial and trade centre, Singapore plays a crucial role in facilitating international commerce and investment. Hong Kong, akin to Singapore, operates as a city-state with unique economic characteristics. It stands out as one of the world's most densely populated cities, with a population of seven million packed into the city's 426 square miles. Hong Kong's strategic location and economic vibrancy make it a crucial player in global trade and finance, contributing to the dynamic landscape of East Asian economies (Emerging Asian Economies, 2017).

While Singapore, Hong Kong, Japan, and South Korea are highly developed economic powerhouses in Asia, India, positioned in South Asia, is a rapidly growing economy and the world's fifth-largest by nominal GDP. As one of the most populous countries globally, India's economic landscape is diverse, featuring a robust services sector, a thriving industrial base, and a significant agricultural presence. The nation's economic trajectory has garnered attention on the global stage, making it a key player in shaping regional and international dynamics. Sri Lanka, an island nation in South Asia, has shown economic resilience and potential, with a focus on sectors like tourism and agriculture. Thailand thrives on a strong tourism industry and robust agriculture, the Philippines stands out with its business process outsourcing and remittance-driven economy, and Taiwan distinguishes itself as a global technological leader with a unique geopolitical status. These nations represent a spectrum of economic development stages, contributing to the rich diversity of the Asian economic landscape.

1.3 A Review of Cross-Country Consumption Studies

Static Demand Analysis

There is a large body of consumption economics literature on modelling consumer demand. The literature on cross-country consumption goes back to the pioneering work of Houthakker (1957), which represents the first study to compare the expenditure elasticities for different countries—developed and developing. The study estimated expenditure elasticities for food, clothing, housing, and miscellaneous items based on double-log Engel curves using cross-sectional data from 30 countries. The results revealed that elasticities are similar across commodities but not equal. Since the study utilized cross-sectional data that does not capture price variation, the study eschews the estimation of price elasticities. Houthakker (1965) performed a similar study to Houthakker (1957) using time series data for the period 1948–1959 for 13 OECD countries. The results suggested that while price elasticities show no uniformity across the commodities (food, clothing, rent, durables, and miscellaneous), the expenditure elasticities are consistent.

Goldberger and Gamaletsos (1970) analysed the consumer expenditure patterns of 13 OECD countries for food, clothing, rent, and durables over the period 1950–1961, employing the Linear Expenditure System (LES) introduced by Stone (1954) and the Constant Elasticity Demand System (CEDS) used by Houthakker (1965). Parks and Barten (1973) hypothesized that some of the differences in demand behaviour between countries could be explained by differences in the age composition of the population. The study estimated LES using time series data of five commodities (food, clothing, housing, durables, others) for the years 1950–1967 for 14 OECD countries. The results revealed that population composition has a significant effect on the parameters of the demand model after correcting for the difference associated with the level of real income across the countries. The results also found that income elasticities are positive and own-price elasticities are negative in all countries.

Lluch and Powell (1975) estimated the LES for eight commodity groups using data from 19 countries. The cross-country analysis revealed some discernible patterns in the variation of price and expenditure elasticities as a function of GNP per head. Moreover, the study noted that the own-price and expenditure elasticity of food appeared to decline in absolute value as real income increases. Overall, the own-price elasticities and cross-price elasticities of food appear to account for most of the total price responsiveness (about 80%). Lluch et al. (1977) employed an extended LES where total consumption expenditure was assumed to be endogenous across 17 developing countries between 1955 and 1969. The study considered eight commodities (food, clothing, housing, durables, personal care, transport, recreation, and miscellaneous) and found food and housing to be necessities, clothing to be borderline, and durables, personal care, transport, recreation, and miscellaneous goods to be luxuries.

Many advances in the area of demand model applications have been achieved due to the cross-country database made available through the International Comparison Program (ICP) sponsored by the United Nations and the World Bank since the early 1970s. Pioneering studies that applied a cross-country demand system to ICP data include Clements et al. (1979), Theil et al. (1980), Finke et al. (1983), Seale et al. (2003), and Seale and Regmi (2009). Another leading work on cross-country application was conducted by Theil (1987) using the ICP data compiled by Kravis et al. (1982). These data covered 34 countries and provided comparable price and volume indices for more than 100 detailed categories of consumption.

Selvanathan and Selvanathan (1993) analysed the consumption of ten commodities across 18 OECD countries from 1960 to 1981. The study revealed that OECD consumers spend about half of their income on food, housing, and transport. The results also found that food, housing, and medical care are necessities and clothing, durables, transport, and recreation are luxuries in most OECD countries. The demand for all goods considered was found to be price inelastic.

Clements and Theil (1996) used cross-sectional data from Kravis et al. (1978) from 16 countries to estimate a common system of demand equations for all countries. Compared to the usual time series application for a given country, countries here played the role of time periods. This idea was introduced by Theil et al. (1981), which suggested that tastes are to be the same across countries. Although a rather bold assumption, it is the one advocated by Stigler and Becker (1977), who hypothesized that tastes neither change capriciously nor differ importantly between people. In the international context, this hypothesis implies that consumers in different countries have similar tastes irrespective of differences in language, religion, culture, and geography. Pollak and Wales (1987) tested this using the quadratic expenditure system with time series/cross-country data for Belgium, the UK, and the USA. Based on likelihood ratios and nonparametric (revealed preference) tests, the study concluded that the data from these countries could not be pooled to estimate a common demand system. Hence, the study rejected the hypothesis of identical tastes. Selvanathan and Selvanathan (1993) also found that OECD consumption data do not support Stigler and Becker's (1977) hypothesis using consumption data for 18 OECD countries.

Chen and Clements (1996) analysed consumption patterns in 13 emerging/developing economies to identify key empirical regularities using a system-wide approach. Chen (2001) extended the work of Selvanathan and Selvanathan (1993) by adding 13 less-developed countries (giving a total of 31) during the same time period. Clements and Ye (2003) estimated a double-log model for 18 wealthy (OECD) countries and 13 developing countries. The study concluded that differences in income and relative prices explained a significant share of the variation in international consumption patterns. Selvanathan and Selvanathan (2003b) investigated the consumption patterns of the five strongest Asian economies (Hong Kong, Japan, Korea, Singapore, and Taiwan). The results based on the Rotterdam model revealed that the consumption data of these five countries supported a number of empirical regularities, including the law of demand and Engel's law. Clements et al. (2006) constructed a new database that built upon that of Selvanathan and Selvanathan (2003a) and estimated the CBS model to analyse the extent to which the consumption basket was diversified, how this changed with income and whether a simple utility maximizing model was capable of explaining the diversity of consumption patterns internationally. In a recent study, Rathnayaka et al. (2022) examined the similarities in consumption patterns in ten Asian countries, using the Rotterdam, CBS and AIDS models. The study noted a less diversified consumption basket for consumers in developing countries than those in relatively wealthy countries in Asia. The demand elasticity estimates suggested that food and housing are necessities, and clothing, durables, and transport are luxuries for Asian consumers. The demand for all goods was found to be price inelastic.

In a recent book, Selvanathan et al. (2023) presented a cross-country analysis of consumption patterns involving 45 countries grouped into 27 developed and 18 developing countries (with similar lifestyles within each group) and provided convincing evidence regarding the consumption patterns of consumer goods. The book presented an extensive three-dimensional analysis on the consumption patterns of 12 consumer goods across 45 countries and over time using the Rotterdam and Almost Ideal Demand Systems.

A list of major cross-country consumption studies and their summary findings is presented in Table 1.1. In summary, the major findings from previous studies are that, in most countries, food, clothing, and housing are necessities. Consumers from developed countries spend about half of their income on food, housing, and transport combined while consumers in developing countries spend more than half of their income on food. Consumers in developing countries have a less diversified consumption basket than those in relatively wealthy countries. Also, the demand for all goods considered was found to be price inelastic.

Dynamic Demand Analysis

The above cross-country consumption studies assume that consumers immediately and fully adjust to a new equilibrium when either income or prices change, and their elasticity estimations are based on static demand systems. However, consumers are unlikely to have adjusted to equilibrium in each time period; hence the assumption of instantaneous adjustments by consumers is potentially incorrect. Therefore, a number of studies, predominantly single-country studies, have recognized the importance of including dynamic adjustments in demand systems and have adopted a number of approaches.

For instance, several consumer demand studies have introduced dynamic nature into the well-known AIDS by including the lagged budget share $w_{i,t-1}$ on the right-hand side of the AIDS equation (see Blanciforti & Green, 1983; Blanciforti et al., 1986, for the USA; Karagiannis & Velentzas, 1993, for Greece; and Molina, 1994, for Spain). Furthermore, a few other studies have estimated a more general dynamic AIDS model by including its own past budget shares and the budget shares of all other goods (e.g. Alessie & Kapteyn, 1991, for the Netherlands; Kesavan et al., 1993, for the USA; Edgerton, 1997, for Sweden; and Klonaris & Hallam, 2003, for Greece).

Relatedly, Anderson and Blundell (1983) for the UK, Balcombe and Davis (1996) for Bulgaria, Edgerton et al. (1996) for Sweden, and Karagiannis and Velentzas (1997) for Greece have incorporated dynamic elements into AIDS by relying on the statistical properties of the data. This has led to the application of the error-corrected linear approximated AIDS (EC-LA-AIDS) in a number of recent studies on demand for nondurable goods, such as food subcategories. For example, using EC-LA-AIDS, Karagiannis et al. (2000) analysed the demand for meat in Greece. Eakins and Gallagher (2003) analysed the dynamics of alcohol expenditure in Ireland, while Fanelli and Mazzocchi (2002) estimated the demand for meat in Italy and Nzuma and Sarker (2010) estimated the demand for major cereals consumed in Kenya. Singh et al. (2011) employed EC-LA-AIDS to estimate demand for major crustaceans at a disaggregated level in the USA. More recently, Rathnayaka et al.

Table 1.1 Major studies in cross-country consumption patterns

Study	Countries	Type of data	Number of goods	Model	Main findings
(1)	(2)	(3)	(4)	(5)	(6)
Chen and Clements (1996)	13 developing countries	Cross-country	9	Double-log	Demand elasticities for the broad aggregates are the same in both rich and poor countries, except that of transport
Chai et al. (2023)	90 rich and poor countries	Cross-sectional		Entropy index	National expenditure hierarchies are relatively similar across countries among necessities
Clements et al. (2006)	45 developed and developing countries	Time-series	8	CBS	Consumption baskets have a distinct tendency to become more diversified as income rises, indicating a positive income elasticity of the demand for variety
Clements and Ye (2003)	18 OECD and 13 poor countries	Cross-country	8	Double-log	Transport is less income elastic in poor countries and is more price elastic in the rich countries
Clements and Theil (1996)	16 developed and developing countries	Cross-country	4	Working's model	Frisch's (1959) conjecture—the income elasticity of the marginal utility of income takes negative values which increase toward zero as the consumer becomes more affluent—is verified

(continued)

Table 1.1 (continued)

Study	Countries	Type of data	Number of goods	Model	Main findings
(1)	(2)	(3)	(4)	(5)	(6)
Houthakker (1957)	30 developed and developing countries	Cross-sectional	4	Double-log	Expenditure elasticities are similar across the 30 countries but not equal
Houthakker (1965)	13 OECD countries	Time-series (1948–1959)	5	Double-log	Food is a necessity for all the countries. For most of countries durables is a luxury
Kravis et al. (1982)	34 countries	Cross-country	103 and 25	Double-log and LES	The higher the level of aggregation the more similar demand equations are for Asian and European consumers and therefore the more similar the tastes
Lluch et al. (1977)	17 countries	Time-series (1955–1978)	8	Extended LES	Food expenditure elasticity declines on average from 0.93 to 0.38 over time. Own-price elasticities for food display a wide range of variation, from − 0.85 to − 0.16 over time
Lluch et al. (1977)	17 developing countries	Time-series (1955–1969)	8	ELES	Food and housing are necessities while durables, personal care, transport and recreation are luxuries

(continued)

Table 1.1 (continued)

Study	Countries	Type of data	Number of goods	Model	Main findings
(1)	(2)	(3)	(4)	(5)	(6)
Parks and Barten (1973)	14 OECD countries	Time-series (1950–1967)	5	LES	Income elasticities are positive, own price elasticities are negative in all countries
Pollak and Wales (1987)	Belgium, UK and US	Time-series	3	QES	The hypothesis of identical tastes between consumers in the three countries is rejected. Caution is required in pooling international consumption data
Rathnayaka et al. (2022)	10 Asian countries	Time series	8	CBS, AIDS, Rotterdam	Food and housing are necessities, and clothing, durables and transport are luxuries. The demand for all goods was found to be price inelastic
Seale et al. (2003)	Cross-country	Cross-sectional	5	Florida model	Low-income countries are more responsive to changes in income and food prices
Seale and Regmi (2009)	114 countries	1996 ICP data	9	Florida model	Income elasticity of food varies from 0.85 to 0.71 in low-income countries, from 0.71 to 0.57 in middle-income countries, and from 0.56 to 0.35 in high income countries

(continued)

Table 1.1 (continued)

Study	Countries	Type of data	Number of goods	Model	Main findings
(1)	(2)	(3)	(4)	(5)	(6)
Selvanathan and Selvanathan (1993)	18 OECD countries	Time-series (1960–1981)	10	Rotterdam under PI	In most countries, food, housing and medical care are necessities and clothing, durables, transport and recreation are luxuries
Selvanathan and Selvanathan (2003a)	23 OECD and 23 LD countries	Time-series (1970–1999)	9	CBS	OECD consumers allocate a lesser proportion of their income on food and higher proportion on housing, medical care, transport and recreation. LD consumers consider food, housing and medical care as necessities
Selvanathan and Selvanathan (2003b)	5 Asian countries	Time-series (1970–1999)	8	Rotterdam model	In most countries, food, housing and medical care are necessities while clothing, durables and transport are luxuries
Selvanathan et al. (2023)	27 developed and 18 developing countries	Time series (varying data range)	12	Rotterdam and AIDS	Supports empirical regularities in most countries including the Engel's law; law of demand; demand homogeneity; and Slutsky symmetry. Also found that consumers' tastes are preference independent

(continued)

Table 1.1 (continued)

Study	Countries	Type of data	Number of goods	Model	Main findings
(1)	(2)	(3)	(4)	(5)	(6)
Selvanathan et al. (2024)	40 countries	Time series (varying data range)	8	LA-AIDS, dynamic LA-AIDS, EC-LA-AIDS	Food and housing are necessities; durables, transport, and recreation are luxuries in developed and developing countries in the long-run and short-run
Theil and Clements (1987)	34 countries	1975 ICP data	10	Rotterdam and Working's model	Food, clothing and education are necessities. Beverages, housing, durables, medical care, transport and recreation are luxuries. Income flexibility is − 0.5
Theil et al. (1981)	15 countries	Cross-country	8	Working's model	Income elasticities are mostly closer to 1 and Divisia variances are smaller
van Driel et al. (1997)	USA and the Netherlands	Time-series (1929–1988)	6	CBS	Income elasticity of food is 0.75, own price elasticity of food is − 0.45 in the USA. Income elasticity of food is 0.65 and own price elasticity of food is − 0.20 in Netherlands

(2019) modelled the dynamic behaviour of Sri Lankan consumers in consuming eight broad commodity groups employing EC-LA-AIDS. In another very recent study, Selvanathan et al. (2024) modelled the static and dynamic patterns of consumption behaviour in 40 developed and developing countries using the static-LA-AIDS, dynamic LA-AIDS, and error-corrected LA-AIDS models and the most up-to-date time series data. Overall, the dynamic LA-AIDS model appeared to be the preferred model for most countries, followed by the EC-LA-AIDS model. The implied elasticities reveal that, in general, there are some differences between the long-run and short-run elasticities, and between developed and developing countries. A few studies have also employed EC-LA-AIDS to model the demand for tourism across countries (Durbarry & Sinclair, 2003; Wu et al., 2012).

In addition to the above studies based on the dynamic versions of AIDS, Bushehri (2003) introduced a generalized dynamic Rotterdam model. A few consumption studies have employed this approach (see, for example, Muhammad & Jones, 2009; Muhammad et al., 2015 for the USA; Greear & Muhammad, 2021 for Japan). The dynamic demand modelling techniques facilitate distinguishing long- and short-run effects of income and prices on demand for various commodity groups.

1.4 Aims of the Book

The main objective of this book is to analyse consumption patterns in Asian countries that are at different stages of economic development and to look at the similarities and disparities of consumption patterns across countries using a system-wide framework.

This overarching objective is supported by the following specific objectives.

- To review the economic theory of consumer demand and provide a comprehensive review of cross-country consumption studies.
- To estimate the income and price elasticities for different commodities in Asian countries and to test whether there are similarities among Asian consumers.
- To model the dynamic behaviour of consumption patterns and to test whether there are differences in short- and long-term consumer responses.
- To analyse the demand for the animal-derived food group comprising meat (chicken, beef, pork, and mutton), eggs and fish, and derive conditional and unconditional income and price elasticities and to decompose the changes in consumer demand.

In a departure from previous studies in the literature which mainly present only single-country analysis, this book aims to provide a comprehensive analysis of cross-country consumption patterns considering several Asian countries, using the most recent consumption expenditure data for aggregate commodity groups. In comparing consumption patterns across countries, we use unit-free measurements such as budget shares and changes in logarithms of price and quantities, thus avoiding problems associated with exchange rate conversions.

1.5 A Preview of the Book

This book presents a comprehensive analysis of the consumption patterns of consumers in 10 Asian countries which can be used as a representative sample of all the Asian countries at various levels of development. The study uses time series data and various popular and up-to-date demand models to present the analysis. The findings of this book can be used as inputs by policy analysts and researchers since the knowledge of price and income responses is undoubtedly an important element in the formulation of fiscal policy or any other type of economic control. This is primarily because consumption absorbs more than 60% of GDP in most economies and is the largest macroeconomic aggregate; it thus has great significance for the state of an economy as a whole. Estimated income and price elasticities in this book will be useful inputs for various applications about policy issues such as taxation, the cost-of-living index, and the formation of international trade policies between Asia and other countries. For instance, the findings may be used as input parameters in partial equilibrium and general equilibrium models, which in turn can project such matters as tariff changes and the effect of import, export, and domestic prices. Moreover, deep insights into consumption patterns in transforming Asia will be beneficial for international operators wanting to expand their business investments in a wide range of sectors.

This chapter presents an overview of changes in consumption patterns of Asian countries over the years and discusses the impact of the economic success of Asia, the integration of global consumer markets, and globalization on Asian consumers. The literature on cross-country consumption goes back to the pioneering work of Hendrik Houthakker in 1957. This chapter also presents a review of past studies that have analysed cross-country consumption patterns using both time series and cross-sectional data and provides a comparison of income and own-price elasticities for the consumption of the broad commodity groups in Asian countries reported by previous studies.

Chapter 2 reviews the theory of demand and presents various demand models commonly used in the applied-demand analysis. The chapter commences by introducing directly specified demand systems such as the double-log demand equations and the Working's model; it then discusses directly specified demand equations derived from specific forms of utility functions such as the linear expenditure system (LES); this is followed by presenting an indirectly specified utility demand function, as in the trans-log demand function of Christensen et al. (1975). It then considers the derivation of a demand system from the specification of the cost function, such as the popular AIDS model of Deaton and Muellbauer (1980). Finally, Theil's (1975/76) approach is used to derive several other well-known demand systems such as the Rotterdam, CBS and CBS/PI demand models, and Selvanathan's (1985) 'Even Simpler Demand System'. To analyse the demand for individual commodities within a group, this chapter presents demand equations under *block-independent preference*. Hence, given the demand for a group, the issue will be how the expenditure will be allocated to the commodities within the group. This question can be answered by the *conditional demand equations* which will also be discussed in detail.

Chapter 3 presents summary characteristics of Asian consumers and a preliminary data analysis of the consumption patterns of Asian consumers using time series data for 10 Asian countries and 8 broad commodity groups. We also investigate several empirical regularities in consumption economics, supported by the cross-country data: (1) Quantity variance exceeds price variance; (2) Demand curve slopes downwards; (3) Income flexibility tends towards − 0.5; and (4) Budget share of food declines with increasing income. The chapter also presents preliminary income and price elasticity estimates by estimating a double-log demand system.

Chapter 4 uses three well-known demand systems—Rotterdam, CBS, and AIDS—to study the consumption patterns of consumers in ten Asian countries. The chapter first estimates the three demand models using the consumption and price data for 8 broad commodity groups for the 10 Asian countries and tests whether the cross-country data support the demand theory hypotheses of demand homogeneity, Slutsky symmetry, and preference independence. We then select the most preferred demand model for each economy using the goodness of fit measure, which involves analysing information inaccuracies and estimating the income and price elasticities of the eight commodities for the ten countries using the preferred model per economy. In addition, we formally test the hypothesis of similarity in the consumption patterns of Asian consumers.

In Chap 5, we isolate food from other broad commodity groups and analyse the demand for the animal-derived food group comprising meat (chicken, beef, pork, and mutton), eggs and fish, and derive income and price elasticities in Asian countries. As you will see, the food sector accounts for around 30% of the world's total energy consumption and accounts for around 22% of total Greenhouse gas emissions. As a global community, we are facing the significant challenge of feeding nine billion mouths in 2050 within the means of the global ecosystem (De Bakker & Dagevos, 2012; Godfray et al., 2010; Steinfeld et al., 2006). The production and consumption of animal proteins are among the most environmentally harmful components of the food package. Therefore, consumption trends of meat, eggs, and fish in the Asian region should also be a matter of interest to environmental economists and ecologists. We estimate the group demand elasticities and conditional and unconditional demand elasticities for the above animal-derived food items using the system-wide approach and the most recent consumption and price data. Firstly, we briefly review previous studies analysing the demand for meat and fish products in Asian countries. Next, we present a preliminary analysis of the data, and we test empirical regularities in the consumption patterns of animal-derived food in Asian countries. We then test the demand theory hypotheses, estimate the group demand equation, conditional demand equations and unconditional demand responses, and obtain the implied group and conditional demand elasticities. Next, we decompose the growth in chicken, beef, pork, mutton, eggs, and fish consumption into the effect of changes in consumer taste, income effect, own-price effect, and cross-price effect for each of the seven countries. The results of the decomposition analysis, which show the effect of simultaneous changes in prices, income, and tastes, can be applied to policy considerations.

Chapter 6 models the dynamic behaviour of consumption patterns in the Asian countries using annual time series data for eight commodity groups. First, we present three versions of the AIDS prior to testing for stationarity and cointegration of the model variables, then estimate the three demand models and test demand theory hypotheses. We then select the preferred demand model using the goodness-of-fit measure to establish any information inaccuracy. Finally, in this chapter, we estimate the short-run and long-run demand elasticities. Using the estimation results, we investigate whether habit persistence plays a major role in the consumption of goods and services and if there are any differences in short- and long-run demand elasticities. The deviations between the short- and long-run demand elasticities indicate the need to adopt a dynamic approach when estimating demand elasticities that can be used in the computations of optimal taxation, tax reform and in applied computable general equilibrium models.

The final Chap 7 consolidates and summarizes the findings of all chapters to provide an overall picture of consumption patterns in Asian countries. The chapter also discusses the important policy implications arising from the findings of this study. Finally, this chapter briefly presents the possible limitations of this study and future research directions that could be explored to further investigate consumption patterns.

References

ADB. (2023). *Asian development outlook, economic forecasts: Subregions, September 2023*. Asian Development Bank.

Alessie, R., & Kapteyn, A. (1991). Habit formation, interdependent preferences and demographic effects in the almost ideal demand system. *The Economic Journal, 101*(406), 404–419.

Anderson, G., & Blundell, R. (1983). Testing restrictions in a flexible dynamic demand system: An application to consumers' expenditure in Canada. *The Review of Economic Studies, 50*(3), 397–410.

Balcombe, K. G., & Davis, J. R. (1996). An application of cointegration theory in the estimation of the almost ideal demand system for food consumption in Bulgaria. *Agricultural Economics, 15*(1), 47–60.

Blanciforti, L. A., & Green, R. D. (1983). An almost ideal demand system incorporating habits: An analysis of expenditures on food and aggregate commodity groups. *The Review of Economics and Statistics*, 511–515.

Blanciforti, L. A., Green, R. D., & King, G. A. (1986). *U.S. consumer behaviour over the postwar period: An almost ideal demand system analysis*. Paper Monographs Series st 40, Giannini Foundation, University of California, Davis.

Bushehri, M. A. (2003). Dynamic generalization of the Rotterdam model. *Applied Economics Letters, 10*(5), 303–306.

Chai, A., Stepanova, E., & Moneta, A. (2023). Quantifying expenditure hierarchies and the expansion of global consumption diversity. *Journal of Economic Behaviour and Organization, 214*, 860–886.

Chen, D., & Clements, K. W. (1996). Empirical regularities in consumption patterns in emerging economies. *The Developing Economies, 34*(3), 219–246.

Chen, D. L. (2001). *World consumption economics*. World Scientific.

Christensen, L. R., Jorgenson, D. W., & Lau, L. J. (1975). Transcendental logarithmic utility functions. *American Economic Review, 65*, 367–383.

Clements, K. W., & Chen, D. L. (1996). Fundamental similarities in consumer behaviour. *Applied Economics, 28*(6), 747–757.

Clements, K. W., Suhm, F. E., & Theil, H. (1979). A cross-country tabulation of income elasticities of demand. *Economics Letters, 3*(2), 199–202.

Clements, K. W., & Theil, H. (1996). A cross-country analysis of consumption patterns (Chap. 7). In H. Theil (Ed.), *Studies in global econometrics*. Springer, US.

Clements, K. W., Wu, Y., & Zhang, J. (2006). Comparing international consumption patterns. *Empirical Economics, 31*(1), 1–30.

Clements, K. W., & Ye, Q. (2003). The economics of global consumption patterns. *Journal of Agricultural and Applied Economics, 35*, 21–37.

De Bakker, E., & Dagevos, H. (2012). Reducing meat consumption in today's consumer society: Questioning the citizen-consumer gap. *Journal of Agricultural and Environmental Ethics, 25*, 877–894.

Deaton, A. S., & Muellbauer, J. (1980). An almost ideal demand system. *American Economic Review, 70*, 312–326.

Durbarry, R., & Sinclair, M. T. (2003). Market shares analysis: The case of French tourism demand. *Annals of Tourism Research, 30*, 927–941.

Eakins, J. M., & Gallagher, L. A. (2003). Dynamic almost ideal demand systems: An empirical analysis of alcohol expenditure in Ireland. *Applied Economics, 35*(9), 1025–1036.

Edgerton, D. L. (1997). Weak separability and the estimation of elasticities in multistage demand systems. *American Journal of Agricultural Economics, 79*(1), 62–79.

Edgerton, D. L., Assarsson, B., Hummelmose, A., Laurila, I. P., Rickertsen, K., & Vale, P. H. (1996). *The econometrics of demand systems: With applications to food demand in the Nordic countries*. Kluwer Academic Publishers.

Emerging Asian Economies. (2017). *Business in Asia*. Leading Edge Alliance Global.

Fanelli, L., & Mazzocchi, M. (2002). A cointegrated VECM demand system for meat in Italy. *Applied Economics, 34*(13), 1593–1605.

Finke, R., Rosalsky, M. C., & Theil, H. (1983). A new cross-country tabulation of income elasticities of demand. *Economics Letters, 12*(3–4), 391–396.

Frisch, R. (1959). A complete scheme for computing all direct and cross demand elasticities in a model with many sectors. *Econometrica, 27*, 177–196.

Godfray, H. C. J., Beddington, J. R., Crute, I. R., Haddad, L., Lawrence, D., Muir, J. F., Pretty, J., Robinson, S., Thomas, S. M., & Toulmin, C. (2010). Food security: The challenge of feeding 9 billion people. *Science, 327*(5967), 812–818.

Goldberger, A. S., & Gamaletsos, T. (1970). A cross-country comparison as consumer expenditure patterns. *European Economic Review, 1*(3), 357–400.

Greear, E. K., & Muhammad, A. (2021). Tariff elimination and the competitiveness of wine-exporting countries in Japan. *Agricultural and Resource Economics Review, 50*(1), 76–98.

Houthakker, H. S. (1957). An international comparison of household expenditure patterns, commemorating the centenary of Engel's law. *Econometrica, 25*(4), 532–551.

Houthakker, H. S. (1965). New evidence on demand elasticities. *Econometrica, 33*(2), 277–288.

Hubacek, K., Guan, D., & Barua, A. (2007). Changing lifestyles and consumption patterns in developing countries: A scenario analysis for China and India. *Futures, 39*(9), 1084–1096.

IMF. (2023). *The regional economic outlook: Asia and Pacific, October 2023*. International Monetary Fund, Publication Services.

Karagiannis, G., Katranidis, S., & Velentzas, K. (2000). An error correction almost ideal demand system for meat in Greece. *Agricultural Economics, 22*(1), 29–35.

Karagiannis, G., & Velentzas, K. (1993). Habits and empirical analysis of demand for six aggregate commodity groups in Greece. *Spoudai, 43*, 139–154.

Karagiannis, G., & Velentzas, K. (1997). Explaining food consumption patterns in Greece. *Journal of Agricultural Economics, 48*(1–3), 83–92.

Kesavan, T., Hassan, Z. A., Jensen, H. H., & Johnson, S. R. (1993). Dynamics and long-run structure in US meat demand. *Canadian Journal of Agricultural Economics, 41*(2), 139–153.

Klonaris, S., & Hallam, D. (2003). Conditional and unconditional food demand elasticities in a dynamic multistage demand system. *Applied Economics, 35*(5), 503–514.

Kravis, I. B., Heston, A. W., & Summers, R. (1978). *International comparisons of real product and purchasing power*. United Nations, Statistical Office, World Bank.

Kravis, I. B., Heston, A. W., & Summers, R. (1982). *World product and income: International comparisons of real gross product*. World Bank.

Lluch, C., & Powell, A. (1975). International comparisons of expenditure patterns. *European Economic Review, 6*(3), 275–303.

Lluch, C., Powell, A. A., Williams, R. A., & Betancourt, R. R. (1977). *Patterns in household demand and saving*. Oxford University Press.

Molina, J. A. (1994). Food demand in Spain: An application of the almost ideal demand system. *Journal of Agricultural Economics, 45*, 252–258.

Muhammad, A., & Jones, K. G. (2009). An assessment of dynamic behavior in the US catfish market: An application of the generalized dynamic Rotterdam model. *Journal of Agricultural and Applied Economics, 41*(3), 745–759.

Muhammad, A., Zahniser, S., & Fonsah, E. G. (2015). A dynamic analysis of US banana demand by source: A focus on Latin American suppliers. *International Journal of Trade and Global Markets, 8*(4), 281–296.

Nzuma, J. M., & Sarker, R. (2010). An error corrected almost ideal demand system for major cereals in Kenya. *Agricultural Economics, 41*(1), 43–50.

Parks, R. W., & Barten, A. P. (1973). A cross-country comparison of the effects of prices, income and population composition on consumption patterns. *The Economic Journal, 83*(331), 834–852.

Pollak, R. A., & Wales, T. J. (1987). Specification and estimation of non separable two-stage technologies: The Leontief CES and the Cobb–Douglas CES. *Journal of Political Economy, 95*(2), 311–333.

Rathnayaka, S. D., Selvanathan, E. A., & Selvanathan, S. (2022). Modelling the consumption patterns in the Asian countries. *Economic Analysis and Policy, 74*, 277–296.

Rathnayaka, S. D., Selvanathan, S., Selvanathan, E. A., & Kler, P. (2019). Modelling Sri Lankan consumption patterns using error corrected LA-AIDS. *Economic Modelling, 80*, 185–191.

Seale, J. L., Jr., & Regmi, A. (2009). International consumption patterns: Evidence from the 1996 international comparison programme (Chap. 12). In S. Ghatak & P. Levine (Eds.), *Development macroeconomics: Essays in memory of Anita Ghatak*. Routledge.

Seale, J. L., Regmi, A., & Bernstein, J. (2003). *International evidence on food consumption patterns*. Economic Research Service, US Department of Agriculture.

Selvanathan, E. A. (1985). An even simpler differential demand system. *Economics Letters, 19*, 343–347.

Selvanathan, E. A., & Selvanathan, S. (2003a). *International consumption comparisons: OECD versus LDC*. World Scientific.

Selvanathan, E. A., & Selvanathan, S. (2003b). Similarities in the consumption patterns of the five Asian tigers. *Asian Economic Journal, 17*, 297–323.

Selvanathan, E. A., Selvanathan, S., & Jayasinghe, M. (2023). *Household demand for consumer goods in developing countries: A comparative perspective with developed countries*. Routledge Studies in Development Economics. Routledge, UK.

Selvanathan, S., Jayasinghe, M., Selvanathan, E. A., & Rathnayaka, S. D. (2024). Dynamic modelling of consumption patterns using LA-AIDS: A comparative study of developed versus developing countries. *Empirical Economics, 66*(1), 75–135.

Selvanathan, S., & Selvanathan, E. A. (1993). A cross-country analysis of consumption patterns. *Applied Economics, 25*(9), 1245–1259.

Singh, K., Dey, M. M., & Thapa, G. (2011). An error corrected almost ideal demand system for crustaceans in the United States. *Journal of International Food and Agribusiness Marketing, 23*(3), 271–284.

Steinfeld, H., Wassenaar, T., & Jutzi, S. (2006). Livestock production systems in developing countries: Status, drivers, trends. *Revue Scientifique et Technique, 25*(2), 505–516.

Stigler, G. J., & Becker, G. S. (1977). De gustibus non est disputandum. *American Economic Review, 67*, 76–90.

Stone, R. (1954). Linear expenditure systems and demand analysis: An application to the pattern of British demand. *The Economic Journal, 64*(255), 511–527.

Theil, H. (1975/76). *Theory and measurement of consumer demand*. North-Holland Publishing Company.

Theil, H. (1987). The econometrics of demand system (Chap. 3). In H. Theil & K. W. Clements (Eds.), *Applied demand analysis: Results from system-wide approaches*. Ballinger Publishing Company.

Theil, H., & Clements, K. W. (1987). *Applied demand analysis: Results from system-wide approaches*. Ballinger Publishing Company.

Theil, H., Suhm, F. E., & Meisner, J. F. (1980). Statistical inference in cross-country demand systems. *Economics Letters, 5*(4), 383–387.

Theil, H., Suhm, F. E., Suhm, F. H., & Meissner, J. F. (1981). *International consumption comparisons: A system-wide approach* (Vol. 30). North-Holland.

van Driel, H., Nadal, V., & Zeelenber, K. (1997). The demand for food in the United States and the Netherlands: A systems approach with the CBS model. *Journal of Applied Econometrics, 12*(5), 509–532.

Wu, D. C., Li, G., & Song, H. (2012). Economic analysis of tourism consumption dynamics: A time-varying parameter demand system approach. *Annals of Tourism Research, 39*(2), 667–685.

Chapter 2
A Review of Consumer Demand

2.1 Introduction

A sound understanding of consumption theory is crucial for any consumer demand study. Consumption theory is concerned with how a rational consumer makes consumption decisions. Interest in the theory and measurement of consumer behaviour dates as far back as the nineteenth century, as evidenced by the works of Cournot (1838), Edgeworth (1881), Engel (1857), and Fisher (1892). Major works on the determinants of consumer demand include Working (1943), Stone (1954), Leser (1960), Houthakker (1960), Philps (1974), Christensen et al. (1975), Barten (1977), Deaton and Muellbauer (1980a), Theil (1975/76, 1980, 1996), Theil and Clements (1987), Pollak and Wales (1992), Selvanathan (1993), Selvanathan and Clements (1995), Selvanathan and Selvanathan (2003, 2004, 2006), and Clements et al. (2006). These past works on consumer theory, married with data have contributed strongly to the field of applied econometrics (Selvanathan & Clements, 1995): they have greatly informed policy-making by governments as well as the investment decisions of international organizations.

Demand analysis involves the study of how consumers allocate their income among different commodities. Consumers' choices for these commodities are represented by their demand function for each of the commodities. The demand function for a single commodity explains how changes in income and the prices of all goods affect the quantity of a commodity consumed. Thus, the measurements of a consumer's response to these changes, represented in income and price elasticities, become important. The objective of this chapter is to describe the theory of the utility-maximizing consumer, the derivation of demand functions and the theoretical restrictions on these functions, and the derivation of implied income and price elasticities from these demand functions.

S. D. Rathnayaka et al., *Economic Development and Consumption Patterns in Asian Countries*, https://doi.org/10.1007/978-981-97-2628-8_2

More importantly, we discuss (chronologically) several methods for deriving demand equations. In early studies, demand equations were directly specified without any reference to utility functions. An example is the double log demand system. A subsequent approach derived demand equations by specifying the direct utility function: the specification of the indirect utility function or the specification of the cost function, either by maximizing the consumer utility function or minimizing the cost function. A third approach for generating demand equations is the differential approach. This approach requires no initial algebraic specification of utility or cost functions, so it can be considered more mathematical and flexible compared to the first two approaches. Demand systems generated from the third approach include the Rotterdam model and Working's model, which is a parameterization of the former (see Selvanathan & Clements, 1995; Sulgham, 2006).

The rest of this chapter will be structured thus: Sect. 2.2 defines the concepts of budget and marginal shares, income and price elasticity of demand, and the Divisia indexes. Section 2.3 formulates the general form of the system of demand equations by maximizing the consumer's utility function. This section will also introduce the constraints on demand equations: (1) demand equations must satisfy the budget constraints for all values of income and prices; (2) demand homogeneity; (3) Slutsky symmetry; and (4) the $n \times n$ matrix of compensated price derivatives being negative semi-definite. The differential approach to demand system is discussed in Sects. 2.4 to 2.6, wherein Sect. 2.4 provides Barten's (1964) fundamental matrix equation and an in-depth review of preference independence (or strong additivity). Section 2.7 introduces five other differential demand systems. Section 2.8 discusses block independence and group demand equations and Sect. 2.9 introduces the conditional demand equation. Section 2.10 concludes this chapter.

The Appendix to this chapter discusses some directly specified demand systems such as the double-log demand equations and Working's model, examples of directly specified demand equations derived from specific forms of utility functions, such as the linear expenditure system (LES), indirectly specified utility demand functions, particularly the trans-log demand function of Christensen et al. (1975), the derivation of a demand system from the specification of the cost function, such as the popular AIDS model of Deaton and Muellbauer (1980a, 1980b), the Quadratic Almost Ideal Demand System (QUAIDS) and the dynamic demand systems.

2.2 Basic Concepts in Consumer Demand

This section defines basic concepts in consumer demand, such as income, budget shares, marginal shares, demand elasticities and Divisia Indexes, which will be used in subsequent sections.

Total Expenditure or Income

Let q_i be the quantity demanded of good i, p_i be the price of good i ($i = 1, 2, \ldots, n$) and n be the number of commodities, then the total expenditure M, also termed as *income* in short, is given by

$$M = \sum_{i=1}^{n} p_i q_i. \tag{2.2.1}$$

Budget Shares and Marginal Shares

The proportion of income allocated to good i is known as the *budget share*, and it can be defined as

$$w_i = \frac{p_i q_i}{M}, \quad i = 1, \ldots, n. \tag{2.2.2}$$

Budget shares are always positive and, according to (2.2.1) and (2.2.2), have a unit sum, where

$$\sum_{i=1}^{n} w_i = 1. \tag{2.2.3}$$

When income increases by \$1, how much of this is spent on commodity i is measured by its marginal share. The marginal share of good i, θ_i, can be written as

$$\theta_i = \frac{\partial(p_i q_i)}{\partial M}, \quad i = 1, \ldots, n. \tag{2.2.4}$$

Total expenditure derives from income which is totally spent on n consumer goods; the marginal shares have a unit sum. By differentiating both sides of (2.2.1) by M, it can be seen that

$$\sum_{i=1}^{n} \theta_i = 1. \tag{2.2.5}$$

In contrast to budget shares, marginal shares are not always positive; if good i is an inferior good, then the marginal share (θ_i) will be negative. This is because when income increases, demand for an inferior good falls.

Income Elasticity of Demand

Income elasticity of demand measures the responsiveness of demand due to an increase or decrease in consumer income. The income elasticity of commodity i, η_i, is the percentage change in the consumption of commodity i when income increases by 1%; that is

$$\eta_i = \frac{\partial q_i / q_i}{\partial M / M} = \frac{\partial(\log q_i)}{\partial(\log M)}, \quad i = 1, \ldots, n. \tag{2.2.6}$$

If we divide the marginal share (2.2.4) by the budget share (2.2.2), then

$$\frac{\theta_i}{w_i} = \frac{\partial(p_i q_i)/\partial M}{p_i q_i/M} = \frac{\partial q_i/q_i}{\partial M/M} = \eta_i, \qquad i = 1, \ldots, n.$$

Therefore, income elasticity can be expressed as a ratio of the marginal share to its corresponding budget share, as in

$$\eta_i = \frac{\theta_i}{w_i}, \quad i = 1, \ldots, n. \tag{2.2.7}$$

Commodities with income elasticities less than unity are called *necessities*, while those with income elasticities greater than unity are known as *luxuries*. If the income elasticity is negative, then the good is said to be *inferior*: as people get richer, they spend less on inferior goods and switch to better quality goods and consumption falls with increasing income.

Marginal shares have a unit sum, so it follows from (2.2.7) that a budget-share-weighted average of the income elasticities is equal to unity:

$$\sum_{i=1}^{n} w_i \eta_i = \sum_{i=1}^{n} \theta_i = 1 \tag{2.2.8}$$

Own Price Elasticity of Demand

Own price elasticity of demand measures how a percentage change in the price of good *i* will affect the demand for it:

$$\eta_{ii} = \frac{\partial q_i/q_i}{\partial p_i/p_i} = \frac{\partial(\log q_i)}{\partial(\log p_i)}, \qquad i = 1, \ldots, n. \tag{2.2.9}$$

Demand is price inelastic if it does not respond much to price changes (i.e. $|\eta_{ii}| < 1$) and elastic if demand changes a lot when the price changes (i.e. $|\eta_{ii}| > 1$). Necessities tend to have inelastic demand, and luxuries, elastic demand. In addition, demand is elastic when there are close substitutes. Economists refer to demand as inelastic when the price elasticity of demand is less than 1 in absolute terms. In other words, goods are said to be inelastic if the percentage change in the quantity demanded changes by less than the percentage change in price. Demand is price elastic when the price elasticity of demand is greater than 1. When the price elasticity of demand is 1, we say that demand has unitary elasticity.

Cross-Price Elasticity of Demand

The quantity demanded of a particular good also varies according to the price of other goods. Cross-price elasticity of demand is a measure of how much the quantity demanded of one good *i* responds to a change in the price of another good *j*:

$$\eta_{ij} = \frac{\partial q_i / q_i}{\partial p_j / p_j} = \frac{\partial (\log q_i)}{\partial (\log p_j)}, \qquad i \neq j, \quad i, j = 1, \ldots, n. \tag{2.2.10}$$

Two goods, which are substitutes, will have a positive cross-price elasticity (i.e. $\eta_{ij} > 0$ for $i \neq j$). Two goods, which are complements, will have a negative cross-price elasticity (i.e. $\eta_{ij} < 0$ for $i \neq j$).

Divisia Indexes

Divisia indexes are useful for summarizing price and quantity data. The differential of the budget constraint (2.2.1) is

$$dM = \sum_{i=1}^{n} p_i dq_i + \sum_{i=1}^{n} q_i dp_i.$$

Dividing both sides by M and, using the identity, $dx/x = d(\log x)$ and $w_i = p_i q_i / M$, we can obtain

$$d(\log M) = d(\log Q) + d(\log P), \tag{2.2.11}$$

where

$$d(\log Q) = \sum_{i=1}^{n} w_i d(\log q_i), \tag{2.2.12}$$

is the *Divisia volume index* and

$$d(\log P) = \sum_{i=1}^{n} w_i d(\log p_i), \tag{2.2.13}$$

is the *Divisia price index.*

Equation (2.2.11) decomposes the change in income into volume and price indexes. The volume index defined in (2.2.12) is a budget share-weighted average of the n logarithmic quantity changes, $d(\log q_1), \ldots, d(\log q_n)$. Similarly, the price index (2.2.13) is a budget-share-weighted average of the n logarithmic price changes, $d(\log p_1), \ldots, d(\log p_n)$. These two indexes, Divisia quantity and price indexes, can be viewed as a first-order moment of the quantity and price changes.

The corresponding second-order moments are the *Divisia quantity variance,*

$$K = \sum_{i=1}^{n} w_i \left[d(\log q_i) - d(\log Q) \right]^2 = \sum_{i=1}^{n} w_i \left[d \left[\log \frac{q_i}{Q} \right] \right]^2, \tag{2.2.14}$$

and the *Divisia price variance*

$$\Pi = \sum_{i=1}^{n} w_i \left[d(\log p_i) - d(\log P)\right]^2 = \sum_{i=1}^{n} w_i \left[d\left[\log \frac{p_i}{P}\right]\right]^2. \tag{2.2.15}$$

The Divisia price variance Π, vanishes when all prices change proportionately and increases when the prices change more disproportionately. In other words, Π is *a measure of the changes in relative prices.*

The comovement of prices and consumption can be measured by the *Divisia price-quantity covariance*

$$\Gamma = \sum_{i=1}^{n} w_i d\left[\log \frac{p_i}{P}\right] d\left[\log \frac{q_i}{Q}\right], \tag{2.2.16}$$

and the corresponding *price-quantity correlation* is

$$\rho = \frac{\Gamma}{\sqrt{\Pi K}}. \tag{2.2.17}$$

While covariance can reveal the direction and movement between prices and quantities, correlation measures the direction of the comovement of prices and quantities as well as the strength of the relationship. A normal good possessing above-average price increases would tend to experience below-average increases in consumption and vice versa, Γ and ρ are usually expected to be negative.

2.3 Utility-Based Demand System

Unlike approaches using the traditional directly-specified demand equation, neoclassical consumer theory assumes that a consumer's satisfaction with the purchase of a set of goods can be captured by a utility function. Here, a consumer maximizes utility subject to his/her budget constraint

$$u = u(q_1, q_2, \ldots, q_n) \tag{2.3.1}$$

subject to the budget constraint

$$M = \sum_{i=1}^{n} p_i q_i \tag{2.3.2}$$

where u is the utility function of the consumer at consumption levels $q_1, q_2, \ldots, q_n$, M is total income or expenditure, and p_i^s and q_i^s are prices and quantities, respectively. A special case of the general form of utility function is that of *preference independence*. Under this, the total utility can be written as the sum of n subutility functions, one for each good. That is,

$$u(q_1, q_2, \ldots, q_n) = \sum_{i=1}^{n} u_i(q_i) \tag{2.3.3}$$

We shall discuss preference independence in more detail in the following section and in the next chapter.

A set of demand equations can be derived by utility maximization of (2.3.1) subject to budget constraint (2.3.2) via a Lagrangian function to show the quantity demanded of each commodity as a function of price and income:

$$q_i = q_i(M, p_1, p_2, \ldots, p_n) \tag{2.3.4}$$

This demand function, based on utility maximization, is the Marshallian or uncompensated demand function. If the utility function is differentiable and there is non-satiation, each marginal utility will be positive

$$\frac{\partial u}{\partial q_i} > 0 \qquad i = 1, \ldots, n. \tag{2.3.5}$$

Furthermore, if we assume that there is generalized diminishing marginal utility, the Hessian matrix of the utility function will be negative definite. As Hessians are symmetric, then

$$\boldsymbol{U} = \left[\frac{\partial^2 u}{\partial q_i \partial q_j}\right] \tag{2.3.6}$$

will be a symmetric negative definite $n \times n$ matrix.

Mathematically, the demand equation for a good can be derived from utility maximization based on the Lagrangian method. The Lagrangian function for the consumer utility maximization problem can be written as

$$L(\boldsymbol{q}, \lambda) = u(q_1, \ldots, q_n) + \lambda\left(M - \sum_{i=1}^{n} p_i q_i\right) \tag{2.3.7}$$

The first-order conditions for a maximum of the function L is $\partial L/\partial q_i = 0$, for $i = 1, \ldots, n$, and $\partial L/\partial \lambda = 0$, which yield

$$\frac{\partial u}{\partial q_i} = \lambda p_i \qquad i = 1, \ldots, n \tag{2.3.8}$$

and

$$M = \sum_{i=1}^{n} p_i q_i \tag{2.3.9}$$

Equation (2.3.8) implies that all marginal utility from good i is proportional to the corresponding prices. As the prices are positive, it follows from (2.3.5) that λ must be greater than zero. By dividing both sides by p_i, we can represent (2.3.8) as

$$\frac{\partial u}{\partial (p_i q_i)} = \lambda \tag{2.3.10}$$

Equation (2.3.10) shows that a \$1 increase in income causes utility to rise by λ when this income is spent on any of the n goods. Thus, λ, the Lagrangian multiplier, can be interpreted as the marginal utility of income.

The first-order conditions in Eqs. (2.3.8) and (2.3.9) constitute $n + 1$ equations, which can be solved for the $n + 1$ unknowns, $q_1, \ldots, q_n$, and λ. The resulting quantities are unique and positive for the relevant values of prices and income. The optimal quantities depend on income and prices, so the demand functions may be written as

$$q_i = q_i(p_1, p_2, \ldots, p_n, M), \qquad i = 1, \ldots, n. \tag{2.3.11}$$

This is a system of n demand equations. These n equations contain n income slopes $\partial q_i/\partial M$ or income elasticities

$$\eta_i = \frac{\partial q_i}{\partial M}\frac{M}{q_i}$$

as well as n price slopes $\partial q_i/\partial p_i$ or price elasticities

$$\eta_{ii} = \frac{\partial q_i}{\partial p_i}\frac{p_i}{q_i}.$$

With the introduction of the utility function, demand analysis becomes richer in both its implications and applications. Examples are that the utility framework can be the basis for index number theory which includes the measurement of real income; that it can be the measurement of the effects of distortions such as that of commodity taxation; and that goods can be divided into subgroups which are closely related. More importantly, the utility function provides the basis for the following restrictions on demand analysis: demand equations are homogeneous of degree-zero in income and prices; the symmetry of the substitution effects; and that the substitution matrix is negative semi-definite.

The Constraints on the Demand Equation

There are several constraints, resulting directly from the utility maximization problem, which the demand Eq. (2.3.11) must satisfy. They are formulated in terms of the income and price derivatives of (2.3.11) and are written in vector and matrix form as

$$\frac{\partial \boldsymbol{q}}{\partial M} = \left[\frac{\partial q_1}{\partial M} \cdots \frac{\partial q_n}{\partial M}\right]' \tag{2.3.12}$$

$$\frac{\partial \boldsymbol{q}}{\partial \boldsymbol{p}'} = \begin{bmatrix} \frac{\partial q_1}{\partial p_1} & \frac{\partial q_1}{\partial p_2} & \cdots & \frac{\partial q_1}{\partial p_n} \\ \vdots & \vdots & & \vdots \\ \frac{\partial q_n}{\partial p_1} & \frac{\partial q_n}{\partial p_2} & \cdots & \frac{\partial q_n}{\partial p_n} \end{bmatrix} \tag{2.3.13}$$

Differentiating the budget constraint (2.3.2) with respect to M and p_j, we obtain

$$\sum_{i=1}^{n} p_i \frac{\partial q_i}{\partial M} = 1 \quad \text{or} \quad \boldsymbol{p}' \frac{\partial \boldsymbol{q}}{\partial M} = 1 \tag{2.3.14}$$

$$\sum_{i=1}^{n} p_i \frac{\partial q_i}{\partial p_j} = -q_j \quad \text{or} \quad \boldsymbol{p}' \frac{\partial \boldsymbol{q}}{\partial \boldsymbol{p}'} = -\boldsymbol{q}', \tag{2.3.15}$$

where $\boldsymbol{p}' = (p_1, p_2, \ldots, p_n)$ and $\boldsymbol{q}' = (q_1, q_2, \ldots, q_n)$ are the price and quantity vectors.

First Constraint

The first constraint (2.3.14) means that the marginal shares sum to 1.

Second Constraint

The second constraint (2.3.15) is termed *demand homogeneity*, which arises from the fact that the demand functions are homogeneous of degree-zero. The economic interpretation of this is that an equi-proportionate change in income and prices leaves the consumption of each good unchanged; in other words, the consumer does not suffer from money illusion. Thus, if we apply Euler's theorem to (2.3.11), we obtain

$$M \frac{\partial q_i}{\partial M} + \sum_{j=1}^{n} p_j \frac{\partial q_i}{\partial p_j} = 0, \qquad i = 1, \ldots, n. \tag{2.3.16}$$

Premultiplying both sides of (2.3.16) by $1/q_i$ yields

$$\frac{\partial q_i/q_i}{\partial M/M} + \sum_{j=1}^{n} \frac{\partial q_i/q_i}{\partial q_j/q_j} = 0, \qquad i = 1, \ldots, n.$$

Thus, demand homogeneity can be expressed in elasticity form as

$$\eta_i + \sum_{j=1}^{n} \eta_{ij} = 0, \qquad i = 1, \ldots, n. \tag{2.3.17}$$

The *Slutsky equation* decomposes the total substitution effect of a price change in commodity j on the demand for commodity i as

$$\frac{\partial q_i}{\partial p_j} = \frac{\partial q_i^*}{\partial p_j} q_j \frac{\partial q_i}{\partial M}, \qquad i, j = 1, \ldots, n \tag{2.3.18}$$

where the superscript * denotes that utility remains constant, that is

$$\frac{\partial q_i^*}{\partial p_j} = \left. \frac{\partial q_i}{\partial p_j} \right|_{\partial u = 0}.$$

Holding utility constant is equivalent to keeping real income unchanged, so $\partial q_i^*/\partial p_j$ in (2.3.18) is known as the *substitution effect of a change in the price of commodity j on the demand for i.* The remaining term on the right of (2.3.18), $-q_j \partial q_i/\partial M$, is the effect on the demand for i due to a fall in real income resulting from the increase in the price of j, with nominal income M being held constant. This term is known as the *income effect of a change in the price of j on the demand for i.*

Equation (2.3.18) can be expressed in elasticity form as

$$\frac{\partial q_i/q_i}{\partial p_j/p_j} = \frac{\partial q_i^*/q_i}{\partial p_j/p_j} - \frac{p_j q_j}{M} \frac{\partial q_i/q_i}{\partial M/M}.$$

That is,

$$\eta_{ij} = \eta_{ij}^* - w_j \eta_i, \qquad i, j = 1, \ldots, n, \tag{2.3.19}$$

where

$$\eta_{ij}^* = \frac{\partial (\log q_i^*)}{\partial (\log p_j)}$$

is called the *compensated price elasticity of i with respect to the price of j.* If $\eta_{ij}^* > 0$ (< 0), then the pair of goods i and j are called *net substitutes* (*net complements*). If we sum both sides of (2.3.19) over $j = 1, \ldots, n$, and then use (2.3.17) and $\sum_{j=1}^{n} w_j$, the demand homogeneity (2.3.17) can also be expressed in terms of the compensated price elasticities as

$$\sum_{j=1}^{n} \eta_{ij}^* = 0, \qquad i = 1, \ldots, n. \tag{2.3.20}$$

Third Constraint

The third constraint is the *Slutsky symmetry*. This states that, when real income is held constant, the effect of an increase in the price of commodity j on the demand for commodity i is equal to the effect of a price increase of i on the demand for j. In other words, as the commodity subscripts can be interchanged, the substitution effects are symmetric in i and j:

$$\frac{\partial q_i^*}{\partial p_j} = \frac{\partial q_j^*}{\partial p_i}, \qquad i, j = 1, \ldots, n. \tag{2.3.21}$$

In elasticity form, this constraint becomes

$$w_i \eta_{ij}^* = w_j \eta_{ji}^*, \qquad i, j = 1, \ldots, n. \tag{2.3.22}$$

Fourth Constraint

The final constraint is that the $n \times n$ matrix of compensated price derivatives is negative semi-definite. That is, for any n-vector $\boldsymbol{x}$, the quadratic form is negative

$$x' \frac{\partial q^*}{\partial p'} x \leq 0 \quad \text{or} \quad \sum_{i=1}^{n} \sum_{j=1}^{n} x_i x_j \frac{\partial q_i^*}{\partial p_j} \leq 0. \tag{2.3.23}$$

If $\boldsymbol{x}$ is proportional to $\boldsymbol{p}$, using (2.3.20), it can easily be shown that the above quadratic equation is equal to zero. With (2.3.23), if $\boldsymbol{x} = \boldsymbol{e}_i$, a n-vector with 1 in the ith place and zeros in the rest, then

$$\boldsymbol{e}_i' \frac{\partial \boldsymbol{q}^*}{\partial \boldsymbol{p}'} \boldsymbol{e}_i = \frac{\partial q_i^*}{\partial p_i} < 0 \quad \text{or} \quad \eta_{ii}^* < 0, \tag{2.3.24}$$

where the second step follows from the negative semi-definiteness of $\partial q^* / \partial p'$. Hence, the implication is that an increase in the price of a commodity will never result in an increase in the demand for that commodity when real income is held constant.

Rearranging (2.3.20) gives

$$\sum_{j \neq i} \eta_{ij}^* = -\eta_{ii}^* > 0,$$

where the second step follows from (2.3.24) in elasticity form. This suggests that, on average, all pairs of goods are net substitutes.

Combining (2.3.20) and (2.3.22) gives $(1/w_i) \sum_{j=1}^{n} w_j \eta_{ji}^* = 0$. Multiplying this by w_i and exchanging subscripts gives

$$\sum_{i=1}^{n} w_i \eta_{ij}^* = 0, \quad j = 1, \ldots, n. \tag{2.3.25}$$

Rearranging (2.3.19) to give $\eta_{ij}^* = \eta_{ij} + w_j \eta_i$, and substituting in (2.3.25) gives

$$\sum_{i=1}^{n} w_i(\eta_{ij} + w_j\eta_i) = 0$$

or

$$\sum_{i=1}^{n} w_i\eta_{ij} + w_j = 0, \qquad j = 1, \ldots, n, \tag{2.3.26}$$

which follows from $\sum_{i=1}^{n} w_i\eta_i = \sum_{i=1}^{n} \theta_i = 1$. Equations (2.3.25) and (2.3.26) are known as *Cournot aggregation*.

2.4 Differential Approach to Demand Systems Derivation

Barten's Fundamental Matrix Equation

In a demand function, $q_1, \ldots, q_n$ and λ are the endogenous variables and $p_1, \ldots, p_n$ and M are the exogenous variables. This gives rise to the issue of how the values of endogenous variables respond to changes in the exogenous variables. The first-order conditions of (2.3.8) and (2.3.9) can be used to answer the above question.

Here, we first differentiate the budget constraint (2.3.9) with respect to p_j and M, deriving

$$\sum_{i=1}^{n} p_i \frac{\partial q_i}{\partial p_j} = -q_j, \quad j = 1, \ldots, n, \quad \sum_{i=1}^{n} p_i \frac{\partial q_i}{\partial M} = 1.$$

These can be expressed in matrix form as

$$\boldsymbol{p}'\frac{\partial \boldsymbol{q}}{\partial \boldsymbol{p}'} = -\boldsymbol{q}' \text{ and } \boldsymbol{p}'\frac{\partial \boldsymbol{q}}{\partial M} = 1, \tag{2.4.1}$$

where $\partial\boldsymbol{q}/\partial\boldsymbol{p}' = [\partial q_i/\partial p_j]$ is the $n \times n$ matrix of price derivatives of the demand functions and $\partial\boldsymbol{q}/\partial M = [\partial q_i/\partial M]$ is the vector of n income slopes of the demand functions.

Then, we differentiate the proportionality conditions (2.3.10) with respect to p_j and M, which gives

$$\sum_{k=1}^{n} \frac{\partial^2 u}{\partial q_i \partial q_k} \frac{\partial q_k}{\partial p_j} = \lambda\delta_{ij} + p_i \frac{\partial \lambda}{\partial p_j}, \quad i, j = 1, \ldots, n,$$

where δ_{ij} is the Kronecker delta ($= 1$ if $i = j$, 0 otherwise) and

$$\sum_{k=1}^{n} \frac{\partial^2 u}{\partial q_i \partial q_k} \frac{\partial q_k}{\partial M} = p_i \frac{\partial \lambda}{\partial M}, \quad i = 1, \ldots, n.$$

We write these in matrix form as

$$\boldsymbol{U}\frac{\partial \boldsymbol{q}}{\partial \boldsymbol{p}'} = \lambda \boldsymbol{I} + \boldsymbol{p}\frac{\partial \lambda}{\partial \boldsymbol{p}'} \quad \text{and} \quad \boldsymbol{U}\frac{\partial \boldsymbol{q}}{\partial M} = \frac{\partial \lambda}{\partial M}\boldsymbol{p}, \tag{2.4.2}$$

where **U** is the Hessian matrix defined by (2.3.6), $\boldsymbol{I}$ is the $n \times n$ identity matrix and $\partial\lambda/\partial\boldsymbol{p}' = [\partial\lambda/\partial p_i]$ is a row vector of order n.

Thirdly, we combine (2.4.1) and (2.4.2) and get,

$$\begin{bmatrix} \boldsymbol{U} & \boldsymbol{p} \\ \boldsymbol{p}' & \boldsymbol{0} \end{bmatrix} \begin{bmatrix} \partial \boldsymbol{q}/\partial M & \partial \boldsymbol{q}/\partial \boldsymbol{p}' \\ -\partial\lambda/\partial M & -\partial\lambda/\partial \boldsymbol{p}' \end{bmatrix} = \begin{bmatrix} \boldsymbol{0} & \lambda \boldsymbol{I} \\ 1 & -\boldsymbol{q}' \end{bmatrix}. \tag{2.4.3}$$

This equation is known as *Barten's fundamental matrix equation in consumption theory* (see Barten, 1964).

The matrix immediately to the left of the equal sign includes the derivatives of all endogenous variables with respect to all exogenous variables. The inverse of the matrix on the far left of (2.4.3) is

$$\begin{bmatrix} \boldsymbol{U} & \boldsymbol{p} \\ \boldsymbol{p}' & \boldsymbol{0} \end{bmatrix}^{-1} = \frac{1}{\boldsymbol{p}'\boldsymbol{U}^{-1}\boldsymbol{p}} \begin{bmatrix} \left(\boldsymbol{p}'\boldsymbol{U}^{-1}\boldsymbol{p}\right)\boldsymbol{U}^{-1} - \boldsymbol{U}^{-1}\boldsymbol{p}\left(\boldsymbol{U}^{-1}\boldsymbol{p}\right)' & \boldsymbol{U}^{-1}\boldsymbol{p} \\ \left(\boldsymbol{U}^{-1}\boldsymbol{p}\right)' & -1 \end{bmatrix}$$

and, using this inverse, gives the solution to (2.4.3) as

$$\begin{bmatrix} \partial \boldsymbol{q}/\partial M & \partial \boldsymbol{q}/\partial \boldsymbol{p}' \\ -\partial\lambda/\partial M & -\partial\lambda/\partial \boldsymbol{p}' \end{bmatrix} = \frac{1}{\boldsymbol{p}'\boldsymbol{U}^{-1}\boldsymbol{p}} \begin{bmatrix} \left(\boldsymbol{p}'\boldsymbol{U}^{-1}\boldsymbol{p}\right)\boldsymbol{U}^{-1} - \boldsymbol{U}^{-1}\boldsymbol{p}\left(\boldsymbol{U}^{-1}\boldsymbol{p}\right)' & \boldsymbol{U}^{-1}\boldsymbol{p} \\ \left(\boldsymbol{U}^{-1}\boldsymbol{p}\right)' & -1 \end{bmatrix} \begin{bmatrix} \boldsymbol{0} & \lambda \boldsymbol{I} \\ 1 & -\boldsymbol{q}' \end{bmatrix}$$

Carrying out the matrix multiplication block by block, we obtain

$$\frac{\partial \boldsymbol{q}}{\partial M} = \frac{1}{\boldsymbol{p}'\boldsymbol{U}^{-1}\boldsymbol{p}}\boldsymbol{U}^{-1}\boldsymbol{p} \tag{2.4.4}$$

$$\frac{\partial \boldsymbol{q}}{\partial \boldsymbol{p}'} = \lambda\boldsymbol{U}^{-1} - \frac{\lambda}{\boldsymbol{p}'\boldsymbol{U}^{-1}\boldsymbol{p}}\boldsymbol{U}^{-1}\boldsymbol{p}\left(\boldsymbol{U}^{-1}\boldsymbol{p}\right)' - \frac{1}{\boldsymbol{p}'\boldsymbol{U}^{-1}\boldsymbol{p}}\boldsymbol{U}^{-1}\boldsymbol{p}\boldsymbol{q}' \tag{2.4.5}$$

$$\frac{\partial \lambda}{\partial M} = \frac{1}{\boldsymbol{p}'\boldsymbol{U}^{-1}\boldsymbol{p}} \tag{2.4.6}$$

$$\frac{\partial \lambda}{\partial \boldsymbol{p}'} = -\frac{\lambda}{\boldsymbol{p}'\boldsymbol{U}^{-1}\boldsymbol{p}}\left(\boldsymbol{U}^{-1}\boldsymbol{p}\right)' - \frac{1}{\boldsymbol{p}'\boldsymbol{U}^{-1}\boldsymbol{p}}\boldsymbol{q}'. \tag{2.4.7}$$

To simplify the above expressions, we can use (2.4.6) to substitute for $\partial\lambda/\partial M$ for the reciprocal of $p'U^{-1}p$ in (2.4.4), (2.4.5), and (2.4.7). Equation (2.4.4) then becomes

$$\frac{\partial \boldsymbol{q}}{\partial M} = \frac{\partial\lambda}{\partial M}\boldsymbol{U}^{-1}\boldsymbol{p}. \tag{2.4.8}$$

Replacing $\boldsymbol{U}^{-1}\boldsymbol{p}$ in (2.4.5) and (2.4.7) with $\partial\boldsymbol{q}/\partial M$ and dividing by $\partial\lambda/\partial M$ will yield

$$\frac{\partial \boldsymbol{q}}{\partial \boldsymbol{p}'} = \lambda\boldsymbol{U}^{-1} - \frac{\lambda}{\partial\lambda/\partial M}\frac{\partial \boldsymbol{q}}{\partial M}\frac{\partial \boldsymbol{q}'}{\partial M} - \frac{\partial \boldsymbol{q}}{\partial M}\boldsymbol{q}' \tag{2.4.9}$$

$$\frac{\partial\lambda}{\partial \boldsymbol{p}'} = -\lambda\frac{\partial \boldsymbol{q}'}{\partial M} - \frac{\partial\lambda}{\partial M}\boldsymbol{q}'. \tag{2.4.10}$$

Equations (2.4.8) and (2.4.9) give the income and price derivatives of the demand functions. If we write Eq. (2.4.7) in scalar form, we get

$$\frac{\partial q_i}{\partial p_j} = \lambda u^{ij} - \frac{\lambda}{\partial\lambda/\partial M}\frac{\partial q_i}{\partial M}\frac{\partial q_j}{\partial M} - \frac{\partial q_i}{\partial M}q_j, \quad i, j = 1, \ldots, n, \tag{2.4.11}$$

where u^{ij} is the (i, j)th element of U^{-1}.

Equation (2.4.11) shows the total effect of a change in p_j on q_i, with income and other prices held constant; it is made up of two terms, the *income effect* and the *total substitution effect*. Here, $-q_j(\partial q_i/\partial M)$ is the income effect of the price change. The total substitution effect, the response of q_i to a change in p_j with real income (and the other prices) held constant, consists of the *specific substitution effect* and the *general substitution effect*. The specific substitution effect is λu^{ij} and it deals with the interaction of goods i and j in the utility function. The general substitution effect is $-\frac{\lambda}{\partial\lambda/\partial M}\frac{\partial q_i}{\partial M}\frac{\partial q_j}{\partial M}$ with the terminology from Houthakker (1960) and is concerned with the competition of all goods for an extra dollar of a representative consumer's income.

For future reference, we write Eq. (2.4.8) in scalar form as

$$\frac{\partial q_i}{\partial M} = \frac{\partial\lambda}{\partial M}\sum_{j=1}^{n} u^{ij}p_j, \qquad i = 1, \ldots, n. \tag{2.4.12}$$

Differential Demand System

The differential approach to demand analysis was introduced by Theil (1965), Barten (1964) and explored by Theil (1967, 1975/76, 1980). This approach is different from other approaches discussed in this chapter because it requires no algebraic specification of the utility function, the indirect utility functions nor of the cost function. Therefore, the coefficients of the demand equations need not be constant.

The solution of a fundamental matrix equation is used to derive a general system of differential demand equations.

The total differential of (2.3.11) is

$$dq_i = \frac{\partial q_i}{\partial M} dM + \sum_{j=1}^{n} \frac{\partial q_i}{\partial p_j} dp_j, \quad i = 1, \ldots, n.$$

Multiplying both sides of the above equation by p_i/M and using $w_i = p_i q_i/M$, it is transformed to a logarithmic-differential form

$$w_i d(\log q_i) = \frac{\partial (p_i q_i)}{\partial M} d(\log M) + \sum_{j=1}^{n} \frac{p_i p_j}{M} \frac{\partial q_i}{\partial p_j} d(\log p_j), \quad i = 1, \ldots, n. \tag{2.4.13}$$

The second term to the right of the above equation can be expressed by substituting (2.4.12) for $\partial q_i/\partial p_j$ to give

$$\sum_{j=1}^{n} \frac{p_i p_j}{M} \frac{\partial q_i}{\partial p_j} d(\log p_j) = \sum_{j=1}^{n} \frac{p_i p_j}{M} \left[\lambda u^{ij} - \frac{\lambda}{\partial \lambda/\partial M} \frac{\partial q_i}{\partial M} \frac{\partial q_j}{\partial M} - \frac{\partial q_i}{\partial M} q_j \right] d(\log p_j).$$

Substituting this in (2.4.12) and rearranging it gives

$$\begin{aligned} w_i d(\log q_i) = {} & \frac{\partial (p_i q_i)}{\partial M} \left[d(\log M) - \sum_{j=1}^{n} w_j d(\log p_j) \right] \\ & + \sum_{j=1}^{n} \left[\frac{\lambda p_i p_j u^{ij}}{M} - \frac{\lambda/M}{\partial \lambda/\partial M} \frac{\partial (p_i q_i)}{\partial M} \frac{\partial (p_j q_j)}{\partial M} \right] d(\log p_j). \end{aligned} \tag{2.4.14}$$

In view of (2.2.11) and (2.2.13), the term in square brackets on the right of the above is the Divisia volume index $d(\log Q)$; using (2.2.13), we derive

$$\frac{\partial (p_i q_i)}{\partial M} \left[d(\log M) - \sum_{j=1}^{n} w_j d(\log p_j) \right] = \theta_i d(\log Q). \tag{2.4.15}$$

To simplify the price substitution term of (2.4.14), we define

$$\phi = \frac{\lambda/M}{\partial \lambda/\partial M} = \left[\frac{\partial \log \lambda}{\partial \log M} \right]^{-1} \tag{2.4.16}$$

as the reciprocal of the income elasticity of the marginal utility of income or, in short, *income flexibility*. We also define

$$v_{ij} = \frac{\lambda}{M} p_i p_j u^{ij}, \quad i, j = 1, \ldots, n, \tag{2.4.17}$$

which satisfy

$$\sum_{j=1}^{n} v_{ij} = \phi\theta_i, \quad i = 1, \ldots, n. \tag{2.4.18}$$

The substitution term of (2.4.14) can then be expressed as

$$\sum_{j=1}^{n} \left[\frac{\lambda p_i p_j u^{ij}}{M} - \frac{\lambda/M}{\partial\lambda/\partial M} \frac{\partial(p_i q_i)}{\partial M} \frac{\partial(p_j q_j)}{\partial M} \right] d(\log p_j)$$

$$= \sum_{j=1}^{n} v_{ij} \left[d(\log p_j) - d(\log P') \right], \tag{2.4.19}$$

where

$$d(\log P') = \sum_{i=1}^{n} \theta_i d(\log p_i), \tag{2.4.20}$$

is the Frisch (1932) *price index* which uses marginal share as the weight. Therefore, this index differs from the Divisia price index (2.2.13), which uses budget shares as a weight.

Demand Equations in Relative Prices

Using (2.4.15) and (2.4.19) in (2.4.13), the demand equation for good i becomes

$$w_i d(\log q_i) = \theta_i d(\log Q) + \sum_{j=1}^{n} v_{ij} d\left[\log \frac{p_j}{P'} \right], \tag{2.4.21}$$

where $d[\log(p_j/P')] = d(\log p_j) - d(\log P')$, $d(\log P') = \sum_{i=1}^{n} \theta_i d(\log p_i)$. Equation (2.4.21) is known as the *differential demand system in relative prices*.

The variable on the left of (2.4.21) has two interpretations. Firstly, it is the quantity component of the change in the ith budget share. This interpretation can be verified by taking the differential of$w_i = p_i q_i / M$,

$$dw_i = w_i d(\log p_i) + w_i d(\log q_i) - w_i d(\log M).$$

It is only the quantity component of this change which is endogenous from a consumer's viewpoint. The second interpretation is the contribution of a good i to the Divisia volume index, $d(\log Q)$, defined in (2.2.12).

The first term to the right of (2.4.21) gives the effect of real income on the demand for good i. This term is a multiple θ_i of the Divisia volume index $d(\log Q)$. This volume index equals $d(\log M) - d(\log P)$, where $d(\log P)$ is the Divisia price index, so it follows that the Divisia price index transforms a change in money income into a change in real income. Furthermore, as the Divisia price index is the budget-share-weighted average of the n price log-changes, it follows that this index measures the income effect of the n price changes on the demand for the ith good.

The second term on the right of (2.4.21), $\sum_j v_{ij} d[\log(p_j/P')]$ deals with the effect of relative prices. The Frisch price index acts as a deflator of each price change, so that we refer to $d[\log(p_j/P')]$ as the change in the *Frisch-deflated price of j*.

In the next section, we show that the substitution term can be written as the difference between $\sum_j v_{ij} d(\log p_j)$, the specific substitution effects of the n prices on the demand for good i, and $\phi\theta_i d(\log P')$, the general substitution effect. As such, the general substitution effect acts as the deflator of the specific effect by transforming absolute prices into Frisch-deflated prices.

In the substitution term of (2.4.21), v_{ij} is the coefficient of the jth relative price, called the (i, j)th price coefficient. These price coefficients satisfy $\sum_i \sum_j v_{ij} = \phi$, which follows from (2.4.18). If $v_{ij} > 0$, then an increase in the Frisch-deflated price of j causes the consumption of i to increase. Consequently, we follow Houthakker (1960) and define goods i and j as specific substitutes (complements) if $v_{ij} > 0$ (< 0). We can show that income flexibility ϕ is negative, using Eqs. (2.4.17) and (2.4.18)

$$\sum_{j=1}^{n} \frac{\lambda}{M} p_i p_j u^{ij} = \phi\theta_i, \quad i = 1, \ldots, n.$$

In view of $\sum_i \theta_i = 1$, summing both sides of the above over $i = 1, \ldots, n$ gives

$$\phi = \frac{\lambda}{M} \sum_{i=1}^{n} \sum_{j=1}^{n} p_i p_j u^{ij}. \tag{2.4.22}$$

The right-hand side of the above equation is proportional to a quadratic form with matrix $\boldsymbol{U}^{-1}$ and vector $\boldsymbol{p}$. In view of (2.3.6), this matrix is negative definite; therefore, the quadratic form is negative. As the factor of proportionality, λ/M on the right of (2.4.22) is positive, so we can conclude that $\phi < 0$.

Demand Equations in Absolute Prices

We now derive the demand system in terms of absolute prices. The substitution term of Eq. (2.4.21) is formulated in terms of deflated prices. We use (2.4.21) to express the substitution term in absolute (or undeflated) prices as

$$\sum_{j=1}^{n} v_{ij} d\left[\log \frac{p_j}{P'}\right] = \sum_{j=1}^{n} \pi_{ij} d(\log p_j),$$

where

$$\pi_{ij} = \left(v_{ij} - \phi\theta_i\theta_j\right), \quad i, j = 1, \ldots, n. \tag{2.4.23}$$

Equation (2.4.23) is the (i, j)th *Slutsky coefficient*. This coefficient gives the total substitution effect on the demand for good i of a change in the jth price. It can be verified that $\left[\pi_{ij}\right]$ is a symmetric negative semi-definite $n \times n$ matrix with rank $n - 1$.

Using the above yields the *demand equation for good i in terms of absolute prices* as

$$w_i d(\log q_i) = \theta_i d(\log Q) + \sum_{j=1}^{n} \pi_{ij} d\left(\log p_j\right) \tag{2.4.24}$$

Dividing both sides of (2.4.24) by w_i gives the income and compensated price elasticities as

$$\eta_i = \frac{\theta_i}{w_i} \quad \text{and} \quad \eta_{ij}^* = \frac{\pi_{ij}}{w_i}, \quad i, j = 1, \ldots, n. \tag{2.4.25}$$

Demand Equations Under Preference Independence

The number of unknown coefficients in a general system of demand equations is of the order of n^2, where n is the number of commodities. This number of coefficients can only be estimated precisely with data when n is very small. Even for moderate-sized systems (n in the vicinity of 6), it is impossible to estimate such a large number of coefficients from the data as they are usually observed. Here, one possible identifying restriction is *preference independence*. In that case, the consumer's utility function is the sum of n subutility functions, one for each good. Thus, under preference independence, the utility function takes the form of

$$U(q_1, q_2, \ldots, q_n) = \sum_{i=1}^{n} u_i(q_i), \tag{2.4.26}$$

implying that the marginal utility of good i is independent of the consumption of good j, $j \neq i$.

Preference independence could be a reasonable working hypothesis for the commodities that are fairly broad groups, such as food, housing, clothing, and so forth. The total utility is then obtained from the utility derived from food, clothing, housing, etc. These commodity groups can be interpreted as representing the basic wants of the consumer which, in turn, could be expected to exhibit little interaction in the utility function. The Johansen (1969) utility function is a special case of the above (2.4.26), please see Eq. (A.2.8) in Appendix.

Under preference independence, the Hessian matrix $\mathbf{U}$ is an $n \times n$ diagonal matrix, as $u_{ij} = 0$ for $i \neq j$. This also implies that, $v_{ij} = 0$ for $i \neq j$ and Eq. (2.4.18) reduces to $v_{ii} = \phi\theta_i$, so that the demand equation in relative prices (2.4.21) takes the form

$$w_i d(\log q_i) = \theta_i d(\log Q) + \phi\theta_i d\left[\log \frac{p_i}{P'}\right] \tag{2.4.27}$$

That is, under preference independence, only the own-Frisch-deflated price appears in each demand equation, ruling out the possibility of either a specific substitute or complement. Moreover, under preference independence, the $[v_{ij}]$ matrix is a negative definite $n \times n$ diagonal matrix with diagonal elements $\phi\theta_1, \ldots, \phi\theta_n$ and all the off-diagonal elements are zero. Since each marginal share θ_i must be positive, the *hypothesis of preference independence rules out inferior goods*.

2.5 The Rotterdam Model

Demand systems in relative and absolute prices have been formulated to account for infinitesimal changes. However, most economic data available are in finite *time intervals* such as annual, quarterly, or monthly. In order to convert the infinitesimal changes in the above relative and absolute price versions of the demand systems into finite-change form, and assuming the coefficients are constant over the period of observation, the Rotterdam model was introduced by Theil (1965) and Barten (1964). The *finite-change version of the model in relative prices* is represented as

$$\overline{w}_{it} Dq_{it} = \theta_i DQ_t + \sum_{j=1}^{n} v_{ij}\left(Dp_{jt} - DP'_t\right), \tag{2.5.1}$$

where $DQ_t = \sum_{i=1}^{n} \overline{w}_{it} Dq_{it}$ is the finite-change version of the Divisia volume index and $DP'_t = \sum_{i=1}^{n} \theta_i Dp_{it}$ is the finite-change version of the *Frisch price index.*

When the coefficients of the above equations θ_i and v_{ij} are treated as constants, it is known as the ith *demand equation of the relative price version of the Rotterdam model.* As noted earlier, the $n \times n$ matrix of price coefficients $[v_{ij}]$ is symmetric and negative definite. These coefficients also satisfy (2.4.18). Constraint (2.4.18) and the constancy of the coefficients v_{ij} and θ_i imply that ϕ is also a constant in the model.

The second version of the Rotterdam model is the *absolute price version.* The finite-change version of the demand equation in absolute prices is

$$\overline{w}_{it} Dq_{it} = \theta_i DQ_t + \sum_{j=1}^{n} \pi_{ij} Dp_{jt}, \tag{2.5.2}$$

where π_{ij} is the Slutsky coefficient defined previously as $\pi_{ij} = \left(v_{ij} - \phi\theta_i\theta_j\right), i, j = 1, \ldots, n.$

When the coefficients θ_i and π_{ij} are specified as constants, (2.5.2) is known as the ith *equation of the absolute price version of the Rotterdam model.* Equation (2.5.2) should satisfy two theoretical restrictions on the parameters. These are (i) Slutsky symmetry and (ii) demand homogeneity.

Slutsky symmetry requires,

$$\pi_{ij} = \pi_{ji}, \quad i, j = 1, \ldots, n. \tag{2.5.3}$$

Demand homogeneity follows from $\sum_{j=1}^{n} v_{ij} = \phi\theta_i$ and $\pi_{ij} = v_{ij} - \phi\theta_i\theta_j$ and requires

$$\sum_{j=1}^{n} \pi_{ij} = 0, \quad i = 1, \ldots, n. \tag{2.5.4}$$

This homogeneity postulates that changing all prices and income in the same proportion will not affect the quantities of goods demanded. As noted earlier in (2.4.23), the Slutsky matrix $[\pi_{ij}]$ is symmetric negative semi-definite with rank $n - 1$.

The Rotterdam model in absolute prices is linear in its parameters, unlike the Rotterdam model in relative prices, which is nonlinear in its parameters. This makes estimation of absolute price version and hypothesis testing straightforward. However, as the number of goods (n) increases, the number of the π_{ij} parameters in the absolute price version increases rapidly. Therefore, for larger models, the relative price version of the model, with suitable restrictions on the v_{ij} parameters can be used. These restrictions assume that certain goods do not interact in the utility function. A special case of this is preference independence where no good interacts with any other. Under preference independence, the Hessian matrix $\mathbf{U}$ is an $n \times n$ diagonal matrix, as $u_{ij} = 0$ for $i \neq j$. This also implies that $v_{ij} = 0$ for $i \neq j$ and $\sum_{j=1}^{n} v_{ij} = \phi\theta_i$, which reduces to $v_{ii} = \phi\theta_i$; the finite-change version of the demand system under preference independence takes the form

$$\overline{w}_{it} Dq_{it} = \theta_i DQ_t + \phi\theta_i \left(Dp_{it} - DP_t'\right), \quad i = 1, \ldots, n, \tag{2.5.5}$$

where $DP_t' = \sum_{j=1}^{n} \theta_j Dp_{jt}$. The number of unconstrained coefficients in (2.5.5) is n comprised of $n - 1$ unconstrained $\theta_i's$ (one is constrained by $\sum_i \theta_i = 1$) and ϕ.

2.6 A Further Parameterization of the Rotterdam Model

In Eqs. (2.5.1), (2.5.2), and (2.5.5), θ_i is specified as a constant. However, this assumption can be relaxed by reparametrizing the marginal shares thus:

$$\theta_{it} = \beta_i + \overline{w}_{it} \tag{2.6.1}$$

Accordingly, the marginal share exceeds the budget share by a constant. As the budget share $\overline{w}_{it}$ is not constant and varies over time, neither is the marginal share defined in (2.6.1).

For example, if we substitute θ_{it} from (2.6.1) in (2.5.2), we get

$$\overline{w}_{it}(Dq_{it} - DQ_t) = \beta_i DQ_t + \sum_{j=1}^{n} \pi_{ij} Dp_{jt} \quad i = 1, \ldots, n \tag{2.6.2}$$

Equation (2.6.2) is known as Working's parameterization of the Rotterdam model in absolute prices. Note that the only difference between (2.6.2) and (2.5.2) is the variable on the left side of the equation. The income elasticity, based on model (2.6.2), is given by

$$\eta_{it} = \frac{\theta_{it}}{\overline{w}_{it}} = 1 + \frac{\beta_i}{\overline{w}_{it}} \tag{2.6.3}$$

Under Working's model parameterization (2.6.1), the preference independence version of the Rotterdam demand system (2.5.5) takes the form

$$\overline{w}_{it}(Dq_{it} - DQ_t) = \beta_i DQ_t + \phi(\overline{w}_{it} + \beta_i)\left[Dp_{it} - \sum_{j=1}^{n} (\overline{w}_{jt} + \beta_j) Dp_{jt}\right] \tag{2.6.4}$$

For brevity, we shall refer to (2.6.4) as *Working's model under preference independence*. Equation (2.6.4) is also termed the CBS/SI model by Keller (1984).

2.7 Other Differential Demand Systems

In the last section, we parameterized the infinitesimal change of the general demand system to apply to finite change data. In this section, we introduce alternative parameterizations to derive the simpler demand systems developed by Keller (1984) and Selvanathan (1985).

In Sect. 2.4, we derived a system of differential demand equations and, in Sect. 2.5, we obtained a finite-change version of this demand system (Rotterdam model). In general, the number of price coefficients to be estimated, in relative or absolute prices, in this system is of the order n^2. When n is large it becomes impractical to estimate the number of coefficients with most data sets. The usual resolution to this problem is to impose constraints on the structure of preferences, such as preference independence, to limit the number of free coefficients.

In this section, we present an alternate approach. Instead of resolving this problem using the utility function, we formulate constraints on the price coefficients directly.

Of course, the difference in approaches should not be over-emphasized because constraints on the utility function imply constraints on the price coefficients and vice versa. The approach in this section was initiated by Keller (1984) and Selvanathan (1985) in the context of differential demand equations.

We now consider Eqs. (2.5.1), (2.5.2) and (2.5.5). If we divide both sides of (2.6.1) by $\overline{w}_{it}$, we get $\theta_i/\overline{w}_{it}$ as the income elasticity of demand for good *i* and $F_{ij} = v_{ij}/\overline{w}_{it}$ as the (*i*, *j*)th *Frisch-price elasticity*. This F_{ij} is the elasticity of demand for good *i* with respect to the Frisch-deflated price of *j*; this elasticity involves a relative, or deflated, price. Under preference independence, Eq. (2.5.5) implies that $F_{ij} = 0$ for $i \neq j$ and $F_{ii} = \phi\theta_i/\overline{w}_{it}$, which is ϕ times the income elasticity. Using Eq. (2.5.2), the conventional compensated, or Slutsky, price elasticity of demand for *i* with respect to the price of *j* is $\pi_{ij}/\overline{w}_{it}$. This elasticity involves an absolute or undeflated price.

Equation (2.5.2) for $i = 1, \ldots, n$ is the absolute price version of the Rotterdam model. The budget constraint implies that one equation is redundant, so we consider (2.5.2) for $i = 1, \ldots, n - 1$. This model contains $n - 1$ free marginal shares and $(n - 1) \times n$ Slutsky coefficients. The homogeneity constraint (2.5.4) reduces the number of Slutsky coefficients to $(n - 1) \times (n - 1) = (n - 1)^2$, while symmetry (2.5.3) further reduces this number to $1/2\, n(n - 1)$.

For example, if *n* is 10, and with no restrictions, the total number of parameters to be estimated is $(n - 1) = 9$ marginal shares, plus $(n - 1) \times n = 9 \times 10 = 90$ Slutsky coefficients, which is 99. If we impose the homogeneity constraint, this number reduces to $9 + (10 - 1)^2 = 90$. In addition, if we impose symmetry, this number further reduces to $9 + 1/2\ (10 \times 9) = 54$. Furthermore, if we impose preference independence, then the number of parameters to be estimated will only be $9 + 1 = 10$.

Thus, when $n = 10$, the number of parameters to be estimated can be reduced from 99 to 10, a substantial economy in parameterization. The cost of this gain is that the preference independence hypothesis is a fairly restrictive assumption. This is especially so in that preference independence carries with it the implication that the Frisch own-price elasticities F_{ii} are proportional to the corresponding income elasticities.

Therefore, the choice is to use the absolute price version of the Rotterdam model, with too many parameters to estimate, especially for particularly large systems, or to solve the problem by invoking the assumption of preference independence with its rigid structure of price responses. Keller (1984) tried to resolve this dilemma by introducing a variant of the Rotterdam model with more parameters than (2.5.5), albeit one with no link between income and price elasticities.

Taking the differential of $w_i = p_i q_i/M$ will give

$$dw_i = w_i d(\log q_i) + w_i d(\log p_i) - w_i d(\log M). \tag{2.7.1}$$

Substituting $w_i d(\log q_i)$ from Eq. (2.4.24) into (2.7.1) will give

$$dw_i = \theta_i d(\log Q) + \sum_{j=1}^{n} \pi_{ij} d(\log p_j) + w_i d(\log p_i) - w_i d(\log M)$$

$$+ w_i d(\log P) - w_i \sum_{j=1}^{n} w_j d(\log p_j),$$

where we added and subtracted the same term, $w_i d(\log P)$, on the right-hand side and used $d(\log P) = \sum_j w_j d(\log p_j)$. Furthermore, recognizing that

$$d(\log M) - d(\log P) = d(\log(M/P)) = d(\log Q),$$

we can simplify the right-hand side terms as

$$dw_i = (\theta_i - w_i) d(\log Q) + \sum_{j=1}^{n} \left(\pi_{ij} + w_i \delta_{ij} - w_i w_j\right) d\left(\log p_j\right)$$

which can be written as

$$dw_i = \beta_i d(\log Q) + \sum_{j=1}^{n} \gamma_{ij} d\left(\log p_j\right), \tag{2.7.2}$$

where

$$\beta_i = \theta_i - w_i \tag{2.7.3}$$

and

$$\gamma_{ij} = \pi_{ij} + w_i \delta_{ij} - w_i w_j. \tag{2.7.4}$$

Equation (2.7.2) is the differential version of the AIDS model, please see Eq. (A.2.34) in Appendix. If we reparameterise (2.4.24), using (2.7.3) in the form $\theta_i = \beta_i + w_i$, we derive

$$w_i\left[d(\log q_i) - d(\log Q)\right] = \beta_i d(\log Q) + \sum_{j=1}^{n} \pi_{ij} d\left(\log p_j\right). \tag{2.7.5}$$

The above Eq. (2.7.5)has been named by Keller and van Driel (1985), of the Dutch Central Bureau of Statistics (CBS), as the *CBS demand system*. This system includes the AIDS income coefficient, β_i, and the Rotterdam price coefficient, π_{ij}. It is worth noting that Eq. (2.6.2) is the finite change version of (2.7.5).

After rearranging, Eq. (2.7.2) can be written as

$$dw_i + w_i d(\log Q) = \theta_i d(\log Q) + \sum_{j=1}^{n} \gamma_{ij} d(\log p_j). \tag{2.7.6}$$

Equation (2.7.6) has the Rotterdam income coefficients and the AIDS price coefficients as constants. This equation was termed the *NBR system* in Neves' (1987) study.

The restrictions on the new coefficients, β_i's and γ_{ij}'s, are

$$\sum_{i=1}^{n} \beta_i = 0; \quad \sum_{i=1}^{n} \gamma_{ij} = 0; \quad \sum_{j=1}^{n} \gamma_{ij} = 0; \quad \gamma_{ij} = \gamma_{ji}$$

and $\left[\gamma_{ij} + w_i w_j - w_i - w_i \delta_{ij}\right]$ is negative semi-definite. To reduce the number of parameters, π_{ij}'s, which is in the order of n^2, Keller (1984) proposed the following decomposition for π_{ij}:

$$\pi_{ij} = \lambda\left(\Psi_i \delta_{ij} - \Psi_i \Psi_j\right). \tag{2.7.7}$$

Under Eq. (2.7.7), Eq. (2.7.5) becomes

$$w_i\left[d(\log q_i) - d(\log Q)\right] = \beta_i d(\log Q) + \lambda \Psi_i\left[d(\log p_i) - d(\log P_\Psi)\right] \tag{2.7.8}$$

where $d(\log P_\Psi) = \sum_j \Psi_j d(\log p_j)$. Keller (1984) refers to Eq. (2.7.8) as the *CBS substitution independence (CBS/SI) model.*

With specification (2.7.3), the model under preference independence (2.4.27) becomes

$$w_i\left[d(\log q_i) - d(\log Q)\right] = \beta_i d(\log Q) + \phi(\beta_i + w_i)\left[d(\log p_i) - d(\log P')\right], \tag{2.7.9}$$

where $d(\log P') = \sum_j (\beta_j + w_j) d(\log p_j)$. Keller and van Driel (1985) refer to Eq. (2.7.9) as the *CBS preference independence (CBS/PI) model.* Note that should $\Psi_i = \theta_i = \beta_i + w_i$ and $\lambda = \phi$, then Eq. (2.7.8) transforms into (2.7.9). If $\Psi_i = w_i$; Eq. (2.7.8) then becomes

$$w_i\left[d(\log q_i) - d(\log Q)\right] = \beta_i d(\log Q) + \lambda w_i\left[d(\log p_i) - d(\log P)\right] \tag{2.7.10}$$

derived by Selvanathan (1985) which is the *even simpler demand system.*

As most applications of the above models are with finite-change data, we use the finite-change versions of these models for the applications. The finite-change versions of the five demand systems, the CBS demand system (2.7.5), the NBR demand system (2.7.6), the CBS/SI demand system (2.7.8), the CBS/PI demand system (2.7.9), and Selvanathan's even simpler demand system (2.7.10), can be written as follows:

CBS Demand System

$$\overline{w}_{it}(Dq_{it} - DQ_t) = \beta_i DQ_t + \sum_{j=1}^{n} \pi_{ij} Dp_{jt} \quad (2.7.11)$$

NBR Demand System

$$\Delta w_{it} + \overline{w}_{it} DQ_t = \theta_i DQ_t + \sum_{j=1}^{n} \gamma_{ij} Dp_{jt} \quad (2.7.12)$$

CBS/SI Demand System

$$\overline{w}_{it}(Dq_{it} - DQ_t) = \beta_i DQ_t + \lambda\psi_i(Dp_{it} - DP_{\psi t}) \quad (2.7.13)$$

CBS/PI Demand System

$$\overline{w}_{it}(Dq_{it} - DQ_t) = \beta_i DQ_t + \phi(\beta_i + \overline{w}_{it})\left(Dp_{it} - DP_t'\right) \quad (2.7.14)$$

where $DP_t' = \sum_j (\beta_j + \overline{w}_{jt}) Dp_{jt}$.

Even Simpler Demand System

$$\overline{w}_{it}(Dq_{it} - DQ_t) = \beta_i DQ_t + \lambda\overline{w}_{it}(Dp_{it} - DP_t) \quad (2.7.15)$$

where $DP_t = \sum_j \overline{w}_{jt} Dp_{jt}$.

2.8 Block Independence and Group Demand Equations

A weaker version of preference independence is *block independence*. Under block independence, the additive specification is applied to groups of goods rather than to individual goods. Let the n goods be divided into $G < n$ groups, written as $S_1, \ldots, S_G$, such that each good belongs to only one group. Furthermore, let the consumer's preferences be such that the utility function is the sum of G group utility functions, each involving the quantities of only one group.

$$u = \sum_{g=1}^{G} u_g\left(\boldsymbol{q}_g\right) \quad (2.8.1)$$

where $\boldsymbol{q}_g$ is the vector of q_i's that fall under S_g. Under (2.4.26), the marginal utility of a good depends only on the consumption of goods belonging to the same group. When the goods are numbered appropriately, the Hessian of the utility function and its inverse become block-diagonal. Accordingly, this specification (2.4.26) is known as *block-independent preferences*.

In view of (2.4.17), block independence implies that $[v_{ij}]$ is block-diagonal. Therefore, if $i \in S_g$, Eqs. (2.4.18) and (2.4.21) can now be written as

$$w_i d(\log q_i) = \theta_i d(\log Q) + \sum_{j \in S_g} v_{ij} d\left[\log \frac{p_j}{P'}\right], \tag{2.8.2}$$

$$\sum_{j \in S_g} v_{ij} = \phi\theta_i, \quad i \in S_g. \tag{2.8.3}$$

Block independence thus implies that the only deflated prices that appear in the ith demand equation are those of goods belonging to the same group as the commodity in question. As $v_{ij} = 0$ for i and j in different groups, under block independence, no good is a specific substitute or complement of any good that belongs to a different group.

The group budget share and the group marginal share can be written as

$$W_g = \sum_{i \in S_g} w_i \quad \text{and} \quad \Theta_g = \sum_{i \in S_g} \theta_i, \qquad g = 1, 2, \ldots, G. \tag{2.8.4}$$

The group budget share gives the proportion of total consumer expenditure allocated to group S_g. The group marginal share, Θ_g, measures the increase in expenditure on S_g resulting from a \$1 increase in income. The conditional budget share and conditional marginal share for the group S_g are defined as

$$w'_i = \frac{w_i}{W_g} \quad \text{and} \quad \theta'_i = \frac{\theta_i}{\Theta_g}, \quad i \in S_g. \tag{2.8.5}$$

Using (2.8.4) and (2.8.5), we can easily verify that

$$\sum_{i \in S_g} w'_i = 1 \quad \text{and} \quad \sum_{i \in S_g} \theta'_i = 1. \tag{2.8.6}$$

Summing both sides of (2.8.3) over $i \in S_g$ and using (2.8.4), we obtain

$$\sum_{i \in S_g} \sum_{j \in S_g} v_{ij} = \phi\Theta_g. \tag{2.8.7}$$

Since the matrix $[v_{ij}]$ is negative definite, we have $\sum_{i \in S_g} \sum_{j \in S_g} v_{ij} < 0$. Accordingly, since $\phi < 0$, the group marginal share is always non-negative. This means that block independence implies that, although individual members of a group can be inferior, no group as a whole can be inferior.

The group Divisia quantity, Divisia price and Frisch price indexes, respectively, can be defined as

$$d\left(\log Q_g\right) = \sum_{i \in S_g} w_i' d(\log q_i) \tag{2.8.8}$$

$$d\left(\log P_g\right) = \sum_{i \in S_g} w_i' d(\log p_i) \tag{2.8.9}$$

and

$$d\left(\log P_g'\right) = \sum_{i \in S_g} \theta_i' d(\log p_i). \tag{2.8.10}$$

These three indexes will aggregate consistently because the group budget-share-weighted average of $d(\log Q_1)$, ..., $d(\log Q_G)$ equals the Divisia volume index of all the n goods $d(\log Q)$; the group budget-share-weighted average of $d(\log P_1), \ldots, d(\log P_G)$ equals the Divisia price index of all n goods, $d(\log P)$; the group marginal-share-weighted average of $d(\log P_1')$, ..., $d(\log P_G')$ equals the overall Frisch price index $d(\log P')$. That is,

$$d(\log Q) = \sum_{g=1}^{G} W_g d\left(\log Q_g\right) \quad d(\log P) = \sum_{g=1}^{G} W_g d\left(\log P_g\right)$$

$$d\left(\log P'\right) = \sum_{g=1}^{G} \theta_g d\left(\log P_g'\right).$$

Under block independence, summing over $i \in S_g$ on both sides of Eq. (2.8.2) yields the following demand equation for the group S_g as a whole.

$$W_g d\left(\log Q_g\right) = \Theta_g d(\log Q) + \sum_{i \in S_g} \sum_{j \in S_g} v_{ij} d\left[\log \frac{p_j}{P'}\right], \quad g = 1, \ldots, G. \tag{2.8.11}$$

Our objective is to simplify the price substitution term of this equation. As v_{ij} is symmetric in i and j, Eq. (2.8.3) can be expressed as

$$\sum_{i \in S_g} v_{ij} = \phi\theta_j = \phi\Theta_g\theta_j', \quad j \in S_g,$$

so that

$$\sum_{i \in S_g} \sum_{j \in S_g} v_{ij} d\left[\log \frac{p_j}{P'}\right] = \phi\Theta_g \sum_{j \in S_g} \theta_{ij}' d\left[\log \frac{p_j}{P'}\right] = \phi\Theta_g d\left[\log \frac{P_g'}{P'}\right].$$

Accordingly, Eq. (2.8.11) can be expressed as

$$W_g d(\log Q_g) = \Theta_g d(\log Q) + \phi\Theta_g d\left[\log \frac{P'_g}{P'}\right], \quad g = 1, \ldots, G. \tag{2.8.12}$$

Equation (2.8.12) is the *group* or *composite demand equation* for S_g as a group. It shows that, under block independence, the demand for a group of goods as a whole depends on real income, $d(\log Q)$, and the relative price of the group, $d(\log P'_g/P')$. This relative price is the *Frisch-deflated Frisch price index* of the group. It should be noted that the relative prices of goods outside the group in question play no role in Eq. (2.8.12).

Dividing both sides of Eq. (2.8.12) by W_g yields the group income elasticity of demand and the own-price elasticity for the group as

$$\eta_g = \frac{\Theta_g}{W_g} \quad \text{and} \quad \eta_{gg} = \frac{\phi\Theta_g}{W_g}, \quad g = 1, \ldots, G. \tag{2.8.13}$$

The group price elasticity in (2.8.13) is the elasticity of the Divisia volume index of the group with respect to the Frisch-deflated Frisch price index of the group.

2.9 Conditional Demand Equations

As there are G groups of commodities, there will be G composite demand equations, one for each group for each form of Eq. (2.8.12). These equations will give the allocation of income to each of the G groups with the allocation depending only on income and the G relative prices of the groups. Hence, given the demand for a group, the question will be how expenditure will be allocated to the commodities within the group. This question can be answered by the *conditional demand equations.*

We proceed by analysing the form of the conditional demand equations under the assumption of block independence. First, we rearrange (2.8.12) to give

$$d(\log Q) = \frac{W_g}{\Theta_g} d(\log Q_g) - \phi d\left[\log \frac{P'_g}{P'}\right]. \tag{2.9.1}$$

From Eq. (2.4.23) in Sect. 2.8, we know that $\pi_{ij} = (\upsilon_{ij} - \phi\theta_i\theta_j), ij = 1, \ldots, n$. The price coefficients are symmetric in i and j for commodities belonging to the same group

$$\upsilon_{ij} = \upsilon_{ji}, \quad i, j \in S_g. \tag{2.9.2}$$

All the υ_{ij}'s within S_g are also constrained by (2.8.3), namely

$$\sum_{j\in g} v_{ij} = \phi\theta_i = \phi\Theta_g\theta_i', \quad i \in S_g. \tag{2.9.3}$$

In order to derive the conditional demand equation, we first substitute the right side of (2.9.1) for $d(\log Q)$ in the demand Eq. (2.8.2) under block independence, giving

$$\begin{aligned} w_i d(\log q_i) &= \theta_i\left[\frac{W_g}{\Theta_g}d(\log Q_g) - \phi d\left[\log\frac{P_g'}{P'}\right]\right] + \sum_{j\in S_g} v_{ij} d\left[\log\frac{p_j}{P'}\right] \\ &= \theta_i' W_g d(\log Q_g) - \phi\theta_i\left[d(\log P_g') - d(\log P')\right] \\ &\quad + \sum_{j\in S_g} v_{ij}\left[d(\log p_j) - d(\log P')\right], \quad i \in S_g, \end{aligned} \tag{2.9.4}$$

where we have also used

$$\theta_i' = \frac{\theta_i}{\Theta_g}.$$

In view of (2.9.3), the second term on the right of (2.9.4) can be expressed as

$$-\phi\theta_i\left[d(\log P_g') - d(\log P')\right] = -\sum_{j\in S_g} v_{ij}\left[d(\log P_g') - d(\log P')\right] \tag{2.9.5}$$

Applying (2.9.5), (2.9.4) can be simplified to

$$w_i d(\log q_i) = \theta_i' W_g d(\log Q_g) + \sum_{j\in S_g} v_{ij} d\left[\log\frac{p_j}{P_g'}\right], \quad i \in S_g. \tag{2.9.6}$$

Equation (2.9.6) is the *conditional demand equation* for good i within the group S_g, with $\sum_{i\in S_g}\theta_i' = 1$. The conditional marginal share θ_i' answers the question: if income increases by \$1, resulting in a certain additional amount spent on the group S_g, what will be the proportion of this additional amount allocated to commodity $i \in S_g$?

The conditional demand Eq. (2.9.6) is the demand equation for $i \in S_g$, given the demand for the group as a whole $W_g d(\log Q_g)$. This equation shows that the allocation of expenditure to goods within the group S_g depends on the total consumption of the group, as measured by $W_g d(\log Q_g)$, and the relative prices of goods within the group, $d\left[\log\left(p_j/P_g'\right)\right]$. The deflator for these relative prices is the Frisch price index of the group $d\left(\log P_g'\right)$ as defined in (2.8.10). As consumption of other groups and the prices of goods outside S_g do not appear in (2.9.6), it follows that the within-group allocation of expenditure depends only on variables pertaining to the group in question.

If we contrast the conditional demand Eq. (2.9.6) with the corresponding unconditional demand Eq. (2.8.2), we see that the variables on the left side of both equations are the same. However, the real income term in (2.8.2), $\theta_i d(\log Q)$ is replaced by $\theta_i' W_g d(\log Q_g)$ in (2.9.6). Furthermore, the price substitution terms for both are identical, except that the Frisch price index of all goods, $d(\log P)$, acts as the deflator in (2.8.2), while the corresponding group concept $d(\log P_g')$ in (2.9.6) plays this role.

The first term on the right of (2.9.6) gives the effect of real income on the demand for the group. This term is a multiple θ_i' of the Divisia volume index for the group $d(\log Q_g)$. Since this volume index is equal to $d(\log M) - d(\log P_g)$, where $d(\log P_g)$ is the group Divisia price index, it follows that this Divisia price index transforms the change in money income into the change in real income. As the Divisia price index is budget-share-weighted, it means that this index measures the income effect of the group price changes on the demand for the *i*th good.

The second term on the right of (2.9.6), $\sum_{j \in S_g} v_{ij} d\left(\log \frac{p_j}{P_g'}\right)$, deals with the effects of relative prices. As the group Frisch price index acts as a deflator of each price change of the group, we refer to $d\left[\log\left(p_j/P_g'\right)\right]$ as the change in the *Frisch-deflated price of j*.

The substitution term of (2.9.6) can be written as the difference between $\sum_{i \in S_g} v_{ij} d\left(\log p_j\right)$, which is the specific substitution effect of the group prices on the demand for good *i*, and $\phi\theta_i' d(\log P_g')$, which is the general substitution effect. Accordingly, the general substitution effect acts as the deflator of the specific effect by transforming absolute prices into Frisch-deflated prices.

In the substitution term of (2.9.6), v_{ij} is the coefficient of the *j*th relative price, which shall be termed the (*i*, *j*)th price coefficient. These price coefficients satisfy $\sum_{i \in S_g} \sum_{j \in S_g} v_{ij} = \phi\Theta_g$ which follows from (2.8.7). If $v_{ij} > 0$, then an increase in the Frisch-deflated price of *j* causes consumption of *i* to increase. Consequently, we follow Houthakker (1960) in defining goods *i* and *j* as *specific substitutes (complements)* if $v_{ij} > 0$ (< 0).

Block-independent preferences require that the consumer's problem be solved in two steps, thereby creating a decision hierarchy under block independence. The first step relates to the allocation of income to the *G* groups, as described by the *G* group demand equations (2.8.12). Each of these demand equations contains only the real income and relative price of the group in question and not the prices of the individual commodities. The second decision pertains to the allocation of expenditure to the goods within the group for each of the groups. This allocation is described in the conditional demand Eq. (2.9.6); these equations contain total consumption of the group as predetermined by the first step and the relative prices of the goods within the group.

Although the conditional demand Eq. (2.9.6) were obtained under block independence, the results do hold under the weaker condition of blockwise dependence (see, for example, Theil, 1975/76).

Equation (2.9.6) is expressed in relative prices. To obtain the conditional demand equations in absolute prices, we define the (*i*, *j*)th *conditional Slutsky coefficients* as

$$\pi_{ij}^{g} = \upsilon_{ij} - \phi \Theta_{g} \theta_{i}' \theta_{j}', \qquad i, j \in S_{g}. \tag{2.9.7}$$

This coefficient measures the effect of a change in the price of good j on the consumption of good i $(i, j \in S_g)$ under the condition that other prices and total consumption of the group remain constant. The conditional Slutsky coefficients satisfy demand homogeneity

$$\sum_{j \in S_g} \pi_{ij}^{g} = 0, \quad i, j \in S_g, \tag{2.9.8}$$

which follows from (2.9.3) and (2.9.7) and Slutsky symmetry

$$\pi_{ij}^{g} = \pi_{ji}^{g}, \quad i, j \in S_g, \tag{2.9.9}$$

which follows from (2.9.2) and (2.9.7).

Under constraint (2.9.8), an equi-proportional increase in the prices of commodities within the group—the total group consumption remaining unchanged—will have no effect on commodity i. The implication of constraint (2.9.9) is that the substitution effects are symmetric in both i and j.

The Slutsky coefficient π_{ij}^{g} refers to the total substitution effect of a price change. This total effect is made up of a specific and a general substitution effect. The specific substitution effect, with the marginal utility of income held constant, describes the interactions in the utility function among the commodities within the group. We can derive estimates of the specific substitution effects by decomposing the Slutsky coefficients.

The absolute price version of the conditional demand Eq. (2.9.6) can be written as

$$w_i d(\log q_i) = \theta_i' W_g d(\log Q_g) + \sum_{j \in S_g} \pi_{ij}^{g} d(\log p_j), \quad i, j \in S_g. \tag{2.9.10}$$

The conditional income and price elasticities implied by (2.9.10) are

$$\eta_i' = \frac{\theta_i' W_g}{w_i} = \frac{\theta_i'}{w_i / W_g} = \frac{\theta_i'}{w_i'}$$

and

$$\eta_{ij}' = \frac{\pi_{ij}^{g}}{w_i}.$$

Equation (2.9.10) and the constraints are attractive in their simplicity because everything is linear in their parameters.

The variables on the right-hand side of (2.9.10), $d(\log Q_g)$ and $d(\log p_j)$, pertain only to the commodities within the group; consumption of other goods and other prices have no role to play. As such, (2.9.10) refers to the allocation of the group's budget to the commodities within that group. These demand equations hold under the conditions of block independence preference. Under block independence preference, the marginal utility of any member of the group is unaffected by the consumption of other goods.

2.10 Conclusion

In this chapter, we first reviewed the economic theory of consumer demand. We then discussed the differential approach to the demand system. Moreover, three major theoretical restrictions on utility-based consumer demand functions: demand homogeneity, Slutsky symmetry, and the $n \times n$ matrix of compensated price derivatives is negative semi-definite, were verified. We also derived the implied income and price elasticities for each demand model. Demand equations under the restrictive form of the utility structure, preference independence, were also derived. Furthermore, six more differential demand systems were introduced.

We also introduced demand equations under block independence, which are applicable to a group of commodities. Given the demand for a group, the question arises as to how the expenditure on the group is allocated among the commodities within the group, which are the conditional demand equations. Therefore, we have also derived the composite demand equations for the group and conditional demand equations for goods within a group.

As discussed in this chapter, each demand system has its own advantages and drawbacks. Therefore, ranking them is not suitable and, instead, they should be utilized as deemed appropriate given both the available data and the context of the research.

Appendix

This appendix is structured as follows. First, we discuss some directly specified demand systems such as the double-log demand equations and the Working's model, followed by examples of directly specified demand equations derived from specific forms of utility functions, such as the linear expenditure system (LES). Then we introduce the indirectly specified utility demand functions, particularly the trans-log demand function of Christensen et al. (1975), and also consider the derivation of a demand system from the specification of the cost function, including the popular AIDS model of Deaton and Muellbauer (1980a, 1980b). Next, we present a review of the Quadratic Almost Ideal Demand System (QUAIDS), and finally we briefly discuss the dynamic demand systems.

Directly Specified Demand Systems

A directly specified demand system makes no reference to utility. This section discusses two well-known directly specified demand systems, the double-log demand system and Working's model. The following sections consider the demand systems derived from utility or cost functions.

Double-Log Demand System

A popular example of a directly specified demand equation is the *double-log demand system.*

$$\log q_i = \alpha_i + \eta_i \log M + \sum_{j=1}^{n} \eta_{ij} \log p_j, \quad i = 1, \ldots, n \tag{A.2.1}$$

where q_i is the quantity demanded of a good *i*, p_j is the price of the good *j*, $M = \sum_{i=1}^{n} p_i q_i$, is total expenditure/income and α_i, η_i and η_{ij} are constant coefficients.

In Eq. (A.2.1), the coefficient of income is

$$\eta_i = \frac{\partial(\log q_i)}{\partial(\log M)}, \quad i = 1, 2, \ldots, n, \tag{A.2.2}$$

which is known as the income elasticity of demand for good *i* and

$$\eta_{ij} = \frac{\partial(\log q_i)}{\partial(\log p_j)} \quad i = 1, 2, \ldots, n, \tag{A.2.3}$$

is the cross-price elasticity of demand for *i* with respect to the price of *j*.

In a household expenditure survey, all participating families pay approximately the same price for each good, so that the *i*th equation of (A.2.1) reduces to

$$\log q_i = \alpha_i + \beta_i \log M, \qquad i = 1, 2, \ldots, n, \tag{A.2.4}$$

where units are chosen such that the price of each good is a unity, so that $\sum_j \eta_{ij} \log p_j = 0$.

Two attractions of the double-log demand system are its simplicity and its ability to read income and price elasticities directly from the estimated equations without the need for further calculations. However, this system has a serious weakness given that it does not satisfy the adding-up constraint (2.2.1) for all values of income. With constant prices, (A.2.1) suggests that the logarithmic change in expenditure on good *i* is a constant multiple η_i of the change in income, that is,

$$d(\log p_i q_i) = \eta_i d(\log M)$$

Thus, if the income elasticity is greater than unity, it follows that expenditure on good i will increase at a rate that is faster than that of income. If income increases sufficiently, expenditure on good i will eventually exceed income, thereby violating the adding-up constraint.

Working's Model

Another example of a demand system without reference to the utility function is Working's (1943) model. This model is most suitable for household budget data as all households pay the same price; if units are chosen such that the price of each good is equal to unity, then the demand equation can be written as

$$w_i = \alpha_i + \beta_i \log M, \quad i = 1, 2, \ldots, n. \tag{A.2.5}$$

Working's model expresses the budget share of good i, $w_i = p_i q_i / M$ as a linear function of $\log M$. As the sum of the budget shares is unity, it follows from (A.2.5) that $\sum_i \alpha_i = 1$ and $\sum_i \beta_i = 0$. Choosing the income unit such that $M = 1$ for some households, α_i can be interpreted as the budget share of i for that household. Moreover, β_i represents 100 times the change in the budget share of i ($\Delta w_i \times 100$) resulting from a 1% increase in income.

Multiplying (A.2.5) by M, we derive the marginal shares implied by Working's model,

$$p_i q_i = \alpha_i M + \beta_i M \log M, \quad i = 1, 2, \ldots, n.$$

Differentiating both sides with respect to M gives

$$\frac{\partial (p_i q_i)}{\partial M} = \alpha_i + \beta_i (1 + \log M).$$

Using (A.2.4), the above can be written as

$$\theta_i = w_i + \beta_i, \quad i = 1, 2, \ldots, n. \tag{A.2.6}$$

Thus, under Working's model, the ith marginal share exceeds the corresponding budget share by β_i because the budget share is not constant with respect to income, nor is this the marginal share.

We can obtain the income elasticity by applying the ratio of the marginal share (6) to the corresponding budget share.

$$\eta_i = 1 + \frac{\beta_i}{w_i}. \tag{A.2.7}$$

Equation (A.2.7) implies that a good with positive β_i is a luxury (i.e. $\eta_i > 1$) and a good with negative β_i is a necessity (i.e. $\eta_i < 1$). For a luxury good, the budget share increases with rising income, when the price is constant. According to

(A.2.7), increasing income causes the η_i of such a good to fall towards 1. Likewise, the income elasticity of a necessity also drops towards 1 with increasing income under Eq. (A.2.7). Accordingly, under Working's model, as consumers become more affluent, all goods become relatively less luxurious.

Demand Systems Derived from Direct Utility Functions

Additive Utility Function

Demand equations can also be derived by algebraically specifying the forms of the utility function. The algebraic form of one such utility function was proposed by Johansen (1969) and is known as the additive utility function.

$$u(q_1, q_2, \ldots, q_n) = \sum_{i=1}^{n} \frac{\beta_i}{\alpha_i}\left[\left[\frac{q_i - \gamma_i}{\beta_i}\right]^{\alpha_i} - 1\right], \tag{A.2.8}$$

where α_i (< 1), β_i (> 0) and γ_i $(< q_i)$ are constants.

By differentiating (A.2.8) with respect to q_i, we obtain

$$\frac{\partial u}{\partial q_i} = \left[\frac{q_i - \gamma_i}{\beta_i}\right]^{\alpha_i - 1}. \tag{A.2.9}$$

The above equation implies that the marginal utility of good *i* does not depend on the consumption of goods other than good *i*.

By taking the second derivative of (A.2.9), we derive

$$\frac{\partial^2 u}{\partial q_i^2} = \frac{\alpha_i - 1}{\beta_i}\left[\frac{q_i - \gamma_i}{\beta_i}\right]^{\alpha_i - 2} < 0; \quad \frac{\partial^2 u}{\partial q_i \partial q_j} = 0; \quad i \neq j. \tag{10}$$

Therefore, the Hessian matrix of the utility function implied by (A.2.8) is diagonal, and the utility function given by (A.2.8) is said to be in *preference independent form*. Substituting the right-hand side of Eq. (A.2.9) for $\partial u/\partial q_i$ in (2.3.8), we obtain the first-order conditions associated with the utility function (A.2.8),

$$q_i = \gamma_i + \beta_i[\lambda p_i]^{1/(\alpha_i - 1)}, \quad i = 1, 2, \ldots, n. \tag{A.2.11}$$

Stone–Geary Utility Function

The *Stone–Geary utility function* is a special case of the preference independent system, when $\alpha_i = 0$, $i = 1, \ldots, n$, and $\sum_{i=1}^{n} \beta_i = 1$. When α_i tends to zero, applying L'Hospital's rule, the utility function (8) can be written as

$$u(q) = \sum_{i=1}^{n} \beta_i \log(q_i - \gamma_i). \tag{A.2.12}$$

This utility function has also been previously considered by Klein and Rubin (1948).

Linear Expenditure System

If we substitute $\alpha_i = 0$ in (A.2.11) and use the budget constraint (2.3.9) to eliminate λ, we can obtain the algebraic form below of the demand equations associated with the aforementioned Stone–Geary utility function.

$$p_i q_i = p_i \gamma_i + \beta_i \left[M - \sum_{j=1}^{n} p_j \gamma_j \right], \quad i = 1, 2, \ldots, n. \tag{A.2.13}$$

Equation (A.2.13) gives the expenditure on good i as a linear function of the n prices and income and is known as the *linear expenditure system (LES)*. It has been widely used in demand analysis, beginning with Stone (1954).

If the γ_i's are all positive, then (A.2.13) gives the following interpretation: the consumer first purchases γ_i units of good i at a cost of $p_i \gamma_i$ which can be termed the *subsistence consumption* of that commodity. The total cost of the subsistence consumption of all n commodities is $\sum_{j=1}^{n} p_j \gamma_j$ and the remaining income is $(M - \sum_j p_j \gamma_j)$ known as *supernumerary income*. Out of this supernumerary income, a fixed fraction β_i is then spent on commodity i.

If we differentiate both sides of (A.2.13) with respect to M, we obtain the marginal share

$$\theta_i = \frac{\partial (p_i q_i)}{\partial M} = \beta_i, \quad i = 1, 2, \ldots, n, \tag{A.2.14}$$

which is always positive. Consequently, the income elasticity of i will take the form

$$\eta_i = \frac{\beta_i}{w_i}, \quad i = 1, 2, \ldots, n. \tag{A.2.15}$$

Nevertheless, there are two major limitations related to the LES. Firstly, under the LES income elasticity, (A.2.15) is always positive. Accordingly, the *LES does not admit inferior goods*. Secondly, as previously noted, a rise in income, with prices held constant, will result in the budget share of necessities falling and those of luxuries rising. Although the general rule is such, according to Eq. (A.2.15), increasing affluence does cause the income elasticities of necessities to rise while those of luxuries fall and the elasticities of both types of goods become closer to unity. If we consider the case of food as a necessity then, according to the LES, when the consumer becomes richer, the η_i of food increases, causing food to become less of a necessity or more of a luxury. This behaviour of the income elasticity is questionable as food should be less of a luxury for a richer consumer.

If we differentiate (A.2.13) with respect to p_j and multiply both sides by p_j/q_i, we derive the uncompensated price elasticities,

$$\eta_{ij} = \frac{(\gamma_i - q_i)}{q_i}\delta_{ij} - \frac{\beta_i \gamma_j p_j}{p_i q_i}, \quad i, j = 1, 2, \ldots, n,$$

where δ_{ij} is the Kronecker delta. Therefore, the own-price elasticity of commodity i is

$$\eta_{ii} = -1 + (1 - \beta_i)\frac{\gamma_i}{q_i}, \quad i = 1, 2, \ldots, n.$$

Since, $\beta_i > 0$ and $\sum_{i=1}^{n} \beta_i = 1$, we have $0 < \beta_i < 1$. This, together with $0 \leq \gamma_i < q_i$, makes all own-price elasticities fall in the range -1 and 0. Thus, all commodities become *price inelastic under the LES*.

The uncompensated cross-price elasticities are

$$\eta_{ij} = -\frac{\beta_i \gamma_j p_j}{p_i q_i}, \quad i \neq j, i, j = 1, 2, \ldots, n.$$

Since $\gamma_j > 0$ and $\beta_i > 0$, all cross-price elasticities would be negative. Therefore, under LES, *all prices of commodities are gross complements*.

Demand Systems Derived from Indirect Utility Functions

In this section, we derive demand equations from indirect utility functions. Thus, if we substitute the demand Eq. (2.3.4) into the utility function (2.3.1), we obtain this function in terms of income and prices, giving the indirect utility function. This is expressed as

$$u = u\big[\boldsymbol{q}(M, \boldsymbol{p})\big] = u_{\mathrm{I}}(M, \boldsymbol{p}), \tag{A.2.16}$$

where $\boldsymbol{q}$ and $\boldsymbol{p}$ are vectors of n quantities and prices, and function u_{I} $(M, \mathbf{p})$ is termed the indirect utility function.

From (A.2.16), it is evident that indirect utility functions represent the maximum utility attainable that corresponds to given values of income M and prices p. If we apply the chain rule to (A.2.16), we get

$$\frac{\partial u_{\mathrm{I}}}{\partial M} = \sum_{i=1}^{n} \frac{\partial u}{\partial q_i}\frac{\partial q_i}{\partial M}, \tag{A.2.17}$$

$$\frac{\partial u_{\mathrm{I}}}{\partial p_i} = \sum_{j=1}^{n} \frac{\partial u}{\partial q_j} \frac{\partial q_j}{\partial p_i}, \quad i = 1, \ldots, n. \tag{A.2.18}$$

Using first-order conditions, (2.3.8) together with Eqs. (2.3.14) and (2.3.15), we can simplify (A.2.17) and (18) to give

$$\frac{\partial u_{\mathrm{I}}}{\partial M} = \lambda \quad \text{and} \quad \frac{\partial u_{\mathrm{I}}}{\partial p_i} = -\lambda q_i, \quad i = 1, \ldots, n, \tag{A.2.19}$$

where λ is the marginal utility of income. When λ is eliminated from (A.2.18) and (A.2.19), we obtain

$$q_i = -\frac{\partial u_{\mathrm{I}}/\partial p_i}{\partial u_{\mathrm{I}}/\partial M}, \quad i = 1, \ldots, n, \tag{A.2.20}$$

which is known as Roy's (1942) *theorem* or *identity*. Hence, Roy's theorem offers a second way to generate a system of demand equations using a specified algebraic form of the indirect utility function.

A popular form of indirect utility function, introduced by Christensen et al. (1975), is the *translog indirect utility function* given by

$$u_{\mathrm{I}}(M, p) = \sum_{i=1}^{n} \beta_i \log \frac{p_i}{M} + \frac{1}{2} \sum_{i=1}^{n} \sum_{j=1}^{n} \beta_{ij} \log \frac{p_i}{M} \log \frac{p_j}{M}, \tag{A.2.21}$$

where the β_i's and the β_{ij}'s are constants. Application of (A.2.20) to (A.2.21) facilitates the demand equation for commodity i as

$$q_i = \frac{M}{p_i} \frac{\left[\beta_i + \sum_{j=1}^{n} \beta_{ij} \log \frac{p_j}{M}\right]}{\left[\sum_{k=1}^{n} \beta_k + \sum_{k=1}^{n} \sum_{j=1}^{n} \beta_{kj} \log \frac{p_j}{M}\right]}, \quad i = 1, \ldots, n. \tag{A.2.22}$$

Equivalently, the demand equation for commodity i in budget share form can be expressed as

$$w_i = \frac{\beta_i + \sum_{j=1}^{n} \beta_{ij} \log \frac{p_j}{M}}{\sum_{k=1}^{n} \beta_k + \sum_{k=1}^{n} \sum_{j=1}^{n} \beta_{kj} \log \frac{p_j}{M}}, \quad i = 1, \ldots, n. \tag{A.2.23}$$

Demand Systems Derived from the Cost Function

The Marshallian demand function explains how to maximize a consumer's utility subject to budget constraint. However, a consumer's utility problem can also be approached by analysing how to minimize the expenditures or costs to reach a specified level of utility at the given prices of goods. We can express the cost or expenditure function as a function of utility and price and the demand equation can be derived by substituting $C(.)$ for M in the indirect utility function. Doing this for the indirect utility function (A.2.21), we obtain:

$$C(u, \boldsymbol{p}) = \sum_{i=1}^{n} p_i \gamma_i + \mathrm{e}^{u-k} \prod_{i=1}^{n} p_i^{\beta_i}. \tag{A.2.24}$$

Cost functions have the property that

$$\frac{\partial C}{\partial p_i} = q_i, \quad i = 1, \ldots, n. \tag{A.2.25}$$

This is referred to as *Shephard's lemma.*

Almost Ideal Demand System (AIDS)

A third approach to deriving demand equations is to specify the form of the cost function and then apply Shephard's lemma. Deaton and Muellbauer (1980a, 1980b) utilized this approach and suggested

$$C(u, \boldsymbol{p}) = \mathrm{e}^{a(\boldsymbol{p})+ub(\boldsymbol{p})}, \tag{A.2.26}$$

where

$$a(\boldsymbol{p}) = \sum_{i=1}^{n} \alpha_i \log p_i + \frac{1}{2} \sum_{i=1}^{n} \sum_{j=1}^{n} \gamma_{ij} \log p_i \log p_j \tag{A.2.27}$$

and

$$b(\boldsymbol{p}) = \beta_0 \prod_{i=1}^{n} p_i^{\beta_i}. \tag{A.2.28}$$

Here α_i's, γ_{ij}'s, and β_i's are all constants. Deaton and Muellbauer (1980b) applied (A.2.25) to cost function (A.2.26) and derived a demand system in terms of utility and prices. They completed this using the indirect utility function to express utility in terms of income and prices, which results in a demand system in terms of income and prices of the form

$$w_i = \alpha_i + \beta_i \log \frac{M}{P} + \sum_{j=1}^{n} \gamma_{ij} \log p_j, \quad i = 1, \ldots, n, \tag{A.2.29}$$

where

$$\log P = \sum_{i=1}^{n} \alpha_i \log p_i + \frac{1}{2} \sum_{i=1}^{n} \sum_{j=1}^{n} \gamma_{ij} \log p_i \log p_j. \tag{A.2.30}$$

Deaton and Muellbauer (1980b) refer to (A.2.29) as the *Almost Ideal Demand System (AIDS).*

The income and price elasticities implied by the AIDS model are as follows:

$$\eta_i = 1 + \frac{\beta_i}{w_i}, \quad i = 1, \ldots, n, \tag{A.2.31}$$

and

$$\eta_{ij} = -\delta_{ij} + \frac{\gamma_{ij}}{w_i} - \frac{\beta_i w_j}{w_i}, \quad i, j = 1, \ldots, n. \tag{A.2.32}$$

Estimation of (A.2.29) will be more complicated if we use $\log P$ as defined by (A.2.30). Therefore, Deaton and Muellbauer (1980b) proposed an appropriately specified price index that can be defined outside of the AIDS system to replace the nonlinear price index in Eq. (A.2.30). This has resulted in a purely linear system of share equations. They suggested Stone's (1954) *share-weighted geometric mean price index* as an obvious solution:

$$\log P = \sum_{i=1}^{n} w_i d(\log p_i). \tag{A.2.33}$$

With (A.2.30) replaced by (A.2.33), the budget share Eq. (A.2.29) is linear in the parameters α_i, β_i and γ_{ij}, so (A.2.29) becomes

$$w_i = \alpha_i + \beta_i \log Q + \sum_{j=1}^{n} v_{ij} \log p_j, \quad i = 1, \ldots, n. \tag{A.2.34}$$

If we choose $p_i = 1$ for all i, then $\log P = 0$ and the indirect system given by (A.2.29) simplifies to

$$w_i = \alpha_i + \beta_i \log M, \quad i = 1, 2, \ldots, n, \tag{A.2.35}$$

which is the Working's model given by Eq. (5) discussed in Appendix Section.

Quadratic Almost Ideal Demand System (QUAIDS)

Banks et al. (1997) argue that the Engel curve of a commodity can change through income levels and thus propose QUAIDS. They examined the consumption of five commodity groups using the UK's family expenditure survey data. They report a quadratic Engel curve in clothing and alcohol categories. In other words, the expenditure share of clothing and alcohol increases when the income level is low and declines when the income level is high. This finding suggests that some commodities or commodity groups need more dimensions in the Engel curve to represent the quadratic relationship.

Banks et al. (1997) suggested that, in order to maintain the attractive properties of the AIDS model while maintaining consistency with both the Engel curve and relative price effects within a utility maximization framework, a quadratic term in log income should be added to the AIDS model. This leads to the Quadratic AIDS (QUAIDS) model specification that increases the flexibility of the demand system representation.

QUAIDS is derived from an indirect utility function which is given as

$$\ln V = \left(\left[\frac{\ln m - \ln a(p)}{b(p)} \right]^{-1} + \lambda(p) \right)^{-1} \tag{A.2.36}$$

The above indirect utility form reduces to the indirect Almost Ideal Demand System (AIDS) if (p) becomes zero. Adding (p) makes the system rank 3. Applying Roy's identity to Eq. (A.2.36) gives the expenditure share expressed as

$$w_i = \frac{\partial \ln a(p)}{\partial \ln p_i} + \frac{\partial \ln b(p)}{\partial \ln p_i} \ln\left(\frac{m}{a(p)}\right) + \frac{\partial \lambda}{\partial \ln p_i} \frac{1}{b(p)} \left[\ln\left(\frac{m}{a(p)}\right) \right]^2 \tag{A.2.37}$$

Banks et al. (1997) proved that both coefficients of $\ln(m/a(p))$ and $[\ln(m/a(p))]^2$ cannot be independent of prices if the system is to be rank 3. The specifications of $a(p)$, $b(p)$, and $\lambda(p)$ which would make the system rank 3 are given as

$$\begin{aligned} \ln a(p) &= a_0 + \sum_k a_k \ln p_k + \frac{1}{2} \sum_k \sum_j \gamma_{kj} \ln p_k \ln p_j \\ b(p) &= \prod_i p_i^{\beta_i} \\ \lambda(p) &= \sum_i \lambda_i \ln p_i \end{aligned} \tag{A.2.38}$$

Replacing each component in Eq. (A.2.37) by the specifications given in (A.2.38) gives the QUAIDS

$$w_i = \alpha_i + \sum_j \gamma_{ij} \ln p_j + \beta_i \ln\left(\frac{m}{a(p)}\right) + \frac{\lambda_i}{b(p)}\left[\ln\left(\frac{m}{a(p)}\right)\right]^2 \quad \text{(A.2.39)}$$

The form of QUAIDS is identical to the AIDS except for the last quadratic term. This quadratic income term, with a linear income term, represents the Engel curve which is expected to vary across income levels. QUAIDS is quite similar to AIDS and inherits some properties from AIDS. The restrictions imposed on AIDS can be imposed on QUAIDS. They are

Adding up: $\sum \alpha_i = 1,\ \sum \gamma_{ij} = 0,\ \sum \beta_i = 0$ and $\sum \lambda_i = 0$.

Homogeneity: $\sum_j \gamma_{ij} = 0$.

Symmetry: $\gamma_{ij} = \gamma_{ij}$.

To calculate QUAIDS model elasticities, we differentiate Eq. (A.2.39) with respect to ln m and ln p_j, respectively, to give

$$\eta_i = \frac{\partial w_i}{\partial \ln m} = \beta_i + \frac{2\lambda_i}{b(p)} \ln\left(\frac{m}{a(p)}\right) \quad \text{(A.2.40)}$$

$$\eta_{ij} = \frac{\partial w_i}{\partial \ln p_j} = \gamma_{ij} - \mu_i\left(\alpha_j + \sum_k \gamma_{jk} \ln P_k\right) - \frac{\lambda_i \beta_j}{b(p)}\left[\ln\left(\frac{m}{a(p)}\right)\right]^2 \quad \text{(A.2.41)}$$

The budget elasticities are given by $e_i = \frac{\mu_i}{w_i} + 1$ and, with a positive β and a negative λ, will be seen to be greater than unity at low levels of expenditure, eventually becoming less than unity as the total expenditure increases and the term in λ_i becomes more important. Thus, such commodities are luxuries at low levels of total expenditure but are necessities at high levels of total expenditure.

The uncompensated price elasticities are given by $e_{ij}^u = \frac{\mu_{ij}}{w_i} - \delta_{ij}$, where δ_{ij} is the Kronecker delta, which is equal to 1 when $i = j$ and is otherwise 0. The Slutsky equation, $e_{ij}^c = e_{ij}^u + e_i w_j$, is used to calculate the set of compensated elasticities e_{ij}^c; the matrix with elements $w_i\left[e_{ij}^c\right]$ should be symmetric and negative semi-definite.

Dynamic Demand Systems

All the demand systems discussed so far are static and assume that consumers immediately and fully adjust to a new equilibrium when either income or prices change. In reality, consumers are unlikely to have adjusted to equilibrium in each time period and the assumption of instantaneous adjustments by consumers is potentially incorrect. The dynamic demand systems allow for intertemporal rationality of consumer behaviour by explicitly considering the mechanism underlying the short-run adjustment process. Therefore, economists have employed different approaches to explicitly incorporate a dynamic structure into the demand system. For example, the dynamic version of the static AIDS model given in Eq. (A.2.29) has been derived as

$$w_{it} = \alpha_i^* + \sum_{j=1}^{n} \theta_{ij} w_{jt-1} + \beta_i \log \frac{M}{P} + \sum_{j=1}^{n} \gamma_{ij} \log p_j \tag{A.2.42}$$

where we impose $\sum \alpha_i^* = 1$ and $\sum_j \theta_{ij} = 0$ for identification and $\sum_i \theta_{ij} = 0$ for adding up.

In Chap. 6, we will discuss the dynamic demand models in detail and model the dynamic behaviour of consumers.

References

Banks, J., Blundell, R., & Lewbel, A. (1997). Quadratic Engel curves and consumer demand. *Review of Economics and Statistics, 79*(4), 527–539.

Barten, A. P. (1964). Consumer demand functions under conditions of almost additive preferences. *Econometrica, 32*, 1–38.

Barten, A. P. (1977). The systems of consumer demand functions approach: A review. *Econometrica, 45*, 23–51.

Christensen, L. R., Jorgenson, D. W., & Lau, L. J. (1975). Transcendental logarithmic utility functions. *American Economic Review, 65*, 367–383.

Clements, K. W., Wu, Y., & Zhang, J. (2006). Comparing international consumption patterns. *Empirical Economics, 31*(1), 1–30.

Cournot, A. A. (1838). *Recherches sur les Principes Mathématiques de la Théorie des Richesses par Augustin Cournot*. Chez L. Hachette.

Deaton, A. S., & Muellbauer, J. (1980a). *Economics and consumer behavior*. Cambridge University Press.

Deaton, A. S., & Muellbauer, J. (1980b). An almost ideal demand system. *American Economic Review, 70*, 312–326.

Edgeworth, F. Y. (1881). *Mathematical physics: An essay on the application of mathematics to the moral sciences*. Kegan Paul.

Engel, E. (1857). Die Produktions-und Consumtionsverhaltnisse des Königreichs Sachsen, reprinted with Engel. Anlage I, 1–54. *TER, 4*(2), 216–225.

Fisher, I. (1892). *Mathematical investigations in the theory of value and prices*. Augustus M. Kelly Publishers.

Frisch, R. (1932). *New methods of measuring marginal utility*. J.C.B. Mohr.

Houthakker, H. S. (1960). Additive preferences. *Econometrica, 28*, 244–257.

Johansen, L. (1969). On the relationships between some systems of demand functions. *Liiketaloudellinen Aikakauskirga, 1*, 30–41. Reprint Series No. 47. University of Oslo, Institute of Economics, Oslo, Norway.

Keller, W. J. (1984). Some simple but flexible differential consumer demand systems. *Economic Letters, 16*, 77–82.

Keller, W. J., & van Driel, J. (1985). Differential consumer demand systems. *European Economic Review, 27*, 375–390.

Klein, L. R., & Rubin, H. (1948). A constant-utility index of the cost of living. *The Review of Economic Studies, 15*, 84–87.

Leser, C. E. V. (1960). Demand functions for nine commodity groups in Australia. *The Australian Journal of Statistics, 2*, 102–113.

Neves, P. D. (1987). A class of differential demand systems. *Economic Letters, 44*, 83–86.

Philps, L. (1974). *Applied consumption analysis* (2nd ed.). North-Holland Publishing Company.
Pollak, A. A., & Wales, T. J. (1992). *Demand system specification and estimation*. Oxford University Press.
Roy, R. (1942). *De l'utilite*. Hermann et Cie.
Selvanathan, E. A. (1985). An even simpler differential demand system. *Economics Letters, 19*, 343–347.
Selvanathan, E. A., & Clements, K. W. (1995). *Recent developments in applied demand analysis: Alcohol*. Springer-Verlag.
Selvanathan, E. A., & Selvanathan, S. (2003). *International consumption comparisons: OECD versus LDC*. World Scientific.
Selvanathan, E. A., & Selvanathan, S. (2004). Economic and demographic factors in Australian alcohol demand. *Applied Economics, 36*(21), 2405–2417.
Selvanathan, S. (1993). *A system-wide analysis of international consumption patterns*. Advanced Studies in Theoretical and Applied Econometrics. Kluwer Academic Publishers.
Selvanathan, S., & Selvanathan, E. A. (2006). Consumption patterns of food, tobacco and beverages: A cross-country analysis. *Applied Economics, 38*(13), 1567–1584.
Stone, R. (1954). Linear expenditure systems and demand analysis: An application to the pattern of British demand. *The Economic Journal, 64*(255), 511–527.
Sulgham, A. K. (2006). *Econometric essays on specification and estimation of demand systems*. Louisiana State University and Agricultural and Mechanical College.
Theil, H. (1965). The information approach to demand analysis. *Econometrica, 33*, 67–87.
Theil, H. (1967). *Economics and information theory*. North-Holland Publishing Company.
Theil, H. (1975/76). *Theory and measurement of consumer demand*. North-Holland Publishing Company.
Theil, H. (1980). *The system-wide approach to microeconomics*. The University of Chicago Press.
Theil, H. (1996). *Studies in global econometrics*. Kluwer Academic Publishers.
Theil, H., & Clements, K. W. (1987). *Applied demand analysis: Results from system-wide approaches*. Ballinger Publishing Company.
Working, H. (1943). Statistical law of family expenditure. *Journal of the American Statistical Association, 38*, 43–56.

Chapter 3
A Preliminary Data Analysis of Consumption Patterns in Asia

3.1 Introduction

Heterogeneous patterns of consumption across the world are due to varying income levels, demographic factors and cultural factors. For instance, food absorbs more than 50% of the consumption budget in the poorest countries but only about 20% in the most affluent countries (see Clements & Chen, 1996; Selvanathan & Selvanathan, 2003; Selvanathan et al., 2023). On the other hand, citizens of wealthier countries allocate higher proportions of their income to housing and medical care than those in poorer countries. However, rising incomes in Asia, combined with globalization, trade liberalization and technological advancements, have generated a tendency towards the homogenisation or convergence of consumption patterns across countries. Given this background, this chapter undertakes a preliminary analysis of consumption patterns in ten Asian countries,[1] namely Hong Kong, India, Japan, Malaysia, the Philippines, Singapore, South Korea, Sri Lanka, Taiwan, and Thailand using consumption and price data for eight broad commodity groups: food, clothing, housing, durables, medical care, transport, recreation, and miscellaneous, which make up the consumer basket.

This chapter is structured as follows. Section 3.2 presents the summary characteristics of consumers and the economy in the ten Asian countries, and the next section presents a preliminary data analysis of the ten Asian countries' consumption data. In Sect. 3.4, we investigate the four empirical regularities in consumption patterns of consumers in these countries. Section 3.5 utilizes the double-log demand system to obtain preliminary estimates of income and price elasticities for the eight commodity groups and ten countries. Section 3.6 presents concluding comments.

---

[1] Please see detailed discussion in Sect. 1.2 of Chap. 1 regarding the selection of the ten Asian countries for our analysis.

S. D. Rathnayaka et al., *Economic Development and Consumption Patterns in Asian Countries*, https://doi.org/10.1007/978-981-97-2628-8_3

3.2 General Characteristics of Asian Countries

Tables 3.1 and 3.2 provide information on the general geographic and economic characteristics of the ten Asian countries considered in this study. Table 3.1 details, for each economy, the language and religious background of its people, land size, population size, and population growth rate. It shows that these countries are diverse in their size, languages spoken, and religious beliefs. For instance, Singapore has the smallest land size as well as population and India has the largest of both among these ten countries. Japan has the lowest population growth rate (− 0.14%) while the Philippines has the highest (1.7%).

Table 3.2 presents per capita GDP, GDP real-growth rate, rate of inflation, rate of unemployment, the household consumption shares and the food budget shares of these countries. Column (2) shows that Singapore, Hong Kong, and Japan have the highest per capita GDP. Sri Lanka has the highest (3.9%) and Taiwan has the lowest (− 0.8%) rate of inflation while India has the highest (6.5%) and Thailand the lowest (0.7%) rate of unemployment. In terms of household consumption as a percentage of GDP, the Philippines has the highest private consumption share (73.2%) while Singapore spends the lowest proportion of GDP on household consumption (35.3%). According to the last column of the table, the lowest food budget share can be seen in economies that have the highest per capita GDP, such as Singapore (9%), Hong Kong (13.1%), Japan (18%), South Korea (15.4%), and Taiwan (15.5%). Figure 3.1 plots the food budget share against the logarithm of per capita GDP in these ten countries; the solid line depicts the least squares (LS) regression line. As can be seen, a clear inverse relationship exists between the budget share for 'food' and per capita real GDP. This supports Engel's Law, which will be discussed in some detail in Sect. 3.3 of this chapter.

3.3 Consumption Patterns in Ten Asian Countries: A Descriptive Analysis

The annual consumption expenditures (in current and constant prices) of goods and services and population data for each country was drawn from various country-level publications of statistics departments, national economic and social development boards, and central banks. In addition, some earlier years' data were extracted from Selvanathan and Selvanathan (2003). Most previous cross-country consumption studies compiled time series data from the United Nations National Accounts Statistics yearbooks. However, the United Nations stopped publishing individual countries' private consumption expenditure in constant prices after 1996. Therefore, we have used various other data sources for individual countries.[2] Goods and services

[2] When data are extracted from various sources for different time periods, we have corroborated the compatibility of the data sets for various years by comparing data for overlapping years from the various sources.

Table 3.1 General characteristics of ten Asian countries, 2019

Country	Languages	Religions	Land area (km^2)	Population (in million)	Population growth rate (%)
(1)	(2)	(3)	(4)	(5)	(6)
1. Hong Kong	Cantonese, English, Mandarin	Eclectic mixture of local religions Christianity	1050	7.5	0.74
2. India	Hindi, Bengali, Telugu, Marathi, Tamil, English	Hinduism, Islam, Christianity	2,973,190	1383.1	1.03
3. Japan	Japanese	Shintoism, Buddhism, Christianity	364,500	126.6	– 0.14
4. Malaysia	Bahasa Malaysia (official), English, Chinese	Islam, Buddhism, Christianity	328,550	32.8	1.24
5. Philippines	Filipino, English	Catholicism, Islam	298,170	110.4	1.66
6. Singapore	Mandarin (official), English (official), Malay (official), Tamil (official)	Buddhism, Muslim, Hinduism, Taoisim and Catholicism	718	5.7	1.14
7. South Korea	Korean, English	Protestant, Buddhism, Catholicism	97,600	51.8	0.35
8. Sri Lanka	Sinhala, Tamil, other	Buddhism, Hinduism, Islam, Christianity	61,860	21.8	0.61

(continued)

Table 3.1 (continued)

Country	Languages	Religions	Land area (km^2)	Population (in million)	Population growth rate (%)
(1)	(2)	(3)	(4)	(5)	(6)
9. Taiwan	Mandarin Chinese (official), Taiwanese	Buddhism, Taoisim, Christianity	32,260	23.6	0.22
10. Thailand	Thai (official), Burmese, other	Buddhism, Muslim, Christianity	510,890	71.3	0.25

Source The World Fact Book (2019), https://www.cia.gov/library/publications/the-world-factbook/
World development indicators, https://databank.worldbank.org/source/world-development-indicators
Note Population and population growth rate data are for 2019

Table 3.2 Economic characteristics of ten Asian countries, 2019

Country	GDP per capita in $US	GDP real growth rate (%)	Rate of inflation (%)	Rate of unemployment (%)	Household consumption (as a % of GDP)	Food budget share (%)
(1)	(2)	(3)	(4)	(5)	(6)	(7)
1. Hong Kong	48,359	− 1.7	2.0	2.9	69.4	13.1
2. India	2050	3.9	2.4	6.5	60.9	31.2
3. Japan	40,416	− 0.4	0.6	2.4	54.6	18.0
4. Malaysia	11,132	4.4	0.1	3.3	59.8	23.4
5. Philippines	3414	6.1	0.7	2.2	73.2	36.2
6. Singapore	66,070	1.3	− 0.2	3.1	35.3	9.0
7. South Korea	31,902	2.2	− 0.8	3.8	48.6	15.4
8. Sri Lanka	4083	− 0.2	3.9	4.7	62.7	35.7
9. Taiwan	25,903	3.1	0.6	3.7	51.0	15.5
10. Thailand	7629	2.1	1.0	0.7	49.8	25.9

Source World development indicators, https://databank.worldbank.org/source/world-development-indicators
International Monetary Fund, https://www.imf.org/external/datamapper

are classified into ($n = 8$) broad commodity groups as in Table 3.3 and the detailed country-wise database description for the ten Asian countries is shown in Table 3.4.

The proportion of the total expenditure allocated to commodity i is known as the *budget share* of commodity i and is given by $w_{it} = p_{it}q_{it}/M_t$, where p_{it} and q_{it} are the price and consumption of good i in period t and $M_t = \sum_{i=1}^{n} p_{it}q_{it}$ is the total

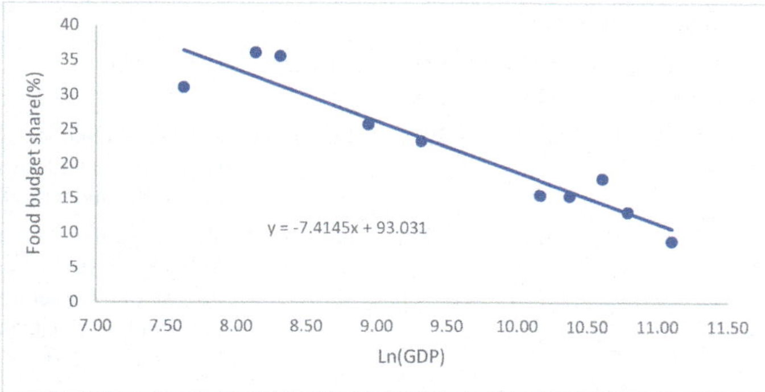

Fig. 3.1 Budget share versus the logarithm of income

Table 3.3 Classification of eight commodity groups

Commodity group	Description
1. Food	Food, non-alcoholic and alcoholic beverages
2. Clothing	Clothing and footwear
3. Housing	Housing, water, electricity, gas and other fuels
4. Durables	Furniture, furnishings, household equipment and operations
5. Medical care	Medical care and health expenses
6. Transport	Personal transport equipment, maintenance, transport services and communications
7. Recreation	Educational, recreational, entertainment and cultural services
8. Miscellaneous	Personal care, expenditure in restaurants, cafes and hotels and other

expenditure (*income* for short). Table 3.5 presents the mean budget share of each commodity averaged over the whole sample period corresponding to each country. The bottom section of the table displays the summary measures of the mean budget share. As can be seen, consumers in Hong Kong, Japan and Singapore allocate less than one fifth of their income to food while South Korean, Malaysian and Taiwanese consumers allocate about one quarter of their income to food. A noticeable difference here is that consumers in India and Sri Lanka spend approximately half of their income on food. This indicates that the proportion of income spent on food is a good indicator of a country's welfare, with an inverse relationship evident between income and food budget share.

Another noticeable observation is that, on average, consumers in Hong Kong, Japan, Malaysia and Taiwan spend approximately one fifth of their income on housing while consumers in India, Sri Lanka, and Thailand spend only about one tenth of their income on housing. The reason for this difference could be that the three latter countries have sizeable rural areas while the former are more urbanized, so housing may be more expensive. Japanese consumer's allocation of income on medical care

Table 3.4 Description of the database

Country	Sample period	Sample size	Base year	Currency	Data source
1. Hong Kong	1971–2019	49	2014	Hong Kong Dollars	Census and Statistics Department and Selvanathan and Selvanathan (2003)
2. India	1970–2019	50	1970	Rupees (Indian)	Various publications of Ministry of Statistics and Programme Implementation, India and Selvanathan and Selvanathan (2003)
3. Japan	1970–2019	50	1990	Yen	OECD database
4. Malaysia	2000–2016	17	2000	Ringgit	Various publications of Department of Statistics, Malaysia, UN database
5. Philippines	1998–2019	22	2000	Pesos	Various publications of Department of Statistics, Philippines and Selvanathan and Selvanathan (2003)
6. Singapore	1963–2019	57	2010	Dollars	Various publications of Department of Statistics, Singapore and Selvanathan and Selvanathan (2003)
7. South Korea	1970–2019	50	2010	Won	OECD database
8. Sri Lanka	1975–2019	45	1975	Rupees (Sri Lankan)	UN database and various publications of Central Bank of Sri Lanka and Selvanathan and Selvanathan (2003)
9. Taiwan	1962–2019	58	2011	Dollars	Various publications of Department of Statistics, Taiwan and Selvanathan and Selvanathan (2003)
10. Thailand	1967–2019	57	2002	Baht	Various publications of National Economic and Social Development Board, Thailand and Selvanathan and Selvanathan (2003)

is around four to five times that of the other Asian countries. This could be because, demographically, Japan has a relatively large older population compared to other countries considered here. The proportion of income allocated to transport varies from 7.8% (Hong Kong) to 19.7% (Malaysia). While consumers in India, the Philippines and Sri Lanka, on average, spend only a small proportion (less than 7%) of their income on recreation and education combined, consumers in the other countries spend a much higher proportion of their income on recreation and education.

Table 3.5 Sample average budget shares for eight commodities, ten Asian countries

Country	Food	Clothing	Housing	Durables	Medical care	Transport	Recreation	Miscellaneous
(1)	(2)	(3)	(4)	(5)	(6)	(7)	(8)	(9)
1. Hong Kong	18.0	16.2	18.0	8.1	3.8	7.8	8.3	19.9
2. India	49.6	8.4	11.6	3.7	3.5	12.0	3.5	7.8
3. Japan	19.7	5.3	21.4	5.2	10.6	11.1	11.6	15.2
4. Malaysia	23.8	2.8	17.0	5.5	2.3	19.7	15.6	13.3
5. Philippines	42.2	1.7	12.2	4.6	2.6	13.7	6.0	17.0
6. Singapore	15.7	6.0	13.1	7.4	4.5	14.6	22.8	16.0
7. South Korea	25.9	7.6	14.8	3.9	3.8	13.0	11.8	19.4
8. Sri Lanka	52.4	7.0	8.5	4.7	1.7	18.1	3.5	4.1
9. Taiwan	23.6	5.8	18.8	4.4	3.7	13.8	15.5	14.6
10. Thailand	33.1	5.9	9.2	4.5	3.7	13.0	22.4	8.3
Mean	30.4	6.7	14.5	5.2	4.0	13.7	12.1	13.5
Standard deviation	13.3	3.9	4.3	1.5	2.5	3.4	7.0	5.2
Coefficient of variation (×100)	43.8	58.6	29.6	28.1	61.0	24.5	58.2	38.6
Minimum	15.7	1.7	8.5	3.7	1.7	7.8	3.5	4.1
Maximum	52.4	16.2	21.4	8.1	10.6	19.7	22.8	19.9
Median	24.8	5.9	13.9	4.7	3.7	13.3	11.7	14.9

This is because high-income countries have a significantly upward bias toward recreation and entertainment relative to low-income countries due to greater disposable incomes. Across all countries, on average, consumers allocate about 30% of their income to food. The remaining income is spent on clothing (6.7%), housing (14.5%), durables (5.2%), medical care (4%), transport (13.7%), recreation (12.1%) and all other goods (13.5%). In general, food, clothing, housing, transport, and recreation absorb about four-fifths of consumer income in these ten Asian countries. The coefficient of variations presented at the bottom section of the table reveal that there is more variation in the budget shares for clothing, medical care, and recreation than the other five commodities across the ten countries.

The price and quantity log-changes are defined as $Dp_{it} = \ln p_{it} - \ln p_{it-1}$ and $Dq_{it} = \ln q_{it} - \ln q_{it-1}$, respectively. When multiplied by 100, these log-changes can be interpreted as percentage changes or growth rates of price and consumption from year $t - 1$ to year t. Here and elsewhere, ln refers to the natural logarithm. Table 3.6 presents the mean (averaged over the sample period and multiplied by 100) of the price and quantity log-changes. As can be seen, Japan, Singapore, and Malaysia have the lowest growth rates in prices and Sri Lanka, South Korea, and India have the highest growth rates in prices for consumer goods across the ten Asian countries. Growth in food prices is very important for consumers in any country, but particularly so for consumers who allocate a larger share of budget to food. As can also be seen from the table, growth in food price is very high in Sri Lanka, India, and South Korea compared to other countries.

The last two rows of each section of Table 3.6 present the means and standard deviations of the mean price and quantity log-changes for each commodity across the ten Asian countries. The average mean price log-change varies between 3.4% (durables) and 5% (housing) across countries. In terms of consumption, food has the lowest annual average consumption growth (1.8%) while transport (5.7%) has the highest.

3.4 Empirical Regularities in the Asian Countries

Various consumption studies have observed a number of empirical regularities in consumption patterns across a number of countries (see, for example, Chen, 2001; Powell, 1974; Rathnayaka et al., 2019; Selvanathan, 1993; Selvanathan & Clements, 1995; Selvanathan & Selvanathan, 1994, 2003; Selvanathan et al., 2023; Theil, 1975/76; Theil & Clements, 1987). The four important empirical regularities are as follows:

1. Quantity variance exceeds price variance;
2. Demand curve slopes downwards;
3. Income flexibility is close to – 0.5; and,
4. Budget share of food declines with increasing income.

In this section, we will investigate whether these empirical regularities are supported by data from the ten Asian countries.

Table 3.6 Average price and quantity log-changes for eight commodities, ten Asian countries (at sample means)

Country	Food	Clothing	Housing	Durables	Medical care	Transport	Recreation	Miscellaneous
(1)	(2)	(3)	(4)	(5)	(6)	(7)	(8)	(9)
	Mean price log-changes ($D\overline{p}_i$)							
1. Hong Kong	5.09	4.42	5.11	0.93	6.19	3.95	5.94	5.44
2. India	7.41	6.08	9.92	5.33	7.68	6.24	6.26	5.82
3. Japan	2.39	2.90	2.07	– 0.12	– 1.12	2.16	0.84	3.00
4. Malaysia	3.25	– 1.05	1.69	1.34	2.25	1.55	1.74	2.01
5. Philippines	3.45	5.98	3.89	1.35	6.35	4.10	5.75	4.76
6. Singapore	2.68	1.37	3.19	2.17	3.24	2.50	0.38	2.28
7. South Korea	7.15	6.85	9.14	6.20	6.10	7.24	8.41	7.84
8. Sri Lanka	9.12	7.55	7.68	10.40	10.94	8.32	7.18	9.48
9. Taiwan	3.73	1.91	3.15	3.16	3.33	2.00	4.42	3.42
10. Thailand	4.50	4.41	4.46	3.64	3.03	4.58	3.68	4.86
Mean	4.88	4.04	5.03	3.44	4.80	4.26	4.46	4.89
Standard deviation	2.28	2.73	2.91	3.15	3.35	2.34	2.75	2.40
	Mean quantity log-changes ($D\overline{q}_i$)							
1. Hong Kong	1.47	3.25	3.74	7.13	3.51	4.62	2.82	4.99
2. India	1.40	3.93	1.83	4.99	4.48	6.96	4.95	7.64
3. Japan	0.36	– 0.73	2.60	2.49	3.44	2.85	3.05	1.82
4. Malaysia	3.15	7.25	3.21	4.94	6.36	6.51	8.38	5.39
5. Philippines	2.62	0.20	2.93	2.54	4.36	4.12	3.16	4.15
6. Singapore	0.66	2.09	3.49	1.98	4.17	3.87	4.71	3.97
7. South Korea	1.73	3.39	3.55	5.18	6.82	6.01	4.60	4.65

(continued)

Table 3.6 (continued)

Country	Food	Clothing	Housing	Durables	Medical care	Transport	Recreation	Miscellaneous
(1)	(2)	(3)	(4)	(5)	(6)	(7)	(8)	(9)
8. Sri Lanka	1.77	3.56	7.46	2.53	2.26	8.00	5.25	3.46
9. Taiwan	2.66	5.57	4.85	6.22	4.88	8.63	5.89	4.80
10. Thailand	2.20	3.08	3.66	4.53	5.84	4.72	3.67	7.37
Mean	1.84	3.15	3.73	3.93	4.73	5.74	4.85	4.81
Standard deviation	0.93	2.46	1.62	1.54	1.44	1.97	1.63	1.83

Empirical Regularity 1: Quantity Variance (K) > Price Variance (Π)

The overall growth in consumption and prices in the ten countries was measured using the finite-change version of the Divisia quantity and price indices defined by Eqs. (2.2.12) and (2.2.13) in Chap. 2, which are reproduced here:

$$DQ_t = \sum_{i=1}^{n} \overline{w}_{it} Dq_{it} \quad \text{and} \quad DP_t = \sum_{i=1}^{n} \overline{w}_{it} Dp_{it},$$

where $\overline{w}_{it} = 1/2(w_{it} + w_{it-1})$ is the arithmetic average of the budget shares in periods t and $t-1$.

These indexes are presented in Tables 3.7 and 3.8. The last row of each table presents the mean values for each country averaged over the sample periods. The last row of Table 3.7 shows that, on average, overall prices have increased, per annum, at a rate of approximately 4.7% in Hong Kong, 7.1% in India, 1.8% in Japan, 2.0% in Malaysia, 4% in the Philippines, 2.1% in Singapore, 7.5% in South Korea, 8.7% in Sri Lanka, 3.3% in Taiwan and 4.2% in Thailand. Accordingly, the lowest and highest annual overall price growth has been experienced in Malaysia and Sri Lanka, respectively. As can be seen from the last row of Table 3.8, overall consumption growth in the Asian region varies between 2% (Japan) and 5.2% (Malaysia).

Table 3.9 gives the mean log-changes of relative prices $(D\overline{p}_{it} - D\overline{P}_t)$ and relative quantities $(D\overline{q}_{it} - D\overline{Q}_t)$ where $D\overline{p}_i = (1/T)\sum_{t=1}^{T} Dp_{it}$ and $D\overline{q}_i = (1/T)\sum_{t=1}^{T} Dq_{it}$. As can be seen, mean relative price log-changes for food, housing, and medical care have a positive price growth, while all other commodity groups have a mostly negative price growth. According to the mean relative quantity log-changes, food consumption has the lowest growth rate (− 1.87%) and transport has the highest consumption growth rate (1.95%). It is also noticeable in Table 3.9 that a significant number of the relative prices and corresponding relative quantity log-changes have opposite signs, reflecting the tendency of consumers, on average, to move away from those goods which have above average price increases.

To measure the overall variability in prices and consumption, we use the Divisia second-order moments, Divisia price variance (Π_t), and Divisia quantity variance (K_t), defined as (see Eqs. (2.2.14) and (2.2.15) in Chap. 2)

$$\Pi_t = \sum_{i=1}^{n} \overline{w}_{it}[Dp_{it} - DP_t]^2 \quad \text{and} \quad K_t = \sum_{i=1}^{n} \overline{w}_{it}[Dq_{it} - DQ_t]^2$$

Tables 3.10 and 3.11 display the Divisia price and quantity variances for the ten sample countries. A comparison of the quantity variances (K_t) with the corresponding price variances (Π_t) reveals that, on average, the quantity variance exceeds that of the price variance. Consumers are price takers and hence prices don't vary as much as consumption varies between consumers. Therefore, one would expect a higher level of variation in relative consumption compared to the variation in relative prices. This

Table 3.7 Divisia price index for the ten Asian countries

Year	Hong Kong	India	Japan	Malaysia	Philippines	Singapore	South Korea	Sri Lanka	Taiwan	Thailand
(1)	(2)	(3)	(4)	(5)	(6)	(7)	(8)	(9)	(10)	(11)
1963									0.63	
1964						0.99			0.91	
1965						0.37			0.75	
1966						1.96			0.24	
1967						2.08			3.81	
1968						1.16			5.69	1.18
1969						0.03			3.57	1.38
1970						1.20			4.05	− 0.26
1971		4.41	5.60			3.65	14.03		1.97	1.45
1972	6.86	11.15	4.91			2.68	12.44		4.00	4.18
1973	17.49	17.41	9.11			13.73	11.60		10.99	13.54
1974	14.57	18.41	19.34			11.84	29.00		30.38	19.44
1975	1.75	− 5.45	10.91			2.27	23.65		5.25	5.27
1976	5.16	2.71	8.74			0.94	16.81	3.30	1.95	1.10
1977	4.74	4.77	7.08			1.94	14.69	4.80	8.49	5.92
1978	5.94	12.92	4.63			3.12	20.30	13.54	7.13	8.09
1979	12.38	7.77	3.46			3.46	17.70	13.16	10.06	10.11
1980	13.23	14.49	6.72			5.86	24.81	21.25	19.59	16.36
1981	11.40	9.12	4.23			4.36	18.05	12.08	13.91	10.95
1982	9.60	6.54	2.51			0.56	5.67	13.73	2.92	5.87
1983	9.56	8.85	3.00			− 0.36	3.46	17.46	1.60	3.65

(continued)

Table 3.7 (continued)

Year	Hong Kong	India	Japan	Malaysia	Philippines	Singapore	South Korea	Sri Lanka	Taiwan	Thailand
(1)	(2)	(3)	(4)	(5)	(6)	(7)	(8)	(9)	(10)	(11)
1984	8.75	5.99	2.54			1.86	4.57	17.35	0.92	0.88
1985	3.10	5.50	2.24			0.24	4.35	2.85	0.69	3.27
1986	5.33	6.85	0.86			0.09	1.81	8.21	0.69	3.63
1987	5.90	7.64	0.56			2.38	4.15	3.49	1.59	2.85
1988	7.15	8.52	0.55			3.74	6.06	11.62	0.99	4.38
1989	7.92	7.02	1.87			4.35	6.41	11.57	3.56	5.64
1990	7.98	9.79	2.35			4.54	9.11	33.48	3.31	5.85
1991	9.06	12.75	2.50			2.21	11.10	15.80	4.06	5.65
1992	7.23	5.86	1.90			1.90	8.07	3.78	3.42	2.53
1993	6.36	7.59	1.32			3.99	6.75	5.88	3.19	2.84
1994	7.84	13.96	0.78			5.54	9.84	7.68	3.58	5.26
1995	7.89	6.34	0.13			1.29	6.66	8.27	3.15	4.35
1996	5.73	4.08	0.35			0.93	6.87	10.73	3.05	5.15
1997	4.76	23.37	1.21			2.23	6.29	2.10	1.37	4.97
1998	0.88	10.55	– 0.76			– 2.08	6.17	6.02	1.47	7.56
1999	– 5.38	4.60	– 0.20		5.86	– 2.36	3.22	7.74	1.02	0.62
2000	– 3.49	2.58	– 0.66		4.05	– 0.95	5.14	7.19	1.04	0.77
2001	– 1.05	2.33	– 1.04	1.24	6.20	– 0.81	4.39	10.22	– 0.25	2.24
2002	– 3.54	1.89	– 1.45	1.72	3.06	– 1.41	3.56	1.98	0.25	0.97
2003	– 2.83	3.86	– 1.20	0.99	3.26	– 0.31	3.38	5.28	– 0.39	1.95

(continued)

Table 3.7 (continued)

Year	Hong Kong	India	Japan	Malaysia	Philippines	Singapore	South Korea	Sri Lanka	Taiwan	Thailand
(1)	(2)	(3)	(4)	(5)	(6)	(7)	(8)	(9)	(10)	(11)
2004	− 0.46	2.08	− 0.25	1.26	6.27	0.54	3.27	8.93	1.29	3.05
2005	1.94	7.28	− 0.23	2.60	6.65	0.01	2.53	9.12	1.16	4.27
2006	1.44	6.09	0.29	2.62	5.33	1.84	1.63	8.18	0.79	4.48
2007	4.06	4.94	− 0.39	1.62	3.30	4.81	1.88	13.24	1.29	2.73
2008	2.51	6.71	1.29	4.13	8.87	5.82	3.93	18.04	2.82	5.53
2009	− 1.14	6.69	− 2.13	1.20	2.00	1.01	2.17	3.65	− 1.15	0.55
2010	1.95	8.16	− 0.75	1.65	3.94	3.79	2.78	5.18	0.79	3.80
2011	4.46	2.01	0.21	2.76	4.83	4.86	3.64	6.48	0.91	3.98
2012	3.64	9.96	0.77	1.58	2.97	3.71	2.11	7.51	1.19	2.52
2013	2.42	7.18	− 0.64	1.69	2.14	1.36	1.11	6.04	0.31	2.10
2014	2.55	3.94	2.08	2.60	2.52	1.23	1.23	3.20	0.67	1.62
2015	1.28	− 1.08	− 0.22	1.83	0.82	0.49	0.91	0.64	− 0.71	− 0.64
2016	1.54	9.39	− 17.18	2.34	1.29	− 0.44	6.68	3.68	0.85	0.33
2017	2.72	3.55	0.00		7.01	− 4.58	1.84	1.93	− 0.66	0.81
2018	3.05	4.28	0.00		2.68	0.48	1.35	3.68	0.96	0.97
2019	2.62	3.78	0.00		0.76	0.76	0.34	3.87	0.58	1.06
Mean	4.73	7.13	1.77	1.99	3.99	2.05	7.50	8.73	3.26	4.17

Note All entries are to be divided by 100

Table 3.8 Divisia quantity index for the ten Asian countries

Year	Hong Kong	India	Japan	Malaysia	Philippines	Singapore	South Korea	Sri Lanka	Taiwan	Thailand
(1)	(2)	(3)	(4)	(5)	(6)	(7)	(8)	(9)	(10)	(11)
1963									3.95	
1964						– 4.41			10.90	
1965						3.32			7.05	
1966						5.58			3.80	
1967						5.01			8.20	
1968						7.00			7.36	3.34
1969						7.58			5.80	3.07
1970						10.87			5.92	5.46
1971		0.63	4.87			7.00	6.30		7.18	3.29
1972	5.68	– 4.41	7.08			7.70	4.36		8.86	3.94
1973	5.65	0.31	7.61			7.87	8.18		10.35	5.42
1974	– 6.14	– 1.50	– 1.58			5.81	4.14		3.27	3.85
1975	0.82	5.10	2.62			1.21	3.44		4.59	3.13
1976	7.54	– 2.31	2.44			3.71	6.35	2.43	5.57	– 4.43
1977	11.81	7.67	2.95			5.07	3.54	9.20	5.72	5.91
1978	13.46	2.48	4.03			7.64	5.64	0.65	7.58	4.56
1979	2.38	– 1.95	5.28			8.73	6.02	8.06	8.61	4.15
1980	5.37	2.83	0.74			7.27	– 1.61	5.46	4.02	3.49
1981	4.95	2.17	0.61			3.91	2.50	1.74	1.97	0.73
1982	3.04	0.69	3.59			0.11	4.75	2.61	3.38	0.50
1983	4.44	4.87	2.44			5.42	7.05	– 1.60	4.76	4.94

(continued)

Table 3.8 (continued)

Year	Hong Kong	India	Japan	Malaysia	Philippines	Singapore	South Korea	Sri Lanka	Taiwan	Thailand
(1)	(2)	(3)	(4)	(5)	(6)	(7)	(8)	(9)	(10)	(11)
1984	4.01	1.53	1.94			1.55	5.09	− 3.55	6.56	2.19
1985	2.90	1.47	2.60			− 2.57	4.89	3.78	3.76	− 0.61
1986	6.65	2.72	2.72			4.50	8.13	− 0.41	5.93	1.12
1987	9.94	1.54	3.52			8.33	7.24	2.90	10.19	6.74
1988	7.77	3.83	4.27			8.38	6.86	3.11	12.07	8.02
1989	2.65	2.21	4.19			5.41	7.82	− 0.52	11.62	8.07
1990	4.54	1.75	4.13			4.85	7.70	− 12.76	7.32	9.59
1991	5.91	− 0.15	2.17			0.45	6.68	− 0.21	6.03	3.59
1992	8.03	1.97	1.67			3.64	5.33	6.96	8.06	8.13
1993	5.28	2.63	0.80			6.84	5.23	6.93	6.55	7.21
1994	3.08	2.29	1.71			1.05	6.79	6.35	6.47	5.51
1995	− 0.59	3.80	2.00			− 0.20	8.32	1.86	2.94	8.13
1996	− 0.43	6.43	1.73			0.46	5.69	2.42	5.66	4.60
1997	2.23	3.68	0.90			0.45	2.96	8.08	6.19	− 2.09
1998	− 8.82	2.49	− 0.51			− 7.30	− 12.17	8.11	4.30	− 9.92
1999	0.54	4.75	1.43		1.76	7.31	9.29	1.79	4.25	2.48
2000	4.59	1.69	1.76		2.92	10.19	6.40	7.70	3.67	5.69
2001	0.83	4.18	2.21	3.30	1.89	− 0.59	4.43	3.80	0.23	4.96
2002	0.26	1.02	1.42	2.02	2.87	1.32	6.75	8.77	2.44	5.50
2003	− 0.35	5.43	1.17	1.45	3.31	1.01	− 1.33	4.61	2.52	5.87

(continued)

Table 3.8 (continued)

Year	Hong Kong	India	Japan	Malaysia	Philippines	Singapore	South Korea	Sri Lanka	Taiwan	Thailand
(1)	(2)	(3)	(4)	(5)	(6)	(7)	(8)	(9)	(10)	(11)
2004	6.67	3.82	0.90	10.79	3.82	5.13	− 0.73	1.69	4.54	6.47
2005	4.07	6.53	1.46	8.19	2.50	1.60	3.34	3.68	2.81	3.51
2006	5.38	6.55	1.33	5.90	2.28	0.98	3.38	7.81	1.23	3.49
2007	8.41	7.12	0.88	10.26	2.97	1.35	4.12	5.01	1.90	1.76
2008	2.04	5.19	− 0.23	6.35	2.02	− 3.45	1.65	6.53	− 2.44	2.41
2009	0.67	5.20	0.31	− 1.01	0.72	− 5.08	0.34	− 4.24	− 0.44	− 2.51
2010	7.45	6.29	1.84	4.19	1.66	7.02	3.28	8.40	3.26	5.57
2011	8.89	7.75	− 0.11	4.11	3.72	2.91	2.52	14.43	3.05	3.72
2012	3.72	3.19	1.88	4.77	4.80	0.03	0.71	8.16	1.56	7.16
2013	5.96	5.32	2.75	5.78	3.90	0.78	0.80	2.74	1.91	2.94
2014	1.58	4.45	− 0.33	9.59	3.80	0.82	1.44	4.82	2.88	− 0.17
2015	1.78	7.15	0.09	2.85	4.55	2.15	2.04	10.08	2.65	4.48
2016	− 0.99	6.79	− 0.82	3.98	5.22	0.55	0.22	− 0.31	3.22	0.15
2017	4.27	4.86	1.63		1.29	3.39	1.42	− 0.80	2.52	4.62
2018	4.91	5.51	1.46		5.94	3.15	2.76	5.06	1.68	3.43
2019	− 4.86	4.04	− 0.07		5.13	1.03	2.49	2.74	2.31	3.33
Mean	3.71	3.30	1.99	5.16	3.19	3.28	3.93	3.73	4.88	3.59

Note All entries are to be divided by 100

Table 3.9 Average relative price and quantity log-changes for the ten Asian countries (at sample means)

Country	Food	Clothing	Housing	Durables	Medical care	Transport	Recreation	Miscellaneous
(1)	(2)	(3)	(4)	(5)	(6)	(7)	(8)	(9)
	Average relative price log-changes ($D\overline{p}_i - D\overline{P}$)							
1. Hong Kong	0.36	− 0.31	0.38	− 3.79	1.46	− 0.77	1.22	0.71
2. India	0.29	− 1.04	2.80	− 1.79	0.56	− 0.89	− 0.87	− 1.31
3. Japan	0.61	1.13	0.30	− 1.89	− 2.89	0.39	− 0.93	1.23
4. Malaysia	1.26	− 3.04	− 0.30	− 0.65	0.26	− 0.44	− 0.25	0.02
5. Philippines	− 0.54	1.99	− 0.10	− 2.64	2.36	0.11	1.76	0.76
6. Singapore	0.63	− 0.68	1.14	0.12	1.19	0.45	− 1.67	0.22
7. South Korea	− 0.35	− 0.65	1.64	− 1.30	− 1.40	− 0.26	0.91	0.34
8. Sri Lanka	0.40	− 1.18	− 1.04	1.68	2.21	− 0.41	− 1.54	0.75
9. Taiwan	0.47	− 1.35	− 0.11	− 0.10	0.07	− 1.26	1.16	0.16
10. Thailand	0.33	0.24	0.29	− 0.53	− 1.14	0.41	− 0.49	0.69
Mean	0.35	− 0.49	0.50	− 1.09	0.27	− 0.27	− 0.07	0.36
Standard deviation	0.50	1.39	1.10	1.55	1.68	0.60	1.24	0.69
	Average relative quantity log-changes ($D\overline{q}_i - D\overline{Q}$)							
1. Hong Kong	− 2.23	− 0.46	0.03	3.42	− 0.20	0.91	− 0.89	1.28
2. India	− 1.90	0.63	− 1.47	1.69	1.18	3.66	1.65	4.34
3. Japan	− 1.63	− 2.72	0.61	0.50	1.45	0.87	1.06	− 0.17
4. Malaysia	− 2.01	2.09	− 1.95	− 0.22	1.20	1.35	3.22	0.23
5. Philippines	− 0.57	− 2.99	− 0.27	− 0.65	1.16	0.93	− 0.03	0.96
6. Singapore	− 2.62	− 1.19	0.21	− 1.30	0.88	0.59	1.42	0.68
7. South Korea	− 2.20	− 0.54	− 0.38	1.25	2.89	2.08	0.67	0.72

(continued)

Table 3.9 (continued)

Country	Food	Clothing	Housing	Durables	Medical care	Transport	Recreation	Miscellaneous
(1)	(2)	(3)	(4)	(5)	(6)	(7)	(8)	(9)
8. Sri Lanka	− 1.96	− 0.17	3.74	− 1.20	− 1.47	4.28	1.53	− 0.26
9. Taiwan	− 2.23	0.69	− 0.03	1.33	0.00	3.74	1.01	− 0.09
10. Thailand	− 1.39	− 0.51	0.07	0.95	2.25	1.13	0.08	3.78
Mean	− 1.87	− 0.52	0.06	0.58	0.93	1.95	0.97	1.15
Standard deviation	0.57	1.53	1.51	1.46	1.24	1.40	1.13	1.62

Note All entries are to be divided by 100. $D\overline{P} = (1/T)\sum_{t=1}^{T} DP_t$, $D\overline{Q} = (1/T)\sum_{t=1}^{T} DQ_t$

means that, at sample means, in general, the quantity variance would exceed the price variance.

Figure 3.2 plots $\sqrt{K_t}$ against $\sqrt{\Pi_t}$ for $t = 1, \ldots, T$, together with the 45° line for individual countries. As can be seen, the majority of the points lie above this line (except for the Philippines which has only a small sample). This indicates that, on average, the quantity variance exceeds the price variance. Figure 3.3 shows the plot for the ten countries combined; again, the majority of the points lie above the 45° line. This agrees with the results that quantity variance (K) exceeds price variance (Π) reported in a number of previous consumption studies (see, for example, Clements & Selvanathan, 1994; Rathnayaka et al., 2019; Selvanathan & Selvanathan, 2004; Selvanathan et al., 2023; Theil, 1975/76, 1987; Wong et al., 2015).

Empirical Regularity 2: Demand Curve Slopes Downwards

The co-movements of price and quantity are measured by the Divisia price-quantity correlation given by (see Eqs. (2.2.16) and (2.2.17) of Chap. 2)

$$\rho_t = \frac{\Gamma_t}{\sqrt{\Pi_t K_t}},$$

and Π_t and K_t are defined as before, where

$$\Gamma_t = \sum_{i=1}^{n} \overline{w}_{it}[Dp_{it} - DP_t][Dq_{it} - DQ_t]$$

is the Divisia price-quantity covariance.

Table 3.12 presents the Divisia price-quantity correlations for the ten Asian countries. Almost 90% of the individual price-quantity correlations are negative. For the sample means, the average correlations vary between − 0.43 and − 0.04. This means that, in general, when prices rise, consumption falls, equating to a downward sloping demand curve.

Empirical Regularity 3: Income Flexibility Is Close to − 0.5

We pool the data across countries and plot the relative consumption $(Dq_{it} - DQ_t)$ against the relative price $(Dp_{it} - DP_t)$, $t = 1, \ldots, T$, for each country, thereby obtaining the slope estimates for all ten countries. These estimates can be interpreted as estimates of income flexibility, ϕ (see Eq. (2.4.16), Chap. 2), for each country. Figure 3.4 presents the plots for the pooled data $(Dq_{it} - DQ_t)$ against $(Dp_{it} - DP_t)$, $t = 1, \ldots T$ and $i = 1, \ldots, n$. for each country. Figure 3.6 highlights the plot for the ten countries combined. According to the plots, the points are scattered around a negatively sloping line. In other words, these figures imply that, in all countries, consumption falls when relative prices rises.

Table 3.13 presents the estimates of income flexibility, ϕ, collected from all the plots in Fig. 3.4 for each country and in Fig. 3.5 for all countries combined. Results show that all the estimates are negative and range between − 0.68 and − 0.30 with

Table 3.10 Divisia price variance for the ten Asian countries

Year	Hong Kong	India	Japan	Malaysia	Philippines	Singapore	South Korea	Sri Lanka	Taiwan	Thailand
(1)	(2)	(3)	(4)	(5)	(6)	(7)	(8)	(9)	(10)	(11)
1963									1.61	
1964						0.42			2.23	
1965						1.25			2.11	
1966						3.81			14.91	
1967						7.42			15.05	
1968						1.75			7.33	0.65
1969						3.74			9.15	1.38
1970						2.56			16.47	3.33
1971		2.18	3.49			4.28	20.25		2.05	9.98
1972	13.51	15.15	4.59			5.29	7.95		5.87	2.25
1973	53.96	19.70	31.41			45.67	10.84		19.98	13.23
1974	35.07	32.60	31.48			20.93	11.89		55.82	11.68
1975	22.26	48.95	8.87			9.45	19.66		8.46	1.80
1976	3.17	6.53	3.42			5.90	23.73	2.30	5.87	50.78
1977	14.90	5.04	4.66			1.73	15.21	5.09	9.69	2.22
1978	2.15	703.52	7.00			1.89	12.35	33.08	7.69	6.73
1979	11.97	12.86	2.81			1.70	7.39	100.56	8.51	18.11
1980	11.34	39.87	5.40			24.34	17.51	118.11	25.48	237.90
1981	8.02	3.44	1.40			18.10	11.39	29.65	22.27	32.81
1982	8.86	5.11	1.97			21.46	22.51	65.87	4.96	5.09
1983	8.31	4.09	10.16			11.43	17.40	36.68	2.33	5.33

(continued)

Table 3.10 (continued)

Year	Hong Kong	India	Japan	Malaysia	Philippines	Singapore	South Korea	Sri Lanka	Taiwan	Thailand
(1)	(2)	(3)	(4)	(5)	(6)	(7)	(8)	(9)	(10)	(11)
1984	3.77	3.13	0.94			3.95	6.63	14.11	7.22	12.06
1985	9.22	2.55	3.98			3.91	4.08	19.25	7.89	13.24
1986	7.66	2.63	0.89			2.07	12.21	8.37	3.31	16.79
1987	2.47	0.99	0.85			2.60	5.16	13.06	3.63	2.54
1988	5.72	6.14	0.33			9.15	1.44	38.00	12.60	3.40
1989	8.68	2.76	0.72			4.75	5.18	61.47	10.12	8.60
1990	6.86	5.60	1.35			5.37	21.51	900.87	12.31	5.19
1991	6.39	11.54	1.48			4.40	20.02	64.77	5.22	1.22
1992	4.66	14.54	1.38			6.17	15.00	69.02	6.55	3.41
1993	5.23	1.79	0.75			5.83	14.09	55.95	5.75	6.14
1994	10.54	109.97	1.63			12.45	12.75	7.44	3.77	7.37
1995	5.97	4.56	1.46			10.77	3.83	23.57	0.85	3.97
1996	6.13	4.52	1.14			5.87	1.18	12.57	2.28	2.53
1997	5.10	514.89	0.69			5.05	5.61	1.07	1.63	5.22
1998	8.25	82.64	5.57			13.20	16.16	12.59	3.47	6.69
1999	22.39	94.71	0.51		4.88	19.81	21.94	18.40	1.10	25.95
2000	12.10	20.01	3.83		13.04	1.70	3.74	17.21	1.50	11.29
2001	2.52	3.55	2.66	1.78	8.36	6.13	3.23	16.98	0.49	0.93
2002	8.77	11.21	1.76	5.23	3.10	2.38	1.69	3.54	3.68	0.67
2003	3.10	14.35	3.66	0.46	4.08	3.51	0.76	10.04	1.10	2.70

(continued)

Table 3.10 (continued)

Year	Hong Kong	India	Japan	Malaysia	Philippines	Singapore	South Korea	Sri Lanka	Taiwan	Thailand
(1)	(2)	(3)	(4)	(5)	(6)	(7)	(8)	(9)	(10)	(11)
2004	8.16	51.07	1.61	1.12	3.35	8.10	2.12	9.47	2.17	2.50
2005	6.01	96.35	1.40	2.66	7.80	6.65	0.80	15.09	3.24	4.98
2006	6.53	4.95	1.07	1.58	2.47	8.71	0.45	12.59	0.77	5.65
2007	13.25	9.63	1.50	1.50	6.12	10.24	0.19	30.80	1.00	6.12
2008	23.01	7.91	1.51	5.91	17.37	68.44	0.62	65.07	3.29	17.25
2009	13.08	24.30	4.75	11.53	4.59	2.76	4.70	12.46	3.79	3.46
2010	2.76	6.02	2.92	0.95	4.64	4.68	1.30	13.11	3.52	11.78
2011	11.01	233.81	3.52	1.31	2.01	13.47	1.77	6.66	1.48	4.57
2012	5.53	11.17	9.59	0.82	0.38	6.27	2.44	12.38	2.29	1.01
2013	9.32	3.56	1.89	1.51	1.11	3.24	1.30	6.86	0.72	2.74
2014	8.63	6.21	2.45	1.56	0.10	1.19	1.58	2.09	2.11	4.06
2015	9.32	4.36	3.08	4.77	1.22	6.93	7.34	49.10	9.26	11.31
2016	4.00	23.93	2211.47	0.71	1.28	9.94	100.13	3.58	7.82	4.15
2017	8.48	3.96	0.00		344.21	558.49	0.57	27.45	30.59	1.84
2018	5.24	3.11	0.00		12.65	12.47	0.95	9.66	0.87	0.93
2019	5.10	1.83	0.00		1.00	1.69	0.94	4.76	1.21	0.96
Mean	9.97	47.01	4.17	2.71	21.13	18.67	10.24	46.38	7.31	12.05

Note All entries are to be divided by 10,000

Table 3.11 Divisia quantity variance for the ten Asian countries

Year	Hong Kong	India	Japan	Malaysia	Philippines	Singapore	South Korea	Sri Lanka	Taiwan	Thailand
(1)	(2)	(3)	(4)	(5)	(6)	(7)	(8)	(9)	(10)	(11)
1963									6.18	
1964						11.77			70.70	
1965						3.23			17.22	
1966						24.04			11.22	
1967						28.70			38.70	
1968						8.47			13.82	1.13
1969						22.99			7.83	4.22
1970						7.27			10.89	13.01
1971		20.88	5.53			6.74	25.51		14.31	9.72
1972	23.80	8.28	5.36			4.39	3.21		9.50	1.66
1973	68.50	4.97	12.60			22.93	14.17		35.52	7.33
1974	181.97	22.78	41.22			65.79	5.11		22.10	7.83
1975	24.78	2.69	20.71			12.20	10.88		2.85	9.09
1976	33.84	44.95	10.35			2.81	5.51	59.80	3.54	1610.06
1977	114.73	16.82	7.14			11.65	18.88	57.67	16.16	13.54
1978	61.50	11.13	11.85			15.80	36.95	147.29	32.94	12.13
1979	46.23	16.74	11.51			17.26	22.43	39.04	50.64	6.24
1980	20.01	6.84	15.22			6.04	22.34	94.47	5.43	11.07
1981	15.26	4.40	6.98			31.46	23.57	83.75	3.98	14.47
1982	5.62	11.39	5.97			14.06	37.20	49.88	12.31	7.65
1983	30.54	9.63	4.33			17.03	24.43	53.79	17.24	8.93

(continued)

Table 3.11 (continued)

Year	Hong Kong	India	Japan	Malaysia	Philippines	Singapore	South Korea	Sri Lanka	Taiwan	Thailand
(1)	(2)	(3)	(4)	(5)	(6)	(7)	(8)	(9)	(10)	(11)
1984	15.97	3.78	5.88			12.74	25.88	85.03	7.50	17.42
1985	2.94	11.88	6.92			35.15	33.75	31.51	12.98	15.64
1986	15.61	15.92	10.83			40.39	5.03	60.49	9.33	9.29
1987	22.88	5.21	5.58			45.24	6.54	26.33	13.70	31.63
1988	30.58	5.60	11.04			19.03	4.26	17.54	68.81	22.32
1989	10.10	13.78	11.22			23.33	8.07	88.89	43.09	15.55
1990	11.17	3.73	10.24			44.00	15.32	722.36	14.34	28.32
1991	57.22	12.29	4.51			12.06	7.54	35.47	51.36	11.64
1992	47.64	3.87	5.47			15.37	8.72	105.30	9.42	23.89
1993	17.59	4.91	4.91			19.39	8.25	42.21	6.23	10.08
1994	11.64	13.82	5.86			4.04	18.47	10.68	5.95	4.89
1995	16.18	6.47	2.91			5.54	23.71	5.72	117.17	5.09
1996	8.13	7.13	8.30			7.47	12.22	10.39	19.28	3.57
1997	28.36	48.57	11.35			32.00	11.51	2.38	14.62	35.57
1998	63.50	22.74	8.30			71.05	79.46	329.76	2.10	90.92
1999	9.45	40.17	12.02		0.69	23.34	14.36	22.63	8.01	39.90
2000	22.83	54.51	4.65		1.45	54.55	18.04	197.41	1.88	5.33
2001	13.77	10.85	6.89	21.71	3.68	20.26	14.95	39.97	2.66	4.34
2002	49.12	22.80	5.88	9.52	7.42	14.45	22.14	232.73	7.26	8.84
2003	23.72	10.85	8.45	6.09	1.79	14.28	12.96	54.33	7.00	7.54

(continued)

Table 3.11 (continued)

Year	Hong Kong	India	Japan	Malaysia	Philippines	Singapore	South Korea	Sri Lanka	Taiwan	Thailand
(1)	(2)	(3)	(4)	(5)	(6)	(7)	(8)	(9)	(10)	(11)
2004	15.99	18.88	2.11	104.74	4.28	15.84	4.44	102.35	7.62	10.53
2005	1.90	22.58	3.64	56.33	4.40	2.27	4.16	152.09	4.71	2.00
2006	9.41	37.70	2.13	15.30	1.34	5.40	2.90	57.89	6.63	4.20
2007	31.64	38.51	2.36	14.98	3.54	6.25	5.23	97.67	3.59	2.79
2008	10.62	24.64	5.28	9.22	0.86	1.86	5.12	422.91	14.74	2.01
2009	7.93	31.98	7.10	8.67	0.95	15.83	9.55	335.99	16.35	4.36
2010	35.81	8.60	6.25	5.04	0.55	91.89	3.08	45.63	4.93	19.17
2011	96.58	12.20	3.81	2.34	3.52	24.97	1.73	45.87	10.15	13.27
2012	13.39	10.83	4.89	1.72	2.49	4.13	2.16	24.52	1.43	29.46
2013	40.31	11.47	11.31	1.08	1.20	22.54	1.72	12.92	2.17	23.41
2014	6.56	22.94	2.48	10.26	1.06	2.39	3.10	24.64	2.44	16.55
2015	13.06	26.13	4.94	13.40	4.72	29.11	6.10	51.78	4.52	7.95
2016	26.17	144.72	5.98	2.36	2.11	22.21	6.00	58.09	28.74	3.76
2017	4.84	36.66	1.01		11.44	1.33	1.48	106.37	10.10	7.52
2018	16.80	4.26	0.99		9.38	5.84	1.50	3.46	0.49	2.75
2019	42.61	4.70	0.80		4.29	6.05	2.81	6.77	0.57	2.44
Mean	30.81	48.96	7.65	17.67	3.39	19.75	13.52	96.72	16.58	43.88

Note All entries are to be divided by 10,000

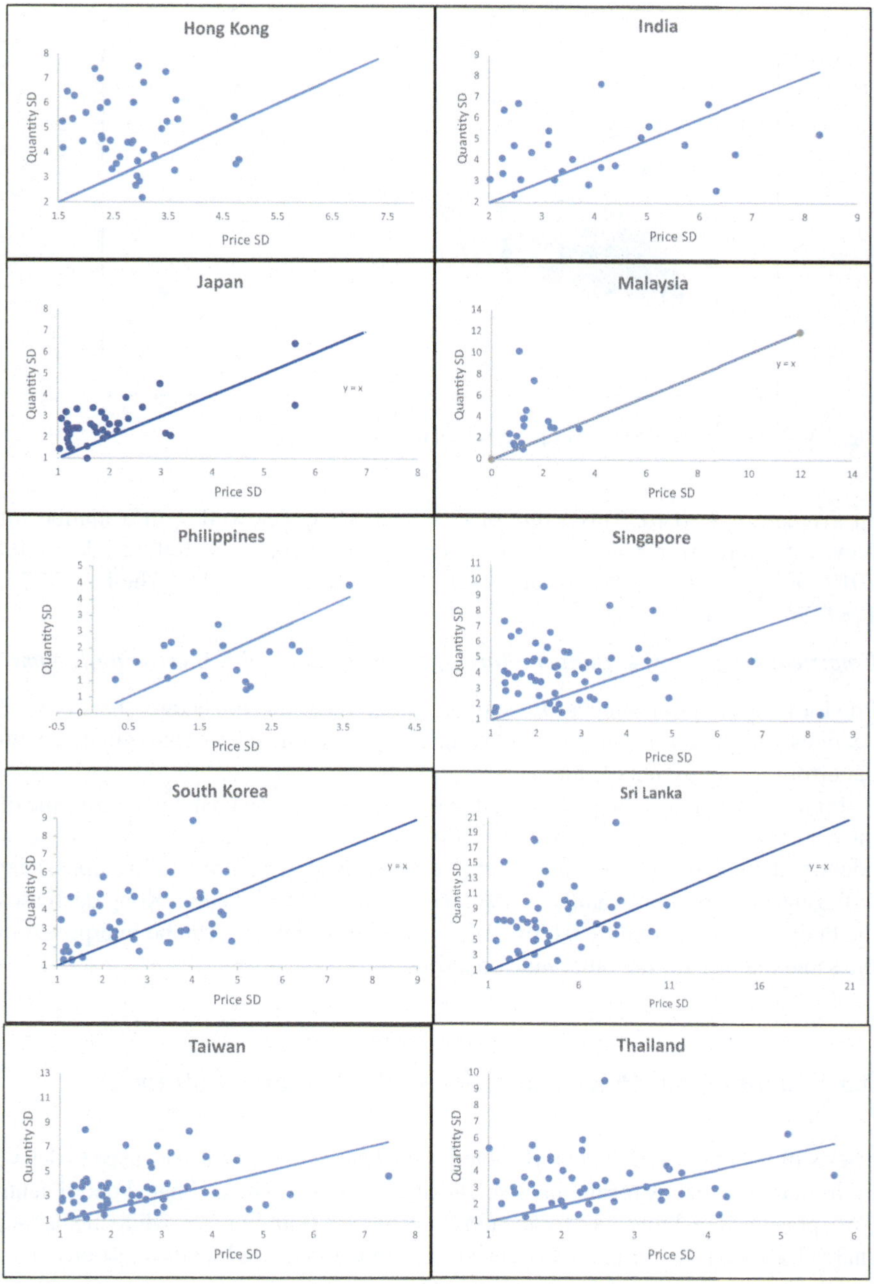

Fig. 3.2 Divisia quantity SD versus price SD, ten Asian countries

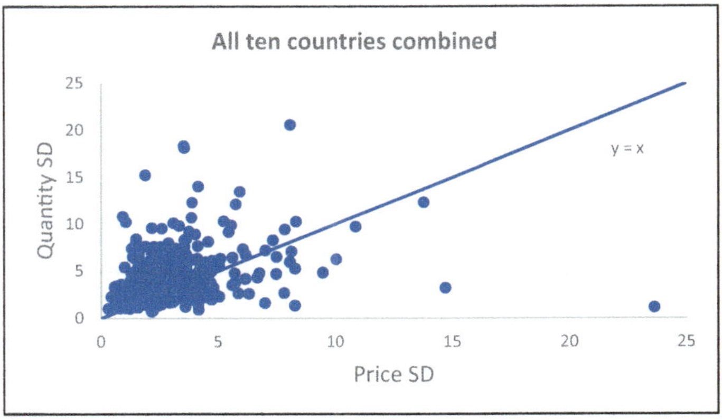

Fig. 3.3 Divisia quantity SD versus price SD, all ten countries combined

an average of − 0.46. This value of $\phi = -0.46$ agrees well with a number of previous studies (for example, Clements & Selvanathan, 1994; Rathnayaka et al., 2019; Selvanathan & Selvanathan, 2004; Selvanathan et al., 2023; Theil, 1975/76, 1987; Wong et al., 2017).

Empirical Regularity 4: Budget Share of Food Declines with Increasing Income

Previous consumption studies also support Engel's Law that the budget share of food declines with increasing income. We now investigate this empirical regularity with data from the ten Asian countries.

Figure 3.6 displays the plot of food budget share (w_{Ft}) against the logarithmic of the per capita consumption expenditure ($\log M_t$) for the ten countries. Irrespective of country, the points are scattered around a negatively sloping straight line, consistent with Engel's Law. For example, a 1% increase in income for Hong Kong decreases the budget share of food by 0.05%. The slope coefficient (β_F) can be interpreted in the same manner for the other nine countries.

3.5 Income and Price Elasticities: Preliminary Estimates

The estimated slope coefficient, β_F noted in the last section can also be used to derive preliminary estimates for the income elasticity for food. The estimated coefficients (β_F), presented in Table 3.14 for the ten countries are from Fig. 3.6, while the budget shares for food ($\overline{w}_i$) for the ten countries are from Table 3.5. Income elasticity (η_F), and the marginal share (θ_F) for each country are computed as $\theta_F = \beta_F + w_F$ and $\eta_F = \theta_F / w_F$, respectively. As evidenced by the table, the income elasticity for food is less than 1; hence, food is a necessity.

As a preliminary analysis for all countries, we estimated the double-log demand equation below for each commodity i (= 1, 2, …, 8) to obtain preliminary estimates

Table 3.12 Divisia price-quantity correlations, ten Asian countries

Year	Hong Kong	India	Japan	Malaysia	Philippines	Singapore	South Korea	Sri Lanka	Taiwan	Thailand
(1)	(2)	(3)	(4)	(5)	(6)	(7)	(8)	(9)	(10)	(11)
1963									0.58	
1964						– 0.41			– 0.55	
1965						– 0.27			– 0.30	
1966						– 0.69			– 0.53	
1967						– 0.47			– 0.22	
1968						– 0.74			– 0.50	– 0.07
1969						0.34			0.13	– 0.17
1970						0.01			– 0.59	0.44
1971		0.76	0.07			– 0.20	– 0.91		– 0.45	0.44
1972	0.38	– 0.96	– 0.42			0.66	– 0.02		– 0.60	– 0.41
1973	– 0.65	– 0.02	– 0.52			– 0.57	– 0.32		– 0.63	– 0.33
1974	– 0.77	– 0.17	– 0.79			– 0.72	0.12		– 0.76	– 0.30
1975	0.61	– 0.64	0.10			– 0.16	– 0.58		– 0.51	– 0.02
1976	0.01	0.22	– 0.76			– 0.30	– 0.51	– 0.85	0.45	0.81
1977	– 0.78	– 0.22	– 0.01			– 0.50	– 0.49	– 0.56	0.14	– 0.29
1978	– 0.80	– 0.12	– 0.19			0.43	– 0.65	– 0.72	– 0.06	– 0.42
1979	– 0.52	– 0.66	0.03			– 0.35	– 0.52	– 0.36	0.49	– 0.60
1980	0.11	– 0.70	– 0.67			– 0.56	0.40	– 0.11	– 0.08	0.32
1981	0.02	0.15	– 0.18			– 0.72	– 0.05	– 0.35	– 0.49	– 0.73
1982	0.21	– 0.26	– 0.44			– 0.77	0.18	– 0.63	– 0.42	0.24
1983	– 0.61	– 0.02	– 0.32			– 0.82	0.13	– 0.48	0.55	– 0.48

(continued)

Table 3.12 (continued)

Year	Hong Kong	India	Japan	Malaysia	Philippines	Singapore	South Korea	Sri Lanka	Taiwan	Thailand
(1)	(2)	(3)	(4)	(5)	(6)	(7)	(8)	(9)	(10)	(11)
1984	− 0.38	− 0.35	− 0.66			− 0.05	0.02	− 0.52	0.28	0.43
1985	0.57	0.59	− 0.72			− 0.30	− 0.05	0.50	− 0.23	− 0.28
1986	0.63	− 0.48	− 0.18			0.27	− 0.08	0.09	− 0.44	− 0.67
1987	0.09	− 0.02	0.09			0.21	0.06	− 0.42	0.61	− 0.69
1988	− 0.67	− 0.34	− 0.53			0.40	0.68	− 0.77	− 0.83	− 0.39
1989	0.03	− 0.31	− 0.19			0.29	0.14	− 0.44	− 0.39	− 0.44
1990	0.08	0.66	− 0.50			− 0.42	0.04	− 0.99	− 0.24	− 0.03
1991	− 0.80	0.26	− 0.61			0.19	− 0.17	− 0.90	− 0.01	− 0.39
1992	− 0.62	− 0.18	0.06			0.28	0.82	− 0.88	− 0.43	− 0.32
1993	0.21	0.09	0.46			0.35	0.45	− 0.87	0.18	0.25
1994	− 0.42	− 0.82	0.46			0.34	− 0.63	− 0.03	− 0.23	− 0.56
1995	− 0.07	0.62	− 0.39			0.71	0.09	0.44	0.23	− 0.75
1996	0.50	− 0.42	− 0.11			0.23	0.71	− 0.40	0.10	− 0.46
1997	− 0.46	0.41	− 0.28			− 0.58	0.39	− 0.68	0.00	− 0.10
1998	0.42	0.04	0.20			− 0.49	− 0.19	− 0.47	− 0.51	− 0.18
1999	0.35	− 0.25	− 0.34		− 0.13	0.06	0.03	− 0.90	− 0.02	− 0.58
2000	0.09	0.23	− 0.21		0.43	− 0.36	− 0.46	− 0.51	0.61	0.26
2001	0.24	− 0.06	− 0.53	0.31	0.53	− 0.26	− 0.31	− 0.90	0.31	0.80
2002	− 0.24	0.78	− 0.23	0.14	− 0.86	− 0.09	− 0.21	− 0.66	− 0.66	0.30
2003	− 0.72	− 0.56	− 0.66	0.30	− 0.44	− 0.22	0.10	− 0.15	− 0.22	0.37

(continued)

Table 3.12 (continued)

Year	Hong Kong	India	Japan	Malaysia	Philippines	Singapore	South Korea	Sri Lanka	Taiwan	Thailand
(1)	(2)	(3)	(4)	(5)	(6)	(7)	(8)	(9)	(10)	(11)
2004	0.67	− 0.54	− 0.34	− 0.66	0.15	− 0.12	− 0.36	− 0.18	− 0.25	− 0.14
2005	0.58	− 0.15	− 0.12	− 0.50	0.29	0.08	− 0.47	− 0.70	− 0.21	− 0.11
2006	− 0.32	− 0.78	− 0.09	− 0.76	− 0.71	− 0.91	0.00	− 0.30	− 0.27	− 0.71
2007	0.56	− 0.29	− 0.63	− 0.59	− 0.18	− 0.76	− 0.28	− 0.57	− 0.68	− 0.57
2008	0.55	− 0.12	− 0.38	− 0.77	0.38	− 0.32	− 0.17	− 0.80	− 0.55	− 0.23
2009	− 0.20	− 0.77	0.37	− 0.08	0.10	0.54	− 0.78	− 0.17	− 0.63	0.05
2010	− 0.09	− 0.72	− 0.67	− 0.72	− 0.27	0.11	− 0.31	− 0.38	− 0.56	− 0.57
2011	− 0.24	− 0.86	− 0.65	− 0.73	− 0.10	− 0.64	− 0.03	− 0.28	− 0.38	− 0.57
2012	− 0.78	− 0.93	− 0.63	− 0.80	− 0.23	− 0.32	− 0.27	0.85	− 0.30	− 0.28
2013	− 0.87	0.14	− 0.63	− 0.44	− 0.47	− 0.36	0.28	− 0.42	− 0.70	− 0.52
2014	0.35	− 0.76	− 0.39	− 0.18	− 0.36	− 0.77	− 0.72	− 0.69	− 0.86	0.80
2015	− 0.06	0.24	0.48	− 0.75	0.06	− 0.27	− 0.60	− 0.77	− 0.23	0.24
2016	0.88	− 0.32	− 0.03	− 0.06	− 0.01	− 0.60	− 0.19	− 0.58	− 0.22	− 0.60
2017	0.71	− 0.85	0.17		0.63	− 0.04	− 0.16	− 0.25	− 0.42	0.92
2018	− 0.54	0.13	0.11		− 0.82	0.41	− 0.05	− 0.04	0.33	0.55
2019	0.70	0.38	− 0.14		− 0.84	0.44	0.33	− 0.10	− 0.43	− 0.17
Mean	− 0.04	− 0.18	− 0.26	− 0.39	− 0.14	− 0.17	− 0.11	− 0.43	− 0.22	− 0.13

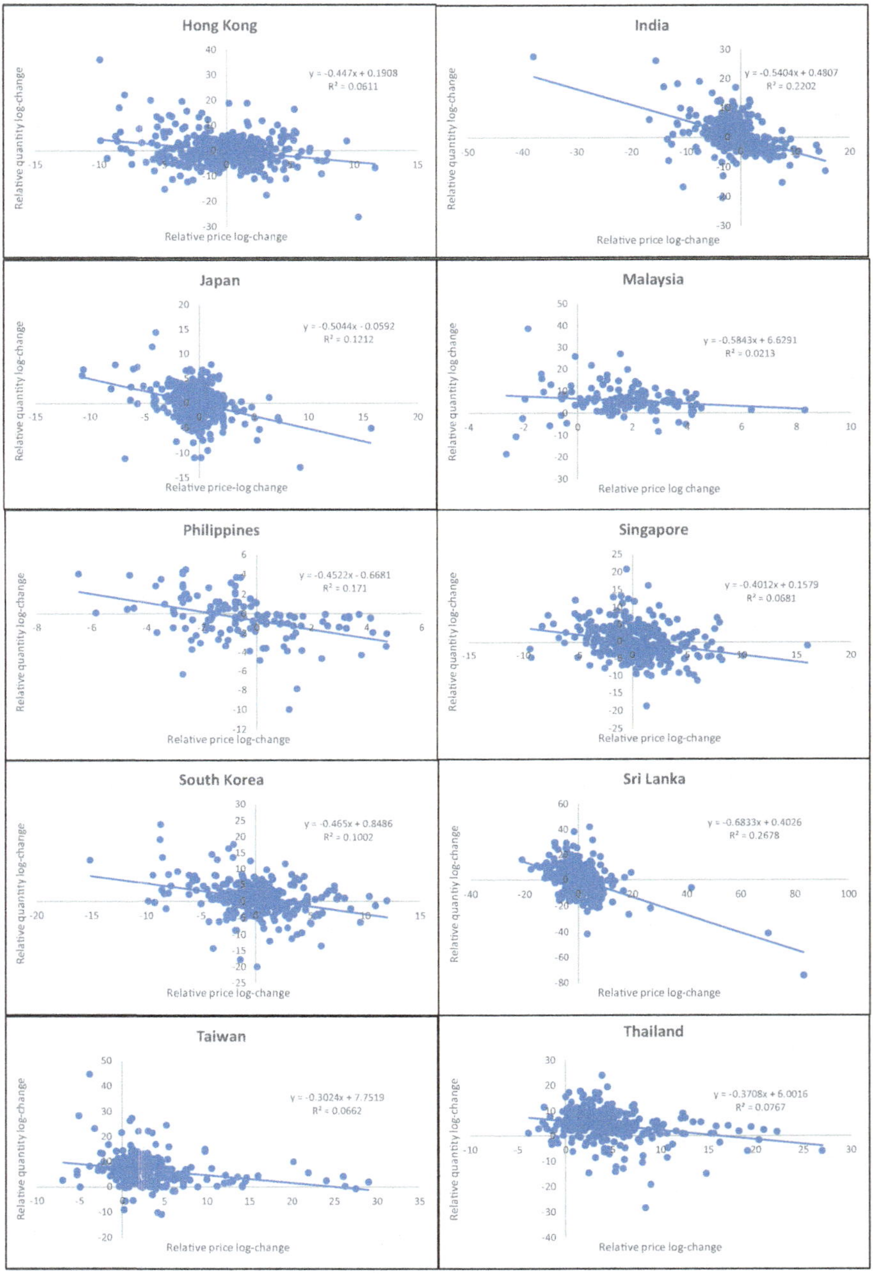

Fig. 3.4 Relative quantity against relative price log-changes, ten Asian countries

Table 3.13 Slope estimates of the demand curve, income flexibility (ϕ), ten Asian countries

Country	Income flexibility
Hong Kong	− 0.45
India	− 0.54
Japan	− 0.50
Malaysia	− 0.58
Philippines	− 0.45
Singapore	− 0.40
South Korea	− 0.47
Sri Lanka	− 0.68
Taiwan	− 0.30
Thailand	− 0.37
All countries	− 0.34
Mean	− 0.46

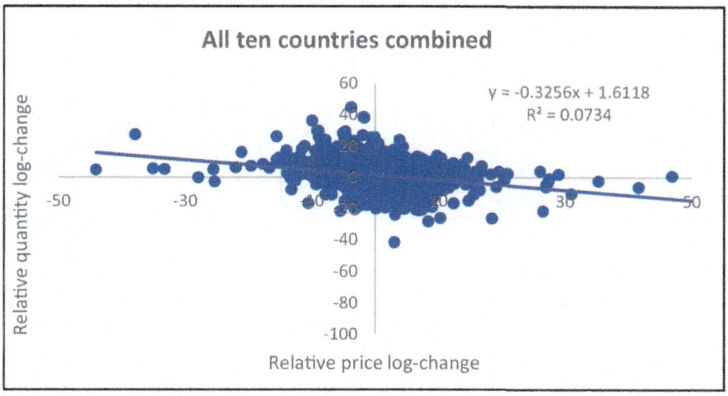

Fig. 3.5 Relative quantity against relative prices, all 10 countries combined

of the income elasticities, η_i, and the own-price elasticities, η_{ii},

$$Dq_{it} = \alpha_i + \eta_i DQ_t + \eta_{ii}[Dp_{it} - DP_t] + \varepsilon_{it} \qquad i = 1, 2, \ldots, 8 \qquad (3.5.1)$$

Tables 3.15 and 3.16 present the LS estimates of income elasticity (η_i) and own-price elasticity (η_{ii}) based on the estimation of (3.5.1) for i = 1, 2, …, 8, for the ten countries. From Table 3.15, it can be seen that the income elasticity of all the commodities for all the countries, except miscellaneous in Thailand, are positive. The income elasticities of food for the ten countries are all less than 1, indicating that it is a necessity and ranges from a low of 0.3 in Malaysia to a high of 0.97 in India and Sri Lanka. For clothing, the income elasticities for the ten countries are very divergent, ranging from 0.1 in Philippines to 3.24 in Malaysia. In terms of housing, all countries have income elasticities less than 1 except for Sri Lanka and

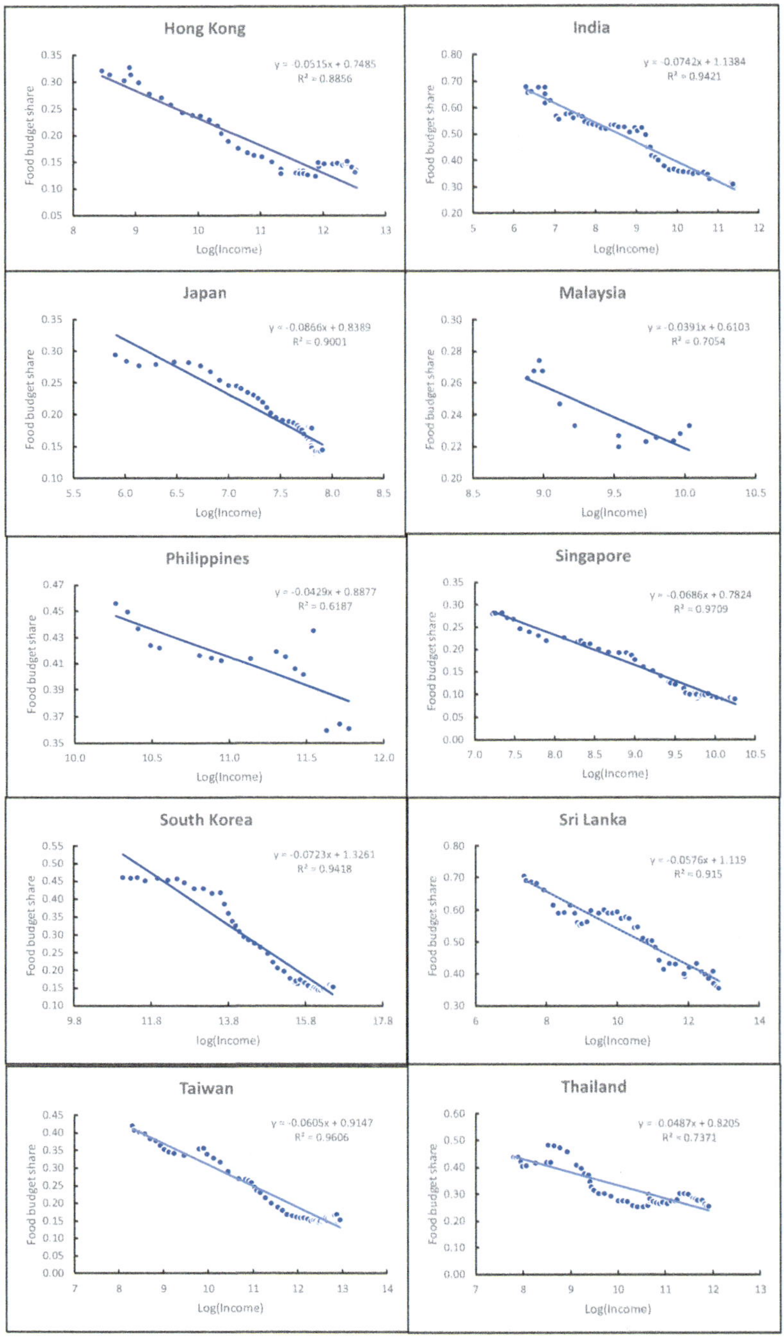

Fig. 3.6 Food budget share against logarithm of per capita consumption expenditure, ten Asian countries

Table 3.14 Preliminary estimates for food, ten Asian countries

Country	β_F	$\overline{w}_t$	θ_F	η_F
Hong Kong	– 0.02	0.18	0.17	0.92
India	– 0.07	0.50	0.43	0.86
Japan	– 0.09	0.20	0.11	0.56
Malaysia	– 0.04	0.24	0.20	0.83
Philippines	– 0.04	0.42	0.38	0.90
Singapore	– 0.07	0.16	0.09	0.56
South Korea	– 0.07	0.26	0.19	0.72
Sri Lanka	– 0.06	0.52	0.47	0.89
Taiwan	– 0.06	0.24	0.18	0.74
Thailand	– 0.05	0.33	0.28	0.85
Mean	– 0.06	0.30	0.25	0.82

the Philippines. On average, durables, transport, and recreation are luxuries in most of the countries. A majority of the own-price elasticities presented in Table 3.16 are negative, as they should be.

Table 3.15 Estimates of income elasticities, double-log demand system, eight commodities, ten Asian countries

	Country	Food	Clothing	Housing	Durables	Medical care	Transport	Recreation	Miscellaneous
	(1)	(2)	(3)	(4)	(5)	(6)	(7)	(8)	(9)
1.	Hong Kong	0.52	2.56	0.14	1.97	0.80	1.03	0.78	0.72
		(0.09)	(0.18)	(0.10)	(0.24)	(0.24)	(0.16)	(0.13)	(0.13)
2.	India	0.97	0.59	0.28	0.97	0.07	0.43	1.10	1.51
		(0.11)	(0.34)	(0.07)	(0.27)	(0.33)	(0.17)	(0.37)	(0.28)
3.	Japan	0.84	1.46	0.72	1.63	0.42	1.51	1.31	1.47
		(0.12)	(0.29)	(0.11)	(0.33)	(0.24)	(0.20)	(0.20)	(0.20)
4.	Malaysia	0.31	3.24	0.42	1.46	0.65	1.27	1.52	1.42
		(0.20)	(0.63)	(0.20)	(0.40)	(0.52)	(0.16)		(0.28)
5.	Philippines	0.58	0.11	1.13	0.89	1.29	1.18	1.18	1.38
		(0.17)	(0.37)	(0.35)	(0.49)	(0.33)	(0.29)	(0.23)	(0.32)
6.	Singapore	0.47	1.33	0.33	0.85	0.67	1.37	1.43	1.33
		(0.09)	(0.17)	(0.13)	(0.11)	(0.16)	(0.18)	(0.12)	(0.15)
7.	South Korea	0.68	1.79	0.36	2.24	0.93	1.44	0.83	1.11
		(0.08)	(0.17)	(0.09)	(0.21)	(0.29)	(0.12)	(0.11)	(0.09)
8.	Sri Lanka	0.97	1.06	1.77	0.50	0.87	0.83	1.90	0.29
		(0.13)	(0.29)	(0.43)	(0.47)	(0.43)	(0.28)	(0.57)	(0.56)
9.	Taiwan	0.57	1.26	0.72	1.39	1.05	2.21	1.08	1.26
		(0.06)	(0.09)	(0.11)	(0.15)	(0.43)	(0.25)	(0.14)	(0.22)
10.	Thailand	0.51	0.68	0.15	1.16	1.12	1.81	1.52	– 0.79
		(0.08)	(0.14)	(0.11)	(0.18)	(0.25)	(0.17)	(0.24)	(0.98)

Standard errors are in parentheses

Table 3.16 Estimates of own-price elasticities, double-log demand system, eight commodities, ten Asian countries

Country	Food	Clothing	Housing	Durables	Medical care	Transport	Recreation	Miscellaneous
(1)	(2)	(3)	(4)	(5)	(6)	(7)	(8)	(9)
Hong Kong	– 0.04	– 0.46	– 0.35	0.02	– 1.16	– 0.27	– 0.31	– 0.26
	(0.12)	(0.12)	(0.11)	(0.30)	(0.32)	(0.17)	(0.17)	(0.15)
India	– 0.14	0.11	0.01	– 0.22	0.06	– 0.10	0.08	– 0.14
	(0.12)	(0.09)	(0.02)	(0.09)	(0.07)	(0.06)	(0.13)	(0.08)
Japan	0.16	– 0.23	– 0.36	– 0.57	– 0.01	– 0.17	– 0.04	0.03
	(0.07)	(0.10)	(0.11)	(0.20)	(0.02)	(0.15)	(0.09)	(0.05)
Malaysia	– 0.95	4.24	– 0.25	– 0.16	– 2.69	– 0.30	– 2.30	– 0.63
	(0.48)	(2.44)	(0.59)	(1.28)	(1.70)	(0.21)		(1.10)
Philippines	0.16	– 0.06	– 0.18	– 0.22	– 0.09	0.17	– 0.05	– 0.13
	(0.06)	(0.04)	(0.16)	(0.19)	(0.06)	(0.12)	(0.06)	(0.08)
Singapore	– 0.28	– 0.18	– 0.17	– 0.66	– 0.16	– 0.27	– 0.04	– 0.22
	(0.14)	(0.19)	(0.12)	(0.18)	(0.21)	(0.16)	(0.08)	(0.15)
South Korea	– 0.10	– 0.31	0.13	– 0.46	– 0.78	– 0.26	0.16	– 0.27
	(0.08)	(0.17)	(0.09)	(0.20)	(0.30)	(0.13)	(0.13)	(0.12)
Sri Lanka	– 0.84	– 0.89	– 0.60	– 1.00	– 0.64	– 0.54	– 1.16	– 1.18
	(0.16)	(0.15)	(0.24)	(0.16)	(0.16)	(0.15)	(0.38)	(0.25)
Taiwan	– 0.13	– 0.36	– 0.12	– 0.08	– 0.25	– 0.39	– 0.44	– 0.70
	(0.06)	(0.09)	(0.22)	(0.10)	(0.37)	(0.28)	(0.11)	(0.31)
Thailand	0.10	0.14	0.00	– 0.50	0.20	– 0.19	0.86	2.05
	(0.10)	(0.14)	(0.06)	(0.22)	(0.28)	(0.15)	(0.31)	(0.76)

Standard errors are in parentheses

3.6 Conclusion

This chapter has presented summary characteristics of ten Asian countries that differ in stages of economic development and provided an empirical analysis of the consumption patterns of those countries. We used budget shares and logarithmic changes in prices and quantities, which are unit-free metrics, to compare consumption patterns across countries. This approach allowed for meaningful comparisons while mitigating issues associated with exchange rate conversions.

In terms of income allocation, we found that consumers in Hong Kong, Japan, and Singapore allocate only about one fifth of their income to food while South Korean, Malaysian, and Taiwanese consumers allocate one quarter; however, consumers in India and Sri Lanka spend half of their budget on food. This implies an inverse relationship between income and food budget share. Japan, Malaysia, and Singapore have the lowest price growth rate for consumer goods and India, South Korea, and Sri Lanka have the highest. Food price growth is highest in India, South Korea, and Sri Lanka. In many countries, food has the lowest consumption growth rate compared to the other seven commodity groups. The consumption expenditure data for the ten countries supported the four important empirical regularities, including the law of demand and Engel's law.

References

Chen, D. L. (2001). *World consumption economics*. World Scientific.

Clements, K. W., & Chen, D. L. (1996). Fundamental similarities in consumer behaviour. *Applied Economics, 28*(6), 747–757.

Clements, K. W., & Selvanathan, S. (1994). Understanding consumption patterns. *Empirical Economics, 19*, 69–110.

Powell, A. A. (1974). *Empirical analytics of demand systems*. Lexington.

Rathnayaka, S. D., Selvanathan, E. A., & Selvanathan, S. (2019). Consumption patterns in Sri Lanka: A decomposition analysis. *Applied Economics, 51*(37), 4056–4072.

Selvanathan, E. A., & Clements, K. W. (1995). *Recent developments in applied demand analysis: Alcohol*. Springer-Verlag.

Selvanathan, E. A., & Selvanathan, S. (2003). *International consumption comparisons: OECD versus LDC*. World Scientific.

Selvanathan, E. A., Selvanathan, S., & Jayasinghe, M. (2023). *Household demand for consumer goods in developing countries: A comparative perspective with developed countries*. Routledge Studies in Development Economics. Routledge.

Selvanathan, S. (1993). *A system-wide analysis of international consumption patterns*. Advanced Studies in Theoretical and Applied Econometrics. Kluwer Academic Publishers.

Selvanathan, S., & Selvanathan, E. A. (1994). *Regional consumption patterns: A system-wide approach*. Ashgate Publishing Company.

Selvanathan, S., & Selvanathan, E. A. (2004). Empirical regularities in South African consumption patterns. *Applied Economics, 36*, 2327–2333.

Theil, H. (1975/76). *Theory and measurement of consumer demand*. North-Holland Publishing Company.

Theil, H. (1987). The econometrics of demand system (Chap. 3). In H. Theil & K. W. Clements (Eds.), *Applied demand analysis: Results from system-wide approaches*. Ballinger Publishing Company.

Theil, H., & Clements, K. W. (1987). *Applied demand analysis: Results from system-wide approaches*. Ballinger Publishing Company.

Wong, L., Selvanathan, E. A., & Selvanathan, S. (2015). Modelling the meat consumption patterns in Australia. *Economic Modelling, 49*, 1–10.

Wong, L. Selvanathan, E. A., & Selvanathan, S. (2017). Empirical analysis of Australian consumption patterns. *Empirical Economics*, *52*(2), 799–823.

Chapter 4
Modelling the Consumption Patterns of the Asian Consumers

4.1 Introduction

Understanding the consumption patterns of broad commodity groups is of paramount importance, as it not only provides insights into consumer behaviour but also serves as, a crucial foundation for shaping effective economic policies, optimizing taxation strategies, and fostering a comprehensive understanding of consumption dynamics across regions. This chapter models the consumption patterns of Asian consumers using a system-wide approach. We also investigate whether the data for the ten selected countries support the demand theory hypotheses, demand homogeneity, Slutsky symmetry, and preference independence. We use the three demand systems introduced in Chap. 2, the Rotterdam demand model, CBS model, and AIDS. The most preferred demand model for each country will then be selected using the goodness of fit measure known as information inaccuracies. The income and price elasticities of the eight commodities for each country will subsequently be estimated using the preferred model.

This chapter is structured as follows. Section 4.2 briefly presents the three demand models, Rotterdam, CBS and AIDS, and tests the demand theory hypotheses of homogeneity and Slutsky symmetry. In Sect. 4.3, we use information inaccuracy measures to select the preferred demand model for each country for further estimations. In the next section, we test for preference independence for the ten countries' data under the preferred model for each country using a Monte Carlo simulation method. Section 4.5 provides the estimation results and the implied demand elasticities derived under the preferred demand models for each country and compares demand elasticities reported by previous consumption studies. In the next section, we test whether there are similarities among Asian consumers by means of a likelihood ratio test. Section 4.7 presents concluding comments.

S. D. Rathnayaka et al., *Economic Development and Consumption Patterns in Asian Countries*, https://doi.org/10.1007/978-981-97-2628-8_4

4.2 The Demand Models

In terms of differential demand systems, the three most popularly utilized in applied demand analysis have been the Rotterdam demand system (Barten, 1964; Theil, 1965), Working's (1943) parameterisation of the Rotterdam model, also termed the CBS demand system (Keller & van Driel, 1985), and the Almost Ideal Demand System, or AIDS (Deaton & Muelbauer, 1980). These three demand models have been respectively described in Sects. 2.5, 2.7 and in the Appendix of Chap. 2. In this section, we briefly re-introduce the three demand systems from Chap. 2 to be used for estimation and then test the demand theory hypotheses in this section.

Rotterdam Model

The basic specification of the Rotterdam model for good *i*, in differentials, takes the form (for example, in Selvanathan, 1993; Selvanathan & Clements, 1995; Theil, 1980) of

$$\overline{w}_{it} Dq_{it} = \alpha_i + \theta_i DQ_t + \sum_{j=1}^{n} \pi_{ij} Dp_{jt} + \varepsilon_{it}, \tag{4.2.1}$$

where $\overline{w}_{it}$, Dq_{it}, Dp_{it} and DQ_t are defined as before and α_i is the constant term of the *i*th demand equation satisfying $\sum_{i=1}^{n} \alpha_i = 0$. The use of the constant terms in the demand equations takes into account any trend-like changes in tastes and the like. The marginal share, θ_i, satisfies

$$\sum_{i=1}^{n} \theta_i = 1.$$

This marginal share, θ_i, answers the question, 'If income increases by $1, how much of this increase will be allocated to commodity *i*?' If $\theta_i < \overline{w}_{it}$, the commodity *i* is classified as a necessity; if it is otherwise, then it is classified as a luxury. The coefficient π_{ij} is the (*i*, *j*)th Slutsky price coefficient which satisfies $\sum_{i=1}^{n} \pi_{ij} = 0$. These coefficients also satisfy

$$\sum_{j=1}^{n} \pi_{ij} = 0, \quad i = 1, 2, \ldots, n. \tag{4.2.2}$$

Constraint (4.2.2) reflects the homogeneity property of the demand system that postulates that a proportionate change in all prices has no effect on the demand for any good under the condition that real income is constant. Accordingly, it is known as *demand homogeneity*.

The Slutsky coefficients are symmetric in *i* and *j*, that is

$$\pi_{ij} = \pi_{ji}, \quad i, j = 1, 2, \ldots, n, \tag{4.2.3}$$

which is known as *Slutsky symmetry*. In other words, when real income is held constant, the effect of an increase in the price of commodity j on the demand for commodity i is equal to the effect of a price increase of i on the demand for j. Thus, as the commodity subscripts can be interchanged, the substitution effects are symmetric in i and j. Furthermore, the Slutsky matrix $[\pi_{ij}]$ is symmetric negative semi-definite with rank $(n-1)$. The term ε_{it} is the disturbance term of the ith demand equation. It is assumed that the disturbance terms, ε_{it}, $i = 1, \ldots, n$, are serially independent and normally distributed with zero means with a contemporaneous covariance matrix.

The income and price elasticities implied by demand system (4.2.1) are given by

$$\eta_{it} = \frac{\theta_i}{\overline{w}_{it}} \quad \text{and} \quad \eta_{ijt} = \frac{\pi_{ij}}{\overline{w}_{it}}.$$

If the income elasticity of good i is less (greater) than 1, then good i is classified as a necessity (luxury). To calculate these elasticities, we use the sample means of the budget shares,

$$\overline{w}_i = \frac{1}{T}\sum_{t=1}^{T}\overline{w}_{it},$$

and calculate

$$\eta_{it} = \frac{\theta_i}{\overline{w}_i} \quad \text{and} \quad \eta_{ijt} = \frac{\pi_{ij}}{\overline{w}_i}. \tag{4.2.4}$$

CBS Model

The basic specification of the second differential demand system, the CBS model, for good i in differentials takes the form (see, for example, Barten et al., 1989; Keller, 1984; Selvanathan, 1993; Selvanathan & Clements, 1995) of

$$\overline{w}_{it}(Dq_{it} - DQ_t) = \alpha_i + \beta_i DQ_t + \sum_{j=1}^{n}\pi_{ij}Dp_{jt} + \varepsilon_{it} \tag{4.2.5}$$

where α_i is the constant term of the ith demand equation satisfying $\sum_{i=1}^{n}\alpha_i = 0$. As above, the use of the constant terms in the demand equations accounts for any trend-like changes in tastes and the like. The income coefficient β_i satisfies $\sum_{i=1}^{n}\beta_i = 0$. If β_i is negative (positive) then the commodity is classified as a necessity (luxury). As before, the coefficient π_{ij} is the (i, j)th Slutsky price coefficient with $\sum_{i=1}^{n}\pi_{ij} = 0$; here, as well, these coefficients satisfy the demand homogeneity property (4.2.2) and Slutsky symmetry (4.2.3). ε_{it} is the disturbance term of the ith equation. The error terms are normally distributed and are independent over time.

Based on the CBS demand system (4.2.5), the implied income and price elasticities are given by

$$\eta_{it} = 1 + \frac{\beta_i}{\overline{w}_{it}} \quad \text{and} \quad \eta_{ijt} = \frac{\pi_{ij}}{\overline{w}_{it}}.$$

If β_i is negative (positive), then the commodity will have income elasticity less (more) than 1 and is classified as a necessity (luxury). As before, we use the sample mean budget shares to calculate the income and price elasticities as

$$\overline{\eta}_i = 1 + \frac{\beta_i}{\overline{w}_i} \quad \text{and} \quad \overline{\eta}_{ij} = \frac{\pi_{ij}}{\overline{w}_i}. \tag{4.2.6}$$

AIDS

Deaton and Muellbauer's (1980) AIDS takes the form

$$w_i = \alpha_i + \beta_i \log \frac{M}{P} + \sum_{j=1}^{n} \gamma_{ij} \log p_j, \quad i = 1, 2, \ldots, n, \tag{4.2.7}$$

where

$$\log P = \sum_{k=1}^{n} \alpha_k \log p_k + \frac{1}{2} \sum_{k=1}^{n} \sum_{j=1}^{n} \gamma_{kj} \log p_k \log p_j. \tag{4.2.8}$$

The estimation of (4.2.7) will prove more complicated if we use log P as defined by (4.2.8). However, *Stone's index* presents a simpler variation of (4.2.8) as

$$\log P = \sum_{k=1}^{n} w_k \log p_k. \tag{4.2.9}$$

With log P in (4.2.7) replaced by (4.2.9), the budget share Eq. (4.2.7) is linear in the parameters α_i, β_i, and γ_{ij}. A weakness of model (4.2.7) is that log P involves w_i, while w_i is also the dependent variable of Eq. (4.2.7); thus, endogeneity could become an issue with the estimation of Eq. (4.2.7).

For applications involving time series data, by adding a subscript to Eq. (4.2.7) and taking the difference between w_{it} and w_{it-1}, we obtain

$$\Delta w_{it} = \beta_i DQ_t + \sum_{j=1}^{n} \gamma_{ij} Dp_{jt}, \tag{4.2.10}$$

where $\Delta w_{it} = w_{it} - w_{it-1}$, $DQ_t = DM_t - DP_t$ and $Dp_{jt} = \ln p_{jt} - \ln p_{jt-1}$ with $DM_t = \ln M_t - \ln M_{t-1}$ and $DP_t = \ln P_t - \ln P_{t-1}$.

Based on the AIDS Eq. (4.2.7), the income and price elasticities can be derived as

$$\eta_{it} = 1 + \frac{\beta_i}{w_{it}} \quad \text{and} \quad \eta_{ijt} = -\delta_{ij} + \frac{\gamma_{ij}}{w_{it}} - \frac{\beta_i w_{jt}}{w_{it}},$$

where $\delta_{ij} = 1$ for $i = j$ and 0 otherwise. We evaluate these elasticities at the sample mean budget shares as

$$\overline{\eta}_i = 1 + \frac{\beta_i}{\overline{w}_i} \quad \text{and} \quad \overline{\eta}_{ij} = -\delta_{ij} + \frac{\gamma_{ij}}{\overline{w}_i} - \frac{\beta_i \overline{w}_j}{\overline{w}_i}. \tag{4.2.11}$$

Pre-estimation, we investigate the stationarity of all the variables in the demand systems to avoid spurious results. We use the augmented Dicky–Fuller unit root test (Dickey & Fuller, 1979) for this purpose. The results indicate that all the variables to be used in the demand systems are stationary.

Testing Demand Theory Hypotheses

We now estimate the three demand systems given by Eqs. (4.2.1), (4.2.5), and (4.2.7) using the seemingly unrelated regression (SUR) procedure (available in Stata 16). Initially, we estimate the three demand systems in their unrestricted form and test the demand theory hypotheses for homogeneity and symmetry.[1] The conventional methods to examine homogeneity and symmetry, and the joint test for both homogeneity and symmetry, are based on the Wald test, the likelihood ratio test, and the Lagrange multiplier test. However, simulation experiments have shown that these tests have considerable bias towards rejecting the null hypothesis, especially when they are applied to large demand systems with relatively few observations (Balcombe & Davis, 1996; Bera et al., 1981; Laitinen, 1978; Meinser, 1979; Selvanathan, 1993; Selvanathan & Clements, 1995). To avoid this, we use the sample size-corrected statistic developed by Court (1968) and Deaton (1974) to test homogeneity, symmetry, as well as homogeneity and symmetry. The test statistic is calculated as follows (see Court, 1968; Deaton, 1974):

$$F = \frac{tr\left(\Omega^R\right)^{-1}\left(\Omega^R - \Omega^U\right)/q}{tr\left(\Omega^R\right)^{-1}\Omega^U/(n-1)(T-k)},$$

where Ω^R and Ω^U denote the estimated residual covariance matrices with and without restrictions imposed, respectively, T is the number of observations, n is the number of equations in the system, k is the number of estimated parameters in each equation, and q is the number of restrictions. The test statistic F is approximately distributed as $F[q, (n-1)(T-k)]$. This test statistic has been used in several empirical studies in the literature (see Baldwin et al., 1983; Chambers, 1990; Li et al., 2004; Rathnayaka et al., 2019; Wu et al., 2012).

[1] In estimating demand models for Sri Lanka, in addition to the income and price variables in all demand systems, we included a dummy variable to account for the impact of civil war (1983–2009) on consumption patterns. Results showed that the war variable does not have any significant impact on the consumption patterns of Sri Lanka. Other countries in the study did not have any long-standing issues.

Test results for demand theory hypotheses under the three demand systems for the ten countries are presented in Table 4.1. The value of the test statistic for testing homogeneity and the critical values for the test of homogeneity, based on finite-sample distributions at the 5% significance level, are presented in columns 3 and 4 of the table. Comparing the observed values of the test statistic with the corresponding critical values, we can conclude that homogeneity is acceptable across the board, except AIDS for Hong Kong and all three models for Japan. Looking at columns 6–8, we see that the Slutsky symmetry is acceptable for almost all the countries, with the exception of AIDS for Japan, Rotterdam, and CBS for South Korea.

4.3 The Preferred Demand Model

The Goodness of Fit of the Models

In this section, the preferred model is selected based on the information criteria of information inaccuracies. By taking the differential of the budget share relationship, $w_i = p_i q_i / M$ in finite changes, we can write (see Theil, 1975/76, vol. 1, pp. 38–39),

$$\Delta w_{it} = \overline{w}_{it} Dp_{it} + \overline{w}_{it} Dq_{it} - \overline{w}_{it} DM_t + O_3,$$

where $\Delta w_{it} = w_{it} - w_{i,t-1}$, and O_3 is the remainder term of the third degree in price, quantity, and income log-changes. As the expectation of the demand model (4.2.1) provides the prediction of $\overline{w}_{it} Dq_{it}$, we have prediction of

$$\overline{w}_{it} Dq_{it} = (\overline{w}_{it} Dq_{it})^{\wedge} = \overline{w}_{it} Dq_{it} - \hat{\varepsilon}_{it}$$

where $\hat{\varepsilon}_{it}$ is the estimated residual from the ith demand equation.

If $\hat{w}_{it}$ is the within sample budget share prediction from the demand model, then it can be shown that (see, for example, Theil, 1975/76, vol., pp. 172, 220–221)

$$\hat{w}_{it} = w_{it} - \hat{\varepsilon}_{it}, \quad i = 1, 2, \ldots, n, \tag{4.3.1}$$

where $\hat{\varepsilon}_{it}$ is the estimated residual from the ith demand equation.

The Information Inaccuracy

Let $w_{1t}, \ldots, w_{nt}$ be the observed budget shares of n commodities in period t and $\hat{w}_{it}, \ldots, \hat{w}_{nt}$ be the predicted budget shares in period t implied by the demand model. The information inaccuracy of these predictions is

$$I_t = \sum_{i=1}^{n} w_{it} \ln\left(\frac{w_{it}}{\hat{w}_{it}}\right). \tag{4.3.2}$$

Table 4.1 Testing demand homogeneity and Slutsky symmetry, ten Asian countries

Country	Model	Homogeneity			Symmetry		
		Test statistic	F_{Critical}	Conclusion	Test statistic	F_{Critical}	Conclusion
(1)	(2)	(3)	(4)	(5)	(6)	(7)	(8)
Hong Kong	Rotterdam	2.37	2.42	Accept	1.11	1.87	Accept
	CBS	2.36	2.42	Accept	1.06	1.87	Accept
	AIDS	2.97	2.42	Reject	1.64	1.87	Accept
India	Rotterdam	1.48	2.25	Accept	1.75	1.85	Accept
	CBS	1.63	2.25	Accept	1.40	1.85	Accept
	AIDS	1.14	2.25	Accept	1.93	1.85	Accept**
Japan	Rotterdam	3.68	2.25	Reject	1.65	1.85	Accept
	CBS	3.93	2.25	Reject	1.73	1.85	Accept
	AIDS	4.11	2.25	Reject	2.16	1.85	Reject
Malaysia*	Rotterdam	0.82	3.20	Accept	0.75	2.44	Accept
	CBS	0.36	3.20	Accept	0.74	2.44	Accept
	AIDS	0.85	3.20	Accept	1.02	2.44	Accept
Philippines	Rotterdam	1.60	2.94	Accept	1.16	2.16	Accept
	CBS	1.21	2.94	Accept	1.35	2.16	Accept
	AIDS	1.16	2.94	Accept	0.93	2.16	Accept
Singapore	Rotterdam	1.92	2.25	Accept	1.76	1.82	Accept
	CBS	2.04	2.25	Accept	1.81	1.82	Accept
	AIDS	1.16	2.25	Accept	1.56	1.82	Accept
South Korea	Rotterdam	2.58	2.71	Accept	2.18	1.93	Reject
	CBS	1.65	2.71	Accept	2.33	1.93	Reject
	AIDS	1.91	2.71	Accept	1.96	1.93	Accept**
Sri Lanka	Rotterdam	0.97	2.72	Accept	0.99	1.94	Accept
	CBS	0.97	2.72	Accept	1.17	1.94	Accept
	AIDS	1.19	2.72	Accept	0.94	1.94	Accept
Taiwan	Rotterdam	0.53	2.70	Accept	0.75	1.91	Accept
	CBS	1.18	2.70	Accept	1.05	1.91	Accept
	AIDS	1.75	2.70	Accept	1.10	1.91	Accept
Thailand	Rotterdam	1.27	2.70	Accept	1.55	1.84	Accept
	CBS	0.95	2.70	Accept	1.55	1.84	Accept
	AIDS	1.84	2.70	Accept	1.36	1.84	Accept

* $n = 7$; the level of significance $\alpha = 0.05$, ** denotes critical value and conclusion at $\alpha = 0.01$

This measures the extent to which the predicted budget shares ($\hat{w}_{it}$) differ from the corresponding observed budget shares (w_{it}). If $\hat{w}_{it} = w_{it}$ for $i = 1, 2, \ldots, n$, then I_t will be equal to zero; otherwise, it will be positive. The larger the I_t is, the poorer the quality of the predicted budget shares $\hat{w}_{1t}, \ldots, \hat{w}_{nt}$.

Based on information inaccuracies, the preferred demand system would be the one with the lowest value of information inaccuracy. Next, we select the demand system with the lowest value of information inaccuracy as our preferred demand system.

Table 4.2 presents these mean information inaccuracies ($\overline{I}$), averaged over the sample period, for all of the ten countries under the three demand systems. We make use of the information inaccuracies displayed in columns 2–4 to select the preferred demand model for each country. For instance, if we consider the calculated information inaccuracies presented for Hong Kong for the three models, we note that the lowest value among the three information inaccuracies is 480, which corresponds to the Rotterdam demand system. Therefore, for Hong Kong, the preferred demand system is the Rotterdam model. A similar comparison leads to the conclusions presented in column (5), which lists the preferred demand system for each country based on the minimum information inaccuracy. The Rotterdam demand system is the preferred demand system for Hong Kong, Malaysia, the Philippines, Singapore, Sri Lanka, and Thailand. However, the preferred demand system for India, Japan, South Korea, and Taiwan is the CBS model.

Table 4.2 Mean information inaccuracies and preferred demand systems, ten Asian countries

Country	Mean information inaccuracy			Preferred demand model
	Rotterdam	CBS	AIDS	
(1)	(2)	(3)	(4)	(5)
Hong Kong	480	591	740	Rotterdam
India	926	646	813	CBS
Japan	213	205	229	CBS
Malaysia	258	315	347	Rotterdam
Philippines	142	151	176	Rotterdam
Singapore	707	772	749	Rotterdam
South Korea	407	274	327	CBS
Sri Lanka	3086	3111	3255	Rotterdam
Taiwan	614	524	555	CBS
Thailand	1060	1364	1628	Rotterdam

4.4 Preference Independence

As the cross-country disaggregated data for the eight commodities are relatively broad aggregates, it would be reasonable to expect each individual commodity to have little interaction with the other commodities in terms of the utility function. As the marginal utility of commodity I is independent of commodity j, for $i \neq j$ it is reasonable to postulate that each commodity is preference independent. We test this property below. The Rotterdam demand model, under preference independence, is given by (2.5.5) of Chap. 2, which we reproduce here with an error term added,

$$\overline{w}_{it} Dq_{it} = \alpha_i + \theta_i DQ_t + \phi\theta_i \left[Dp_{it} - \sum_{j=1}^{n} \theta_j Dp_{jt} \right] + \varepsilon_{it}. \tag{4.4.1}$$

Under preference independence, the Slutsky coefficients take the form

$$\pi_{ij} = \phi(\beta_i + \overline{w}_{it})(\delta_{ij} - \beta_j - \overline{w}_{jt}), \tag{4.4.2}$$

where ϕ is the income flexibility (the reciprocal of the income elasticity of the marginal utility of the income) and δ_{ij} is the Kronecker delta. Substituting (4.4.2) for π_{ij} in (4.2.5), the preference independent version of (4.2.5) can be written as

$$\overline{w}_{it}(Dq_{it} - DQ_t) = \alpha_i + \beta_i DQ_t + \phi(\beta_i + \overline{w}_{it})$$
$$\left[Dp_{it} - \sum_{j=1}^{n} (\beta_j + \overline{w}_{jt}) Dp_{jt} \right] + \varepsilon_{it}. \tag{4.4.3}$$

We use the Monte Carlo simulation procedure, detailed in Selvanathan (1987), to test the preference independence hypothesis for both the Rotterdam and CBS models. Based on the simulation procedure, we reject the null hypothesis of preference independence at the 5% level if the rank of the test statistic, in 1000 simulations, is larger than 950; and reject at the 1% level if the rank is above 990. The simulation results are found in Table 4.3. As can be seen, preference independence is generally acceptable (except for Japan, Philippines, South Korea, and Thailand). Accordingly, the preferred model for Hong Kong, Malaysia, Singapore, and Sri Lanka is the preference independence version of the Rotterdam model whereas, for India, and Taiwan, it is the preference independence version of the CBS model. Nevertheless, the preferred model for Japan and South Korea is the CBS model under the symmetry restriction and for the Philippines and Thailand it is the Rotterdam model under symmetry restriction.

Table 4.3 Test results for preference independence, ten Asian countries

	Country	Rank of the statistic out of 1000 simulations	Decision at the 5% level
1	Hong Kong	971	Accept*
2	India	846	Accept
3	Japan	1000	Reject
4	Malaysia	704	Accept
5	Philippines	997	Reject
6	Singapore	731	Accept
7	South Korea	987	Reject
8	Sri Lanka	969	Accept*
9	Taiwan	499	Accept
10	Thailand	995	Reject

* Decision at the 1% level of significance

4.5 Estimation Results and Demand Elasticities

In this section, we present the estimation results under the preferred demand model for each country. Columns (2) to (9) of Table 4.4 present the estimated marginal shares for each commodity while column (10) displays the estimated income flexibility. We find that all the estimated marginal shares are positive as expected and are statistically significant. A practical interpretation of these numbers indicates that an income increase of $100 will see Hong Kong consumers allocate $9.60 more on food, $41.80 on clothing, $3.60 on housing, $14.90 on durables, $3.30 on medical care, $7.10 on transport, $6.10 on recreation, and the remaining $13.60 on all other goods. All the income flexibility estimates are negative and statistically significant.

The income elasticities and own-price elasticities implied by Table 4.4 parameter estimates and the mean budget shares are presented in Tables 4.5 and 4.6, respectively. From Table 4.5 we note that all the income elasticities are positive, with the average income elasticity for food across all countries being less than 1 (varies in the range of 0.281 for Malaysia to 1.292 for India); this indicates that food is generally a necessity. In addition to food, housing is also generally a necessity. Aside from Taiwan and Thailand, medical care is a necessity. Clothing, durables transport and recreation, with income elasticities greater than 1, are generally luxuries for most countries. The other income elasticities for each country can be interpreted in the same manner. Certain goods, such as food, housing, and durables are expected to have common characteristics across countries. On the other hand, there may be differences in the characteristics (necessity or luxury) from country to country as people react differently when income changes.

For example, in Hong Kong, food, housing, medical care, transport, recreation, and miscellaneous are necessities; only clothing and durables are luxuries.

Table 4.4 Parameter estimates for eight commodities for the ten Asian countries

	Country	Marginal shares								Income flexibility, ϕ
		Food	Clothing	Housing	Durables	Medical	Transport	Recreation	Miscellaneous	
	(1)	(2)	(3)	(4)	(5)	(6)	(7)	(8)	(9)	(10)
1.	Hong Kong	0.096	0.418	0.036	0.149	0.033	0.071	0.061	0.136	− 0.240
		(0.017)	(0.027)	(0.014)	(0.019)	(0.008)	(0.012)	(0.010)	(0.026)	(0.068)
2.	India[a]	0.527	0.041	0.035	0.040	0.008	0.114	0.040	0.194	− 0.092
		(0.061)	(0.024)	(0.009)	(0.009)	(0.011)	(0.026)	(0.014)	(0.032)	(0.028)
3.	Japan[b]	0.094	0.104	0.142	0.084	0.040	0.176	0.146	0.213	
		(0.029)	(0.019)	(0.024)	(0.018)	(0.025)	(0.019)	(0.023)	(0.031)	
4.	Malaysia*	0.067	0.072	0.073	0.080	0.021	0.260		0.427	− 0.357
		(0.043)	(0.017)	(0.024)	(0.018)	(0.009)	(0.028)		(0.048)	(0.116)
5.	Philippines	0.646	0.033	0.283	0.101	0.044	0.265	0.142	0.484	
		(0.064)	(0.007)	(0.044)	(0.025)	(0.008)	(0.045)	(0.015)	(0.048)	
6.	Singapore	0.097	0.08	0.043	0.066	0.022	0.194	0.301	0.198	− 0.137
		(0.017)	(0.010)	(0.014)	(0.010)	(0.006)	(0.028)	(0.030)	(0.023)	(0.052)
7.	South Korea[c]	0.179	0.129	0.051	0.079	0.024	0.19	0.1025	0.237	
		(0.022)	(0.014)	(0.019)	(0.01)	(0.013)	(0.014)	(0.013)	(0.019)	
8.	Sri Lanka	0.486	0.091	0.073	0.068	0.014	0.145	0.06	0.063	− 0.639
		(0.051)	(0.015)	(0.022)	(0.01)	(0.003)	(0.026)	(0.018)	(0.010)	(0.078)
9.	Taiwan[a]	0.119	0.073	0.138	0.057	0.037	0.244	0.153	0.176	− 0.248
		(0.012)	(0.005)	(0.020)	(0.006)	(0.012)	(0.023)	(0.015)	(0.029)	(0.040)
10.	Thailand[d]	0.498	0.111	0.097	0.114	0.079	0.393	0.538	0.170	

(continued)

Table 4.4 (continued)

Country	Marginal shares								Income flexibility, ϕ
	Food	Clothing	Housing	Durables	Medical	Transport	Recreation	Miscellaneous	
(1)	(2)	(3)	(4)	(5)	(6)	(7)	(8)	(9)	(10)
	(0.026)	(0.009)	(0.012)	(0.008)	(0.008)	(0.02)	(0.058)	(0.038)	
Mean	0.281	0.115	0.097	0.084	0.037	0.205	0.172	0.230	– 0.286

Standard errors in parentheses
* Recreation is included in miscellaneous
[a] Estimates based on the preference independent version of the CBS model
[b] Estimates based on the CBS model: symmetry constrained
[c] Estimates based on the CBS model: homogeneity constrained
[d] Estimates based on the Rotterdam model: symmetry constrained

Table 4.5 Income elasticities implied by the preferred demand models, ten Asian countries

	Country	Food	Clothing	Housing	Durables	Medical care	Transport	Recreation	Miscellaneous
		(1)	(2)	(3)	(4)	(5)	(6)	(7)	(8)
1.	Hong Kong	0.534	2.586	0.203	1.843	0.866	0.905	0.738	0.684
2.	India	1.292	0.276	0.233	1.013	0.860	0.816	0.910	1.858
3.	Japan	0.447	1.785	0.800	1.604	0.663	1.584	1.430	0.998
4.	Malaysia*	0.281	2.609	0.429	1.469	0.906	1.316		1.471
5.	Philippines	0.530	0.903	1.320	1.186	0.710	0.928	1.400	1.869
6.	Singapore	0.620	1.338	0.326	0.885	0.493	1.325	1.314	1.246
7.	South Korea	0.694	1.696	0.353	2.063	0.639	1.503	0.874	1.226
8.	Sri Lanka	0.927	1.305	0.863	1.421	0.836	0.804	1.693	1.541
9.	Taiwan	0.513	1.284	0.736	1.288	1.007	1.777	0.981	1.209
10.	Thailand	0.443	0.824	0.113	1.398	1.212	1.940	1.702	1.126
Mean		0.612	1.412	0.444	1.473	0.881	1.489	1.179	1.315

* Recreation is included in miscellaneous

Table 4.6 Own-price elasticities implied by the preferred demand models, ten Asian countries

	Country	Food	Clothing	Housing	Durables	Medical care	Transport	Recreation	Miscellaneous
		(1)	(2)	(3)	(4)	(5)	(6)	(7)	(8)
1.	Hong Kong	– 0.116	– 0.362	0.047	– 0.377	– 0.201	– 0.202	– 0.167	– 0.142
2.	India	– 0.085	– 0.049	– 0.042	– 0.179	– 0.096	– 0.135	– 0.162	– 0.292
3.	Japan	– 0.188	– 0.549	– 0.114	– 0.708	– 0.201	– 0.515	– 0.509	– 0.373
4.	Malaysia*	– 0.094	– 0.864	– 0.142	– 0.482	– 0.317	– 0.348		– 0.301
5.	Philippines	– 0.089	– 0.521	– 0.080	– 0.532	– 0.263	– 0.163	– 0.164	– 0.198
6.	Singapore	– 0.077	– 0.168	– 0.043	– 0.113	– 0.066	– 0.146	– 0.126	– 0.137
7.	South Korea	– 0.128	– 0.356	– 0.019	– 0.335	– 0.750	– 0.138	– 0.127	– 0.260
8.	Sri Lanka	– 0.305	– 0.758	– 0.512	– 0.847	– 0.527	– 0.439	– 1.018	– 0.923
9.	Taiwan	– 0.112	– 0.295	– 0.157	– 0.301	– 0.240	– 0.332	– 0.206	– 0.247
10.	Thailand	– 0.015	– 0.031	– 0.004	– 0.052	– 0.046	– 0.058	– 0.042	– 0.025
Mean		– 0.102	– 0.357	– 0.090	– 0.343	– 0.273	– 0.241	– 0.202	– 0.242

* Recreation is included in miscellaneous

The estimated own-price elasticities, presented in Table 4.6, are all negative and less than 1 in absolute value (except for recreation for Sri Lanka). This means that, in general, the demand for all goods across all the countries is price inelastic. Compared to other countries, consumption in Sri Lanka is the most price sensitive.

Tables 4.7 and 4.8 provide a comparison of income and own-price elasticities for the consumption of the broad commodity groups in Asian countries reported by previous studies.

This study differs from previous studies either on the functional forms employed for estimation or on the sample periods used. However, our income and price elasticities are broadly similar to the results reported in other studies. This lends confidence to our estimates and the selection of the functional forms. Moreover, Figs. 4.1 and 4.2 present the distribution of these income and own-price elasticities collected from previous studies.

4.6 How Similar Are Asian Consumers?

Stigler and Becker (1977) hypothesized that tastes neither change capriciously nor differ importantly between people. In an international context, this hypothesis amounts to stating that consumers in different countries are similar, irrespective of differences in language, culture, and geography. This section tests this hypothesis using the consumption data of the selected ten Asian countries to determine the similarity of Asian consumers. In this section, consumers in different countries are allowed to be idiosyncratic and ten separate systems of demand equations are estimated, one for each country. Further, in this section, it is specified that consumers in different countries are the same and that the parameters of the demand equations are taken to be the same across countries. This involves pooling the data and estimating a common demand system for all countries. (Malaysia was omitted as it has only seven commodity groups.)

Now, the restrictions of the pooled model against the individual country model are formally tested by means of a likelihood ratio test. We reconsider the preference independence version of the Rotterdam model

$$\overline{w}_{it}^c Dq_{it}^c = \alpha_i^c + \theta_i^c DQ_t^c + \phi^c \theta_i^c \left[Dp_{it}^c - \sum_{j=1}^{n} \theta_j^c Dp_{jt}^c \right] + \varepsilon_{it}^c \quad i = 1, \ldots, 8; \quad c = 1, \ldots, 9.$$

When the model is estimated for each country separately, we estimate 7×9 free constant terms (α_i^c), 7×9 free marginal shares (θ_i^c) and 9×1 income flexibilities (ϕ_i^c), which gives 135 free parameters in total. Under pooling, we estimate seven free constant terms (α_i), seven free marginal shares (θ_i), and one income flexibility

Table 4.7 A comparison of income elasticities for eight commodities with previous studies

Study	Data period	Model	Income elasticities							
			Food	Clothing	Housing	Durables	Medical	Transport	Recreation	Miscellaneous
(1)	(2)	(3)	(4)	(5)	(6)	(7)	(8)	(9)	(10)	(11)
Hong Kong										
1. Chen (2001)	1970–1984	Working's	0.51	0.97	1.02	1.20	1.38	1.80	1.33	1.29
2. Selvanathan and Selvanathan (2003a)	1970–1995	CBS	0.48	2.39	0.18	1.13	0.75	1.16	0.68	1.19
3. Selvanathan and Selvanathan (2003b)	1970–1995	Rotterdam	0.49	2.41	0.10	1.12	0.67	1.21	0.63	1.18
4. Rathnayaka et al. (2022)	1971–2016	Rotterdam	0.49	2.62	0.19	1.80	0.91	0.94	0.71	0.61
5. Selvanathan et al. (2024)	1971–2016	ECAIDS (SR)	0.85	3.43	0.43	2.40	1.22	1.13	0.76	1.28
		AIDS (LR)	0.83	0.84	0.60	3.35	1.18	1.05	0.87	0.76
India										
1. Houthakker (1957)	1950	DL	0.94	1.16	0.76					1.40
2. Selvanathan and Selvanathan (2003a)	1980–1995	CBS	0.80	1.08	0.54		1.79	0.09	2.20	1.44
3. Rathnayaka et al. (2022)	1970–2015	CBS	0.73	1.54	0.49	1.54	0.96	1.40	0.98	1.42
4. Selvanathan et al. (2024)	1970–2015	ECAIDS (SR)	0.69	1.51	0.70	1.75	0.80	1.20	1.08	
		AIDS (LR)	0.72	1.43	0.57	1.66	0.91	1.14	1.30	2.60
Japan										
1. Houthakker (1957)	1953	DL	0.65	1.40	0.91					1.39

(continued)

Table 4.7 (continued)

Study	Data period	Model	Income elasticities							
			Food	Clothing	Housing	Durables	Medical	Transport	Recreation	Miscellaneous
(1)	(2)	(3)	(4)	(5)	(6)	(7)	(8)	(9)	(10)	(11)
2. Selvanathan and Selvanathan (1993)	1970–1981	Rotterdam	0.62	1.88	0.22	2.08	0.78	1.35	1.15	1.49
3. Chen (2001)	1970–1981	Working's	0.48	0.92	1.02	1.29	1.23	1.67	1.29	1.13
4. Selvanathan and Selvanathan (2003a)	1970–1997	CBS	0.79	1.80	0.30	1.28	0.81	1.83	0.77	1.42
5. Selvanathan and Selvanathan (2003b)	1970–1996	Rotterdam	0.87	2.12	0.11	1.96	0.35	1.62	1.36	1.13
6. Seale and Regmi (2006)	1996	Florida PI	0.28	0.83	1.16	1.12	1.26	1.18	1.56	1.43
7. Rathnayaka et al. (2022)	1970–2015	CBS	0.47	1.84	0.51	1.37	0.32	1.44	1.21	1.40
8. Selvanathan et al. (2023)	1970–2015	ECAIDS (SR)	0.56	1.31	0.56	1.91	1.02	1.35	1.70	0.94
		AIDS (LR)	0.04	0.32	1.30	0.43	1.34	1.53	1.52	1.26
Philippines										
1. Houthakker (1957)	1954	DL	0.81	1.14	0.87					1.31
2. Lluch and Powell (1975)	1946–1967	LES	0.52	0.74	1.82	2.25	0.08	2.43	1.70	2.11
3. Selvanathan and Selvanathan (2003a)	1983–1995	CBS	1.02	1.23	0.88		1.30			0.92

(continued)

Table 4.7 (continued)

Study	Data period	Model	Income elasticities							
			Food	Clothing	Housing	Durables	Medical	Transport	Recreation	Miscellaneous
(1)	(2)	(3)	(4)	(5)	(6)	(7)	(8)	(9)	(10)	(11)
4. Rathnayaka et al. (2022)	1998–2016	Rotterdam	0.87	0.14	0.45	0.76	1.68	1.19	0.98	1.66
Singapore										
1. Chen (2001)	1967–1984	Working's	0.51	0.93	1.03	1.24	1.77	1.49	1.24	1.10
2. Selvanathan and Selvanathan (2003a)	1963–1995	CBS	0.70	1.32	0.45	0.72	0.64	1.23	1.35	1.40
3. Selvanathan and Selvanathan (2003b)	1963–1995	Rotterdam	0.79	1.40	0.37	0.75	0.54	1.17	1.27	1.38
4. Rathnayaka et al. (2022)	1963–2016	Rotterdam	0.59	1.25	0.32	0.88	0.48	1.40	1.27	1.30
5. Selvanathan et al. (2024)	1967–2016	ECAIDS (SR)	0.56	0.86	0.37	0.71	0.77	1.19	1.45	1.39
		AIDS (LR)	0.27	0.63	0.90	0.66	1.30	1.31	1.37	1.22
South Korea										
1. Lluch and Powell (1975)	1946–1970	LES	0.72	0.75	0.68	2.93	1.98	3.41	1.94	1.86
2. Chen (2001)	1963–1984	Working's	0.72	0.92	1.03	1.43	1.64	1.73	1.36	1.23
3. Selvanathan and Selvanathan (2003a)	1974–1996	CBS	0.83	1.17	0.45	3.07	0.94	1.13	0.83	1.00
4. Selvanathan and Selvanathan (2003b)	1974–1996	Rotterdam	0.73	1.28	0.65	3.23	0.98	1.22	0.81	0.94

(continued)

Table 4.7 (continued)

Study	Data period	Model	Income elasticities							
			Food	Clothing	Housing	Durables	Medical	Transport	Recreation	Miscellaneous
(1)	(2)	(3)	(4)	(5)	(6)	(7)	(8)	(9)	(10)	(11)
5. Seale and Regmi (2006)	1996	Florida PI	0.47	0.84	1.17	1.13	1.29	1.15	1.36	1.31
6. Rathnayaka et al. (2022)	1970–2015	Rotterdam	0.65	1.72	0.33	2.54	0.95	1.50	0.91	1.13
7. Selvanathan et al. (2024)	1970–2019	ECAIDS (SR)	0.74	1.33	0.79	0.65	0.37	1.32	0.94	1.40
		AIDS (LR)	0.31	0.98	1.01	0.93	1.24	1.31	1.50	1.40
Sri Lanka										
1. Houthakker (1957)	1953	DL	0.856	1.108	1.118					1.290
2. Chen (2001)	1963–1984	Working's	0.78	0.90	1.04	1.49	1.93	1.67	1.55	1.78
3. Selvanathan and Selvanathan (2003a)	1974–1995	CBS	0.93	1.10	0.11	1.81	0.85	1.38	0.58	1.37
4. Rathnayaka et al. (2019)	1963–2016	AIDS	0.63	0.86	2.85	0.62	1.79	1.40	1.40	0.97
5. Rathnayaka et al. (2022)	1975–2016	Rotterdam	0.87	1.32	0.93	1.45	0.87	0.89	1.70	1.60
6. Selvanathan et al. (2024)	1975–2016	ECAIDS (SR)	0.29	0.88	0.45	1.62	0.49	2.21	1.36	1.44
		AIDS (LR)	0.31	1.08	1.47	0.62	1.04	1.23	0.91	0.79
Taiwan										

(continued)

Table 4.7 (continued)

Study	Data period	Model	Income elasticities							
			Food	Clothing	Housing	Durables	Medical	Transport	Recreation	Miscellaneous
(1)	(2)	(3)	(4)	(5)	(6)	(7)	(8)	(9)	(10)	(11)
1. Lluch and Powell (1975)	1946–1968	LES	0.58	1.23	1.34		1.55	2.96	1.84	1.80
2. Chen (2001)	1962–1986	Working's	0.71	0.88	1.02	1.42	1.45	2.55	1.28	1.27
3. Selvanathan and Selvanathan (2003a)	1962–1997	CBS	0.75	1.29	0.43	1.16	1.08	2.37	1.14	1.84
4. Selvanathan and Selvanathan (2003b)	1962–1997	Rotterdam	0.58	1.23	0.50	1.17	1.10	2.91	1.28	1.93
5. Rathnayaka et al. (2022)	1962–2016	CBS	0.53	1.31	0.72	1.26	1.01	1.78	0.97	1.22
6. Selvanathan et al. (2024)	1962–2016	ECAIDS (SR)	0.70	1.20	0.83	1.33	1.83	1.26	1.04	1.24
		AIDS (LR)	0.49	1.06	0.79	1.31	1.03	1.99	1.17	0.88
Thailand										
1. Lluch and Powell (1975)	1946–1969	LES	0.91	1.11	1.82	1.45	0.08	2.84	1.56	1.46
2. Chen (2001)	1967–1984	Working's	0.73	0.93	1.04	1.45	1.93	1.67	1.55	1.78
3. Selvanathan and Selvanathan (2003a)	1976–1995	CBS	0.63	1.09	0.54	1.61	1.22	1.84	1.12	1.14
4. Seale and Regmi (2006)	1996	Florida PI	0.65	0.86	1.21	1.15	1.41	1.18	1.56	1.43

(continued)

Table 4.7 (continued)

Study	Data period	Model	Income elasticities							
			Food	Clothing	Housing	Durables	Medical	Transport	Recreation	Miscellaneous
(1)	(2)	(3)	(4)	(5)	(6)	(7)	(8)	(9)	(10)	(11)
5. Rathnayaka et al. (2022)	1967–2015	Rotterdam	0.49	0.85	0.05	1.53	1.21	0.09	1.39	1.13
6. Selvanathan et al. (2024)	1967–2015	ECAIDS (SR)	0.72	0.99	1.29	0.68	1.39	1.17	1.26	0.83
		AIDS (LR)	0.66	0.99	0.9	1.2	1.32	1.48	0.99	1.53
Mean			0.64	1.23	0.77	1.45	1.09	1.52	1.24	1.34
Standard deviation			0.19	0.55	0.49	0.68	0.47	0.62	0.34	0.35

Table 4.8 A comparison of own-price elasticities for eight commodities with previous studies

Study	Data period	Model	Own price elasticities							
			Food	Clothing	Housing	Durables	Medical	Transport	Recreation	Miscellaneous
(1)	(2)	(3)	(4)	(5)	(6)	(7)	(8)	(9)	(10)	(11)
Hong Kong										
1. Chen (2001)	1970–1984	Working's	– 0.13	– 0.23	– 0.25	– 0.31	– 0.37	– 0.46	– 0.35	– 0.35
2. Selvanathan and Selvanathan (2003a)	1970–1995	CBS	– 0.11	– 0.35	– 0.05	– 0.26	– 0.19	– 0.28	– 0.17	– 0.28
3. Selvanathan and Selvanathan (2003b)	1970–1995	Rotterdam	– 0.10	– 0.35	– 0.03	– 0.26	– 0.17	– 0.29	– 0.16	– 0.28
4. Rathnayaka et al. (2022)	1971–2016	Rotterdam	– 0.15	– 0.77	– 0.55	– 0.52	– 0.27	– 0.28	– 0.21	– 0.18
5. Selvanathan et al. (2024)	1971–2016	ECAIDS (SR)	– 0.77	– 1.29	– 0.72	– 1.05	– 1.04	– 1.01	– 0.93	– 0.78
		AIDS (LR)	– 0.76	– 0.29	– 0.21	– 0.68	– 0.58	– 0.18	– 0.78	– 0.20
India										
1. Selvanathan and Selvanathan (2003a)	1980–1995	CBS	– 0.03	– 0.06	– 0.03	– 0.11	– 0.01	– 0.11		– 0.08
2. Rathnayaka et al. (2022)	1970–2015	Rotterdam	– 0.04	– 0.12	– 0.04	– 0.13	– 0.09	– 0.11	– 0.09	– 0.12

(continued)

Table 4.8 (continued)

Study	Data period	Model	Own price elasticities							
			Food	Clothing	Housing	Durables	Medical	Transport	Recreation	Miscellaneous
(1)	(2)	(3)	(4)	(5)	(6)	(7)	(8)	(9)	(10)	(11)
3. Selvanathan et al. (2024)	1970–2015	ECAIDS (SR)	− 0.45	− 0.36	− 0.19	− 0.50	− 0.34	− 0.42	− 0.39	− 0.29
		AIDS (LR)	− 0.44	− 0.22	− 0.14	− 0.57	− 0.25	0.13	− 0.43	0.11
Japan										
1. Selvanathan and Selvanathan (1993)	1970–1981	Rotterdam	− 0.19	− 0.59	− 0.08	− 0.66	− 0.27	− 0.44	− 0.38	− 0.43
2. Chen (2001)	1970–1981	Working's	− 0.12	− 0.25	− 0.25	− 0.35	− 0.32	− 0.42	− 0.33	− 0.28
3. Selvanathan and Selvanathan (2003a)	1970–1997	CBS	− 0.26	− 0.62	− 0.11	− 0.47	− 0.30	− 0.59	− 0.28	− 0.44
4. Selvanathan and Selvanathan (2003b)	1970–1996	Rotterdam	− 0.33	− 0.53	− 0.11	− 0.78	− 0.57	− 0.91	− 0.96	− 0.24
5. Seale and Regmi (2006)	1996	Florida PI	− 0.23	− 0.66	− 0.78	− 0.87	− 0.92	− 0.82	− 1.00	− 0.87
6. Rathnayaka et al. (2022)	1970–2015	Rotterdam	− 0.20	− 0.78	− 0.06	− 0.47	− 0.25	− 0.20	− 0.64	− 0.39

(continued)

Table 4.8 (continued)

Study	Data period	Model	Own price elasticities							
			Food	Clothing	Housing	Durables	Medical	Transport	Recreation	Miscellaneous
(1)	(2)	(3)	(4)	(5)	(6)	(7)	(8)	(9)	(10)	(11)
7. Selvanathan et al. (2024)	1970–2015	ECAIDS (SR)	– 0.48	– 0.40	– 0.20	– 0.91	– 0.65	– 0.88	– 0.74	– 0.91
		AIDS (LR)	– 0.53	– 0.08	– 0.12	– 0.86	– 0.17	– 0.59	– 1.52	– 1.12
Philippines										
1. Lluch and Powell (1975)	1946–1967	LES	– 0.32	– 0.07	– 0.29	– 0.08	– 0.45	– 0.86	– 0.55	– 0.21
2. Selvanathan and Selvanathan (2003a)	1983–1995	CBS	– 0.02	– 0.07	– 0.04		– 0.07			– 0.04
3. Rathnayaka et al. (2022)	1998–2016	Rotterdam	– 0.09	– 0.02	– 0.07	– 0.12	– 0.26	– 0.16	– 0.15	– 0.20
Singapore										
1. Chen (2001)	1967–1984	Working's	– 0.13	– 0.25	– 0.27	– 0.32	– 0.50	– 0.36	– 0.31	– 0.26
2. Selvanathan and Selvanathan (2003a)	1963–1995	CBS	– 0.16	– 0.34	– 0.12	– 0.19	– 0.18	– 0.29	– 0.32	– 0.30

(continued)

Table 4.8 (continued)

Study	Data period	Model	Own price elasticities							
			Food	Clothing	Housing	Durables	Medical	Transport	Recreation	Miscellaneous
(1)	(2)	(3)	(4)	(5)	(6)	(7)	(8)	(9)	(10)	(11)
3. Selvanathan and Selvanathan (2003b)	1963–1995	Rotterdam	– 0.18	– 0.36	– 0.10	– 0.20	– 0.15	– 0.28	– 0.31	– 0.30
4. Rathnayaka et al. (2022)	1963–2016	Rotterdam	– 0.24	– 0.51	– 0.14	– 0.36	– 0.21	– 0.49	– 0.39	– 0.45
5. Selvanathan et al. (2024)	1967–2016	ECAIDS (SR)	– 0.57	– 0.66	– 0.22	– 0.89	– 0.26	– 0.74	– 0.97	– 0.59
		AIDS (LR)	– 0.43	– 0.52	– 0.02	– 0.75	– 0.03	– 0.58	– 0.58	– 1.04
South Korea										
1. Lluch and Powell (1975)	1946–1970	LES	– 0.50	– 0.18	– 0.17	– 0.49	– 0.36	– 0.59	– 0.36	– 0.32
2. Chen (2001)	1963–1984	Working's	– 0.13	– 0.25	– 0.27	– 0.39	– 0.46	– 0.43	– 0.36	– 0.32
3. Selvanathan and Selvanathan (2003a)	1974–1996	CBS	– 0.14	– 0.28	– 0.11	– 0.64	– 0.23	– 0.26	– 0.19	– 0.28
4. Selvanathan and Selvanathan (2003b)	1974–1996	Rotterdam	– 0.12	– 0.28	– 0.14	– 0.62	– 0.22	– 0.25	– 0.18	– 0.20

(continued)

Table 4.8 (continued)

Study	Data period	Model	Own price elasticities							
			Food	Clothing	Housing	Durables	Medical	Transport	Recreation	Miscellaneous
(1)	(2)	(3)	(4)	(5)	(6)	(7)	(8)	(9)	(10)	(11)
5. Seale and Regmi (2006)	1996	Florida PI	– 0.35	– 0.67	– 0.80	– 0.88	– 0.96	– 0.84	– 1.05	– 0.92
6. Rathnayaka et al. (2022)	1970–2015	Rotterdam	– 0.08	– 0.23	– 0.05	– 0.36	– 0.14	– 0.19	– 0.13	– 0.14
7. Selvanathan et al. (2024)	1970–2019	ECAIDS (SR)	– 0.52	– 0.02	– 0.20	– 0.53	– 1.17	– 0.74	– 0.99	– 2.07
		AIDS (LR)	– 0.25	– 0.25	– 0.20	– 0.32	– 2.38	– 0.80	– 0.76	– 2.16
Sri Lanka										
1. Chen (2001)	1963–1984	Working's	– 0.11	– 0.25	– 0.28	– 0.40	– 0.54	– 0.42	– 0.42	– 0.50
2. Selvanathan and Selvanathan (2003a)	1974–1995	CBS	– 0.20	– 0.52	– 0.06	– 0.85	– 0.43	– 0.58	– 0.29	– 0.67
3. Rathnayaka et al. (2019)	1963–2016	AIDS	– 0.67	– 0.66	– 0.88	– 0.65	– 0.99	– 0.74	– 0.73	– 0.61
4. Rathnayaka et al. (2022)	1975–2016	Rotterdam	– 0.29	– 0.75	– 0.54	– 0.84	– 0.54	– 0.47	– 1.00	– 0.94
5. Selvanathan et al. (2024)	1975–2016	ECAIDS (SR)	– 0.55	– 0.99	– 1.03	– 0.98	– 0.99	– 0.92	– 0.98	– 1.00
		AIDS (LR)	– 0.52	– 0.74	– 0.66	– 0.88	– 0.67	– 0.34	– 0.96	– 0.30

(continued)

Table 4.8 (continued)

Study	Data period	Model	Own price elasticities							
			Food	Clothing	Housing	Durables	Medical	Transport	Recreation	Miscellaneous
(1)	(2)	(3)	(4)	(5)	(6)	(7)	(8)	(9)	(10)	(11)
Taiwan										
1. Lluch and Powell (1975)	1946–1968	LES	– 0.44	– 0.40	– 0.53		– 0.45	– 0.86	– 0.55	– 0.60
2. Chen (2001)	1962–1986	Working's	– 0.14	– 0.25	– 0.25	– 0.39	– 0.40	– 0.67	– 0.33	– 0.34
3. Selvanathan and Selvanathan (2003a)	1962–1997	CBS	– 0.12	– 0.27	– 0.09	– 0.25	– 0.23	– 0.44	– 0.22	– 0.36
4. Selvanathan and Selvanathan (2003b)	1962–1997	Rotterdam	– 0.08	– 0.22	– 0.09	– 0.21	– 0.20	– 0.43	– 0.21	– 0.31
5. Rathnayaka et al. (2022)	1962–2016	Rotterdam	– 0.11	– 0.29	– 0.15	– 0.29	– 0.24	– 0.33	– 0.20	– 0.24
6. Selvanathan et al. (2024)	1962–2016	ECAIDS (SR)	– 0.30	– 0.55	– 0.68	– 0.71	0.05	– 0.16	– 0.90	– 0.89
		AIDS (LR)	0.11	– 0.37	– 0.52	– 0.59	0.13	– 1.02	– 0.53	– 1.58
Thailand										
1. Lluch and Powell (1975)	1946–1969	LES	– 0.65	– 0.45	– 0.10	– 0.53	– 0.03	– 1.02	– 0.60	– 0.55

(continued)

Table 4.8 (continued)

Study	Data period	Model	Own price elasticities							
			Food	Clothing	Housing	Durables	Medical	Transport	Recreation	Miscellaneous
(1)	(2)	(3)	(4)	(5)	(6)	(7)	(8)	(9)	(10)	(11)
2. Chen (2001)	1967–1984	Working's	− 0.13	− 0.25	− 0.27	− 0.39	− 0.46	− 0.43	− 0.36	− 0.32
3. Selvanathan and Selvanathan (2003a)	1976–1995	CBS	− 0.10	− 0.21	− 0.11	− 0.31	− 0.25	− 0.32	− 0.23	− 0.22
4. Seale and Regmi (2006)	1996	Florida PI	− 0.41	− 0.68	− 0.85	− 0.90	− 1.08	− 0.87	− 1.23	− 1.05
5. Rathnayaka et al. (2022)	1967–2015	Rotterdam	− 0.06	− 0.11	− 0.01	− 0.30	− 0.05	− 0.08	− 0.38	− 0.22
6. Selvanathan et al. (2024)	1967–2015	ECAIDS (SR)	− 0.45	− 0.48	0.05	− 0.81	− 0.57	− 0.48	− 0.01	− 0.26
		AIDS (LR)	− 0.33	− 0.15	− 0.88	− 0.72	− 0.77	− 0.43	− 0.14	− 1.89
Mean			− 0.27	− 0.39	− 0.27	− 0.53	− 0.43	− 0.49	− 0.51	− 0.54
Standard deviation			0.21	0.26	0.28	0.26	0.41	0.28	0.34	0.49

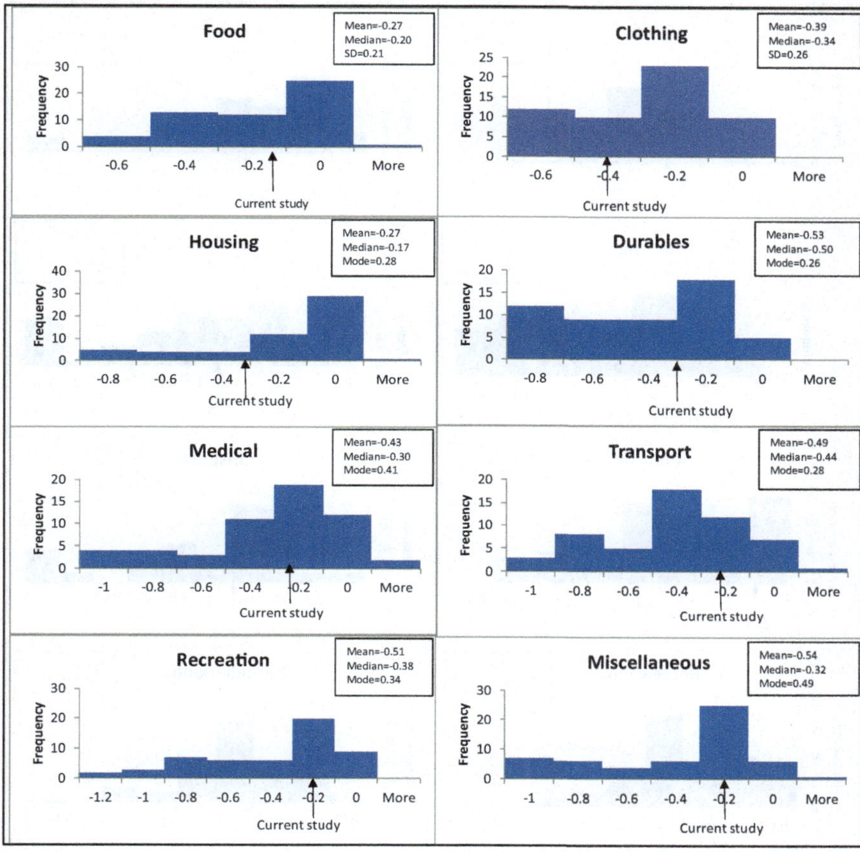

Fig. 4.1 Distribution of income elasticities of eight commodities in Asian countries presented in Table 4.7

(ϕ_i), which gives 15 free parameters in total. These calculations reveal that, relative to nine countries, pooling involves a total of 120 (= 135 − 15) restrictions.

Under the null hypothesis that the demand model parameters are the same across the states (pooling), the test statistics $-2(L_r - L_u)$ follows an asymptotic χ^2 distribution with 120 degrees of freedom. Under the assumption that the observations are independent across countries, the unrestricted log-likelihood value is the sum of the log-likelihood values for the nine countries individually. Therefore,

$$L_u = \sum_{c=1}^{9} L_u^c = 1712.12 + 1837.61 + 2037.30 + 936.85 + 2136.70 + 1999.31 + 1448.28 + 2334.20 + 1928.89 = 16{,}371.27$$

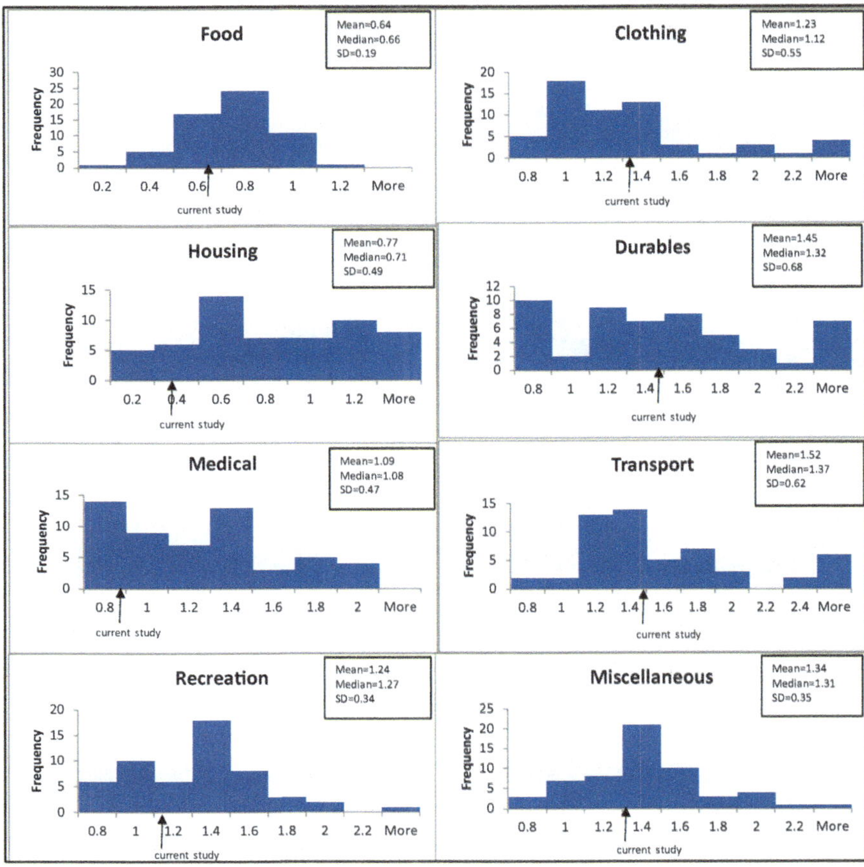

Fig. 4.2 Distribution of own-price elasticities of eight commodities in Asian countries presented in Table 4.8

Under pooling, the restricted log-likelihood value is $L_r = 13{,}836.18$. Thus, the value of the test statistic $-2(L_r - L_u) = -2(13{,}836.18 - 16{,}371.27) = 5070.19$. As this value is too large for $\chi^2_{(0.05,120)} = 144.35$, we are unable to accept the pooled model on the basis of the likelihood ratio test. Therefore, there is insufficient evidence to conclude that consumption patterns are similar across Asian countries. The reason for the rejection of similarity in consumption patterns between the ten countries could be that these countries are at various levels of economic development, so consumer behaviour is expected to be different between rich and poor countries.

4.7 Conclusion

In this chapter, we used the three well-known demand models for the estimations—the Rotterdam model, CBS model and AIDS to model the consumption patterns of consumers in ten Asian countries. First, we estimated demand models using the consumption and price data for eight broad commodity groups for ten Asian countries and tested the demand theory hypotheses. In general, there is support for the demand theory hypotheses of demand homogeneity and Slutsky symmetry. We used the information inaccuracies to select the preferred demand model for each country and found that the Rotterdam demand model performed best for Hong Kong, Malaysia, the Philippines, Singapore, Sri Lanka, and Thailand; the CBS performed best for India, Japan, South Korea, and Taiwan. In addition, we tested for the hypothesis that the eight commodities are separable in the consumption basket and found that preference independence hypothesis is generally acceptable for all countries except Japan and Thailand.

We estimated the income and own-price elasticities under the preferred demand model for each country to explore the price and income responsiveness of consumers in the region. The demand elasticities reveal that, in general, for a typical 'Asian' consumer, food, medical care, and housing are necessities while clothing, durables, and transport are luxuries. Demand for all goods is mostly price inelastic. The demand elasticities presented in this chapter are useful inputs for policy analysts and researchers because the knowledge of price and income responses is a very important element in the formulation of fiscal policy or any other type of economic program. Finally, we conducted a likelihood ratio test to examine the similarity of consumption patterns among Asian consumers. Despite the common belief that globalization, global consumer markets, and economic growth foster similarities in consumption across nations, our study reveals a notable trend. Contrary to expectations, we found more dissimilarities than similarities among the consumption patterns of consumers in the diverse group of Asian countries considered. This outcome is unsurprising given the broad range of development levels within the region, encompassing both developing and highly developed countries.

References

Balcombe, K. G., & Davis, J. R. (1996). An application of cointegration theory in the estimation of the almost ideal demand system for food consumption in Bulgaria. *Agricultural Economics, 15*(1), 47–60.

Baldwin, M. A., Hadid, M., & Phillips, G. D. A. (1983). The estimation and testing of a system of demand equations for the UK. *Applied Economics, 15*(1), 81–90.

Barten, A. P. (1964). Consumer demand functions under conditions of almost additive preferences. *Econometrica, 32*, 1–38.

Barten, A. P., Bettendorf, L., Meyermans, E., & Zonderman, P. (1989). *Users' guide to DEMMOD-3*. Kathlieke Universiteit Leuven.

Bera, A. K., Byron, R. P., & Jarque, C. M. (1981). Further evidence on asymptotic tests for homogeneity and symmetry in large demand systems. *Economics Letters, 8*(2), 101–105.
Chambers, M. J. (1990). Forecasting with demand systems: A comparative study. *Journal of Econometrics, 44*(3), 363–376.
Chen, D. L. (2001). *World consumption economics*. World Scientific.
Court, R. H. (1968). An application of demand theory to projecting New Zealand retail consumption. *The Economic Review, 3*, 401–411.
Deaton, A. S. (1974). The analysis of consumer demand in the United Kingdom, 1900–1970. *Econometrica, 42*, 341–361.
Deaton, A. S., & Muellbauer, J. (1980). An almost ideal demand system. *American Economic Review, 70*, 312–326.
Dickey, D. A., & Fuller, W. A. (1979). Distribution of the estimators for autoregressive time series with a unit root. *Journal of the American. Statistical Association, 74*(366), 427–431.
Houthakker, H. S. (1957). An international comparison of household expenditure patterns, commemorating the centenary of Engel's law. *Econometrica, 25*(4), 532–551.
Keller, W. J. (1984). Some simple but flexible differential consumer demand systems. *Economic Letters, 16*, 77–82.
Keller, W. J., & van Driel, J. (1985). Differential consumer demand systems. *European Economic Review, 27*, 375–390.
Laitinen, K. (1978). Why is demand homogeneity so often rejected? *Economics Letters, 1*(3), 187–191.
Li, G., Song, H., & Witt, S. F. (2004). Modelling tourism demand: A dynamic linear AIDS approach. *Journal of Travel Research, 43*, 141–150.
Lluch, C., & Powell, A. (1975). International comparisons of expenditure patterns. *European Economic Review, 6*(3), 275–303.
Meinser, J. F. (1979). The sad fate of the asymptotic Slutsky test for large systems. *Economics Letters, 2*, 231–233.
Rathnayaka, S. D., Selvanathan, E. A., & Selvanathan, S. (2022). Modelling the consumption patterns in the Asian countries. *Economic Analysis and Policy, 74*, 277–296.
Rathnayaka, S. D., Selvanathan, S., Selvanathan, E. A., & Kler, P. (2019). Modelling Sri Lankan consumption patterns using error corrected LA-AIDS. *Economic Modelling, 80*, 185–191.
Seale, J. L., Jr., & Regmi, A. (2006). Modelling international consumption patterns. *Review of Income and Wealth, 52*(4), 603–624.
Selvanathan, E. A., & Clements, K. W. (1995). *Recent developments in applied demand analysis: Alcohol*. Springer-Verlag.
Selvanathan, E. A., & Selvanathan, S. (2003a). *International consumption comparisons: OECD versus LDC*. World Scientific.
Selvanathan, E. A., & Selvanathan, S. (2003b). Similarities in the consumption patterns of the five Asian tigers. *Asian Economic Journal, 17*, 297–323.
Selvanathan, E. A., Selvanathan, S., & Jayasinghe, M. (2023). *Household demand for consumer goods in developing countries: A comparative perspective with developed countries*. Routledge Studies in Development Economics. Routledge.
Selvanathan, S. (1987). A Monte Carlo test of preference independence. *Economic Letters, 25*, 259–261.
Selvanathan, S. (1993). *A system-wide analysis of international consumption patterns*. Advanced Studies in Theoretical and Applied Econometrics. Kluwer Academic Publishers.
Selvanathan, S., Jayasinghe, M., Selvanathan, E. A., & Rathnayaka, S. D. (2024). Dynamic modelling of consumption patterns using LA-AIDS: A comparative study of developed versus developing countries. *Empirical Economics, 66*(1), 75–135.
Selvanathan, S., & Selvanathan, E. A. (1993). A cross-country analysis of consumption patterns. *Applied Economics, 25*(9), 1245–1259.
Stigler, G. J., & Becker, G. S. (1977). De gustibus non est disputandum. *American Economic Review, 67*, 76–90.

Theil, H. (1965). The information approach to demand analysis. *Econometrica, 33*, 67–87.
Theil, H. (1975/76). *Theory and measurement of consumer demand*. North-Holland Publishing Company.
Theil, H. (1980). *The system-wide approach to microeconomics*. The University of Chicago Press.
Working, H. (1943). Statistical law of family expenditure. *Journal of the American Statistical Association, 38*, 43–56.
Wu, D. C., Li, G., & Song, H. (2012). Economic analysis of tourism consumption dynamics: A time-varying parameter demand system approach. *Annals of Tourism Research, 39*(2), 667–685.

Chapter 5
Demand for Animal-Derived Food in Selected Asian Countries

5.1 Introduction

In recent years, the dietary landscape of Asian consumers has undergone a remarkable transformation, witnessing a significant departure from traditional staples to an increased reliance on protein-rich foods derived from animal and dairy products, fruits, vegetables, as well as fats and oils. This shift in consumption patterns can be ascribed to the rapid economic and income growth experienced by the region, fuelled in part by urbanization, globalization, and the modernization of marketing infrastructures. The studies of Huang and Bouis (1996), Huang and David (1993), Rae (1997, 1998), Pingali (2007), Baker and Friel (2016), and Wu et al. (2021) shed light on the multifaceted factors contributing to this dietary evolution.

The impressive economic progress made by most Asian economies over the past three decades have not only elevated living standards but have also substantially altered food consumption habits. This economic prosperity has led to increased food availability and heightened the purchasing power of individuals, consequently accelerating the nutrition transition. According to FAO (2013), the annual consumption of animal protein per capita in East and Southeast Asia surged from 5.4 kg in 1961 to 23.5 kg in 2013, reflecting the magnitude of this dietary shift. It is crucial to recognize, however, that this region is marked by high diversity, encompassing countries with differing income levels, market maturity, demographics, food expenditures, and dietary preferences. The dynamics of these changes present a complex tapestry that requires nuanced analysis.

Against the backdrop of Asia's economic transformation and the westernization of dietary habits, as elucidated in studies by Huang and Bouis (2001), Pingali (2007), and Hubacek et al. (2007), there emerges a pressing need to examine food demand in Asian countries using more recent data. The evolving socio-economic landscape underscores the importance of gaining deeper insights into contemporary dietary patterns and their implications for public health, economic planning, and sustainable food systems in the region. This chapter, therefore, aims to analyse the demand

S. D. Rathnayaka et al., *Economic Development and Consumption Patterns in Asian Countries*, https://doi.org/10.1007/978-981-97-2628-8_5

for animal-derived food in the Asian region. We consider seven countries, namely Hong Kong, Japan, the Philippines, Singapore, Sri Lanka, Taiwan, and Thailand. We have selected these seven countries mainly based on food consumption and price data availability, especially time series data with enough observations to be able to satisfy the demand model estimation requirements. We analyse the demand for six commodities within the food group derived from animals, namely, chicken, beef, pork, mutton, eggs, and fish. The four food items, chicken, beef, pork, and mutton collectively are also termed as 'meat'. Meat is a good source of high-quality protein, iron and zinc, and of all the B-vitamins except folic acid. Fish is an equally good source of protein and vitamins, including vitamins A and D in fatty fish. Fish also contains a well-balanced supply of minerals, including iodine and, if the bones are eaten, calcium, phosphorous, and fluoride (De Roos et al., 2020; Rathnayaka et al., 2023). Eggs make a useful contribution to the daily intake of vitamin D, retinol, riboflavin, iodine, iron, and protein (Speedy, 2003).

We consider the animal-derived food consumption patterns for the seven countries by estimating demand elasticities using the system-wide approach discussed in Chap. 2. Consumers' budget allocation for animal-derived food commodities is a multistage process. Firstly, consumers determine the amount of money available to spend on food and non-food groups. In the second stage, they divide their food budget among the various food sub-groups such as cereals, fruit and vegetables, animal-derived foods, beverages, and others. In the third stage, consumers then allocate their animal-derived food expenditure to chicken, beef, pork, mutton, eggs, and fish. This three-stage budgeting process is illustrated in Fig. 5.1.

Most empirical studies in the food demand analysis literature only focus on the analysis of a specific commodity group which constitutes only one stage of the multistage budgeting process. Therefore, the demand equations employed in those studies are conditional within a subsystem. Hence, the elasticities published by such studies are conditional in nature and differ from the unconditional elasticities calculated from

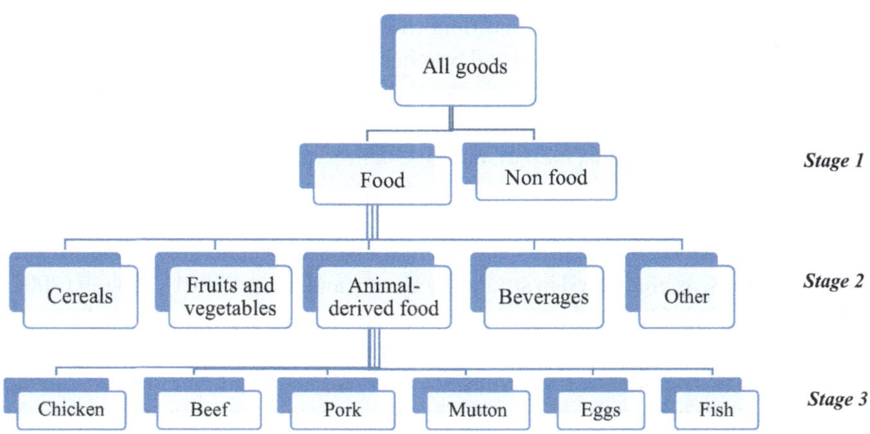

Fig. 5.1 Budget allocation stages for consumer goods

a demand system that includes all goods. As the unconditional demand elasticities are more relevant in welfare analyses and for policy purposes (Edgerton, 1997; Kinnucan et al., 2001; Klonaris & Hallam, 2003; Zheng et al., 2018), our study mainly focuses on unconditional demand equations while also presenting conditional demand analysis. In a departure from the previous studies in the food demand literature, our study, using the conditional and unconditional demand estimates obtains both the implied conditional and unconditional demand elasticities of each animal-derived food commodity for the seven Asian countries. Moreover, we also estimate the group demand equation for the animal-derived food group as a whole. The relationships between conditional and unconditional elasticities in a multistage budgeting process have been explored in combination with AIDS by Edgerton (1997) and Carpentier and Guyomard (2001). However, their approach to estimate conditional and total (or unconditional) elasticities requires a complete set of price and consumption data covering the above three stages. Therefore, in this chapter, we employ the system-wide approach to differential demand systems (for example, see Theil, 1975/76) to estimate conditional and unconditional demand elasticities using consumption and price data of animal-derived food commodities and the price index for all goods. Further, in this chapter, using the growth accounting method, we decompose the growth in consumption of these commodities into the effect of changes in consumer taste, income effect, own-price effect, and cross-price effect for each of the seven countries. We also investigate whether the data for the seven countries support the demand theory hypotheses, namely, demand homogeneity and Slutsky symmetry, based on the conditional demand equations for the animal-derived food items. Moreover, most previous studies are individual country studies and consider only a single commodity such as meat or fish, or both meat and fish combined. However, in this study, we expand the items within the food commodity group and present a simultaneous demand analysis of meat, eggs and fish as one group under the conditional demand analysis framework and also estimate unconditional demand responses. In summary, this study differs from all previous studies in terms of the number of items included in the animal-derived food group, the number of countries included in the analysis, the time period considered, the approach used, the selection of the functional form of the model, and the estimation methods employed.

The significance of the findings in this chapter cannot be overstated, as it furnishes robust econometric estimates for income and price elasticities pertaining to various meat, egg, and fish categories across the seven countries. This valuable information holds immense potential to benefit a diverse range of stakeholders, including producers, food processors, retailers, agricultural policymakers, and trade decision-makers. Additionally, as health policy analysts increasingly recognize the importance of a comprehensive understanding of food demand, these findings become integral to shaping health-related policies.

The impact of this research extends to various sectors; producer organizations and marketers stand to gain valuable insights for strategic planning, marketing initiatives, and price formulation. By providing estimates for market parameters such as own-price, cross-price, and income elasticities of demand, this research equips industry players with a powerful tool for analysing price dynamics within the consumer segment under different scenarios. Given that Asia ranks among the largest food service regions globally, insights into the consumption patterns of animal-derived food products by Asian consumers become not only valuable locally but also offer international operators key information for strategic decision-making.

Food consumption patterns, particularly in the realm of meat and fish, carry potential ramifications for environmental sustainability, a concern emphasized by researchers such as Goodland (1997), White (2000), and Gerbens-Leenes and Nonhebel (2002). The resource-intensive nature of meat production has become a focal point in environmental discourse, with mounting apprehensions regarding its ecological footprint. Studies indicate that producing meat necessitates up to ten times more resources, comprising land, energy, and water, compared to equivalent quantities of vegetarian food, as highlighted by Durning and Brough (1991), Goodland (1997), Dutilh and Kramer (2000), Harrison and Pearce (2000), White (2000), and Gerbens-Leenes and Nonhebel (2002). Similarly, the environmental impact of fish consumption extends to the global stage, contributing to the depletion of natural fish stocks and fostering the expansion of aquaculture (Lucas et al., 2021). The latter, while meeting demand, poses threats to the environment, resulting in the conversion of vital coastal ecosystems like mangroves into fish and shrimp ponds, as observed in studies by Harrison and Pearce (2000), Jackson et al. (2001), Ellis (2003), and Myers and Worm (2003). Given these concerns, the evolving consumption trends of meat, eggs, and fish in the Asian region should be a subject of keen interest not only to economists but also to environmental scientists and ecologists.

The rest of the chapter is organized as follows. Section 5.2 briefly reviews past studies that analyse the demand for animal-derived food products in select countries in the Asian region. Section 5.3 presents a preliminary analysis of the data. In Sect. 5.4, we specify the demand models. In Sect. 5.5, we test the demand theory hypotheses and estimate the group demand equation, conditional demand equations and unconditional demand equations, and obtain the implied group and conditional demand elasticities. The results of the decomposition analysis are reported in Sect. 5.6. Section 5.7 presents the concluding comments and discusses policy implications. Some sections of this chapter are based on our published paper, Rathnayaka et al. (2021).

5.2 A Review of Animal-Derived Food Demand Studies in Selected Asian Countries

The demand for meat has been estimated by many studies utilizing various data and estimation methods (for some recent seminal works, see Karagiannis et al., 2000; Mazzocchi et al., 2006; Selvanathan et al., 2016; Tonsor et al., 2010; Wong et al., 2015; Zheng et al., 2018). Further, Gallet (2010a, 2010b) has performed a meta-analysis of the price and income elasticity of meat and fish reported by previous studies. In alignment with the focus of this chapter on seven select Asian countries, this section reviews previous studies which analyse the demand for animal-derived food only in Asian countries, using both time series and cross-sectional data. Hayes et al. (1990) used the linear approximated (LA) AIDS to estimate the demand for meat in Japan and test three hypotheses (separability, perfect substitutability, and net substitutability) regarding meat consumer behaviour in Japan. They report evidence of net complementarity between chicken and dairy beef as well as between chicken and pork. The results indicated that Japanese wagyu beef was considered a separate commodity to both imported and dairy beef. Hayes et al. (1990) also suggested that fish can be treated as separable in the Japanese meat demand system.

Eales et al. (1997) modelled Japanese fish demand using both ordinary and inverse demand systems, each of which nests several competing specifications. Their results revealed that inverse demand systems dominate the ordinary demand systems in forecasting performance and in non-nested tests. The inverse demand system suggested that Japanese fish prices are less responsive to changes in consumption than found in previous studies. Eales and Wessells (1999) investigated the separability of meat products from fish products using a generalized ordinary differential demand system to gain a better understanding of Japanese consumer choices in protein demand. They note that meat and fish were separable prior to 1990; this is not, however, the case when examined over the entire 1981–1995 study period. Tonsor and Marsh (2007) used national, quarterly data to conduct an empirical analysis of pre-committed meat and fish demand by US and Japanese households using the Generalized Almost Ideal Demand System (GAIDS). According to their findings, US consumers hold significant positive pre-committed demand for beef and pork, while Japanese consumers appear to possess significant, positive pre-committed demand for beef and fish.

Ishida et al. (2010) utilized the AIDS to investigate the impact of Bovine Spongiform Encephalopathy (BSE, widely known as 'mad cow disease') and bird flu (avian influenza) on consumers' meat demand in Japan. BSE and bird flu scares caused a fall in demand for beef and chicken and an upturn in demand for pork and fish products, substitutes for beef and chicken in Japan.

Hayes et al. (1991) analysed meat demand in South Korea using AIDS. They found all own-price elasticities to be negative. Their estimated income elasticities showed beef and marine products to be a luxury, whereas pork and chicken were necessities. Moreover, they simulated the effects of trade liberalization in the South Korean beef sector using some of the parameters of the demand system. The results revealed that South Korea would have reduced its trade surplus by as much as $800 million by 1999 if its beef sector was liberalized. Jung and Koo (2000) estimated fish and meat demand in Korea using the LA-AIDS approach. They found that beef imports would increase as per capita income rose, and that local beef production would decrease. Chicken and pork could retain a market share, but fish could not.

Dharmasena et al. (1990) estimated price and income elasticities for beef, mutton, chicken, fish, and dried fish in Sri Lanka using the Rotterdam model. They reported fish to be a near luxury while others were normal goods. Chicken was price elastic, unlike the other animal protein foods.

Huang and Bouis (2001) investigated the structural changes in the demand for food in Taiwan, including fish, employing AIDS. Their results supported the hypothesis that structural changes in food demand were potentially significant factors driving the rapid changes in dietary patterns seen in other countries in East Asia over the past three decades.

Dey (2000) analysed fish consumption patterns in Bangladesh utilizing quadratic AIDS. Considering fish as a heterogeneous product, the study estimated fish demand elasticities by fish type using individual household expenditure data. Estimated demand elasticities varied across fish type and across income class. Income elasticities for all fish types fell consistently with an increase in per capita expenditure, level of household income; however, none of the fish types become an inferior good at the highest income quartile. Wadud (2006) studied Bangladeshi meat demand with quarterly data from the Household Expenditure Survey for the period 1980–2000. The research considered three meat types (beef, chicken, and mutton) and used LA-AIDS for estimation. The estimated own-price elasticities were − 0.25 (beef), − 0.91 (chicken), and − 0.94 (mutton). Substitutability was found between beef, chicken, and mutton. The income elasticity for chicken (1.46) and mutton (3.08) was greater than 1, indicating that both were luxuries, and negative (− 1.04) for beef, indicating an inferior good.

Capps et al. (1994) compared the demand for meat products in Taiwan, South Korea, and Japan by estimating demand elasticities using the Rotterdam model. They found that demand elasticities for beef, pork, and chicken are different among the various nations in the Pacific Rim.

Rae (1998) analysed the effects of expenditure growth and urbanization on animal-derived food consumption in six Asian countries (China, Indonesia, South Korea, Malaysia, the Philippines, and Thailand). The study found that the urbanization elasticities were always positive, indicating that the process of urbanization had a positive effect on the demand for animal food products. The income elasticities were also positive but often their values are less than they would be if estimated from consumption functions that excluded the effects of urbanization.

Dey et al. (2008) researched the fish demand patterns of nine Asian countries using 2001–2004 data and employing a multistage framework with the quadratic AIDS model. Their results revealed fish to be a clearly heterogeneous product, as shown by the wide variability in the estimated income and price elasticities of different fish types. More specifically, they compared fish demand by income groups to determine how low- and high-income households respond to price and income changes. According to their results, estimated price and income elasticities of all fish types were relatively more elastic among poorer households.

Further, Huang and David (1993), Gale and Huang (2007), Zheng and Henneberry (2010, 2011, 2012), Hovhannisyan and Gould (2014), and Zheng et al. (2018) have also analysed the demand for food in China including the demand for animal-derived food. Table 5.1 presents the income and own-price elasticities reported in the above reviewed studies. As can be seen, among the positive income elasticities, for chicken the elasticities vary between 0.55 and 1.85, for beef 0.03–2.49, for pork 0.49–1.58, mutton 0.22–3.08, and for fish from 0.61 to 1.44. All own-price elasticities are negative and mostly they are less than one in absolute value indicating the demand for chicken, beef, pork, mutton, and fish are generally price inelastic.

Table 5.1 Income and own-price elasticities of meat and fish reported in the reviewed studies

Study	Data period and model	Income elasticity					Own-price elasticity				
		Chicken	Beef	Pork	Mutton	Fish	Chicken	Beef	Pork	Mutton	Fish
Bangladesh											
Wadud (2006)	1980–2000 LA-AIDS	1.46	– 1.04		3.08		– 0.91	– 0.25		– 0.94	
Indonesia											
Forgenie et al. (2023)	2021 QUAIDS	1.07	2.20			1.44	– 1.39	– 1.71			– 1.61
Japan											
Hayes et al. (1990)	1965–1986 LA-AIDS	1.60	2.49	0.53		0.78	– 0.59	– 0.46	– 0.76		– 0.70
Capps et al. (1994)	1962–1991 Rotterdam	1.36	1.10	0.73			– 0.45	1.01	– 0.90		
Eales and Wessells (1999)	1981–1995 CBS	0.69	0.48	0.49		0.89	– 0.49	– 0.52	– 0.35		– 0.75
Tonsor and Marsh (2007)	1976–2001 GAIDS	1.85	0.43	1.58		0.89	– 0.522	– 0.576	– 0.413		– 0.767
Malaysia											
Baharumshah and Mohamed (1993)	1960–1990 AIDS	1.43	0.06	1.15	1.12	1.02	– 3.74	– 0.55	– 0.59	– 0.42	– 0.63
South Korea											
Hayes et al. (1991)	1961–1987 AIDS	0.68	1.13	0.92		1.05	– 0.74	– 0.34	– 1.04		– 0.91
Capps et al. (1994)	1962–1991 Rotterdam	0.78	1.29	0.83			0.47	– 0.94	– 0.65		
Jung and Koo (2000)	1980–1998 LA/AIDS	0.94	1.42	0.85		0.78	– 0.25	– 1.18	– 0.78		– 1.10

(continued)

Table 5.1 (continued)

Study	Data period and model	Income elasticity					Own-price elasticity				
		Chicken	Beef	Pork	Mutton	Fish	Chicken	Beef	Pork	Mutton	Fish
Sri Lanka											
Dharmasena et al. (1990)	1973–1982 Rotterdam	0.55	0.03		0.22	1.34	– 3.33	– 0.24		– 0.96	– 0.80
Taiwan											
Shue (1987)	Single equation						– 0.28	– 1.87	– 0.56		
Capps et al. (1994)	1962–1991 Rotterdam	0.88	1.13	1.01			– 0.45	1.01	– 0.90		
Huang and Bouis (2001)	1981–1991 AIDS					0.61					– 1.64

Forgenie et al. (2023) analysed the demand for animal source food among households in Jakarta, the capital of Indonesia using the data from the 2021 National Socio-Economic Survey. Employing the Quadratic Almost Ideal Demand Systems (QUAIDS) model, they found that all animal source foods except eggs are income elastic, with beef exhibiting the highest income elasticity of demand at 2.20, followed by fish (1.44), and poultry (1.07).

5.3 Preliminary Data Analysis

This chapter uses annual per capita consumption and retail price data for chicken, beef, pork, mutton, eggs, and fish[1] in seven Asian countries, Hong Kong, Japan, the Philippines, Singapore, Sri Lanka, Taiwan, and Thailand. We use the per capita food availability data taken from the Food Balance Sheets (FBS) published by the Food and Agriculture Organization (FAO) of the United Nations (FAO, 2013) as a proxy for per capita food consumption. This measure is computed by dividing the total food supply available for human consumption for each year by the country's population size. The total food supply for human consumption for each year is calculated as (national production + import + stocks) − (exports + feed + non-food usage + usage input for food + wastage + closing stocks). The FAO food balance sheets are the only global source of standardized food consumption data, which allows for time series comparisons to be made.

The retail prices of each food commodity for all countries were drawn from various publications of statistical departments, agri-food and veterinary authorities, agricultural councils, departments of internal trade, and central banks. However, price and consumption data for mutton is available only for Singapore, Sri Lanka, and Taiwan. A description of the database is presented in Table 5.2.

Table 5.3 shows the historical consumption trends for the major food groups: cereals, fruit and vegetables, meat, eggs, fish and seafood, and dairy, in the seven countries. Per capita food consumption data for selected years over the last few decades (1985, 1995, 2005, and 2013) is presented along with their means for each country over the sample period. As can be seen from column (3), per capita consumption of cereal as a staple food has declined over the last four decades in Hong Kong, Japan, and Taiwan. Consumption of fruits, vegetables, and dairy products have increased in all the countries except Japan (both) and the Philippines (fruits and vegetables). As can be seen from column (5) of the table, there is an upward trend in most Asian countries in the total combined consumption of meat, eggs, fish, and seafood over the sample period. The declining intake of cereal during the past few decades has been accompanied by a dramatic increase in the consumption of animal-derived food, illustrating a shift away from carbohydrates to fat and protein. Typically, economists have explained such changes in food consumption

[1] For Japan, Singapore, Taiwan, and Thailand, fish includes different types of fish plus all seafood products. For Hong Kong, the Philippines, and Sri Lanka; fish includes different types of fish only.

Table 5.2 Description of the database, seven Asian countries

Country	Sample period	Sample size	No of commodities	Currency	Data source
1. Hong Kong	1981–2013	33	5	Hong Kong dollars	Publications of Census and Statistics Department FAO Food Balance Sheets
2. Japan	1980–2013	44	5	Yen	Statistics Bureau, Japan
3. Philippines	1990–2013	24	5	Pesos	Publications of Department of Statistics Philippines FAO Food Balance Sheets
4. Singapore	1995–2016	22	6	Dollars	Publications of Agri-Food and Veterinary Authority of Singapore
5. Sri Lanka	1993–2015	23	6	Rupees (Sri Lankan)	Publications of Central Bank of Sri Lanka FAO Food Balance Sheets
6. Taiwan	1993–2015	23	6	Dollars	Council of Agriculture, Taiwan Food Supply and Utilization Annual Reports, Taiwan
7. Thailand	1990–2013	24	5	Baht	Department of Internal Trade, Thailand FAO Food Balance Sheets

as resulting from increases in disposable income, urbanization and integration with global markets, as aforementioned. We find that, at sample means, meat, eggs, fish, and seafood consumption levels vary by country, ranging from 27 kg/per capita/per year in Sri Lanka to 196 kg/per capita/per year in Hong Kong.

Table 5.4 presents the prices (p_{it}) of chicken ($i = 1$), beef ($i = 2$), pork ($i = 3$), mutton ($i = 4$), eggs ($i = 5$), fish ($i = 6$), and the quantities consumed (q_{it}) in log-change form, $Dp_{it} = \ln p_{it} - \ln p_{it-1}$ and $Dq_{it} = \ln q_{it} - \ln q_{it-1}$, at sample means (all are multiplied by 100) for each country. These mean values are the annual average growth rates in the per capita consumption of the six animal-derived food items. Prices presented in the first section of the table show that the prices of all six commodities across countries have a positive rate of growth, except for eggs and fish in Japan.

Looking at the quantity log-changes in the table, it can be seen that per capita chicken and egg consumption has grown positively in all countries. However, the average consumption growth rate of beef is negative in Singapore, Sri Lanka, and Thailand; pork is negative in Singapore and Taiwan; mutton is negative in Sri Lanka; fish is negative in Japan, the Philippines, Singapore and Thailand and positive for Hong Kong and Sri Lanka.

Table 5.3 Annual per capita consumption of food (kg/per capita/year), selected years

Year	Per capita GDP (US $)	Cereals	Fruits and vegetables	Meat, eggs, fish and seafood	Dairy
(1)	(2)	(3)	(4)	(5)	(6)
Hong Kong					
1985	6543	130.0	154.4	153.4	38.1
1995	23,497	115.2	160.5	194.4	61.1
2005	26,650	108.3	172.2	211.3	59.6
2013	38,404	106.0	191.9	237.5	105.9
Mean		113.4	167.1	195.8	62.5
Japan					
1985	11,585	133.3	171.4	120.4	73.6
1995	43,440	122.9	169.8	135.0	82.6
2005	37,218	115.1	168.2	126.3	78.0
2013	40,454	113.4	155.1	117.2	72.1
Mean		120.7	164.0	126.3	77.9
Philippines					
1985	566	130.9	172.3	50.1	13.9
1995	1061	135.4	164.9	58.3	21.7
2005	1195	155.4	157.7	66.2	13.0
2013	2760	163.1	169.4	70.7	15.7
Mean		143.9	168.5	62.3	16.9
Singapore					
1995	24,937	n.a.	155.2	111.9	n.a.
2005	29,870	n.a.	178.0	105.9	n.a.
2016	55,243	n.a.	165.0	108.2	n.a.
Mean			162.7	106.8	
Sri Lanka					
1985	370	141.7	76.0	20.1	28.4
1995	714	147.4	71.9	25.5	31.2
2005	1250	152.5	68.3	25.2	28.9
2013	3609	152.3	82.4	36.7	35.0
Mean		144.6	71.6	27.2	32.2
Taiwan					
1985	3315	105.1	214.9	106.8	32.4
1995	13,129	91.0	239.3	127.3	58.8
2005	16,532	87.3	227.6	123.7	47.4
2013	21,916	81.3	228.6	124.6	43.4
Mean		88.7	237.4	121.5	47.9
Thailand					
1985	747	127.1	135.8	48.9	9.2
1995	2845	123.3	137.8	70.3	25.8
2005	2894	141.9	165.1	70.4	25.6
2013	6168	135.7	154.7	66.5	29.4
Mean		141.0	141.4	54.2	14.7

Source FAO (2013)
n.a. not available

Table 5.4 Price and quantity log-changes of sixanimal-derived food items (at sample means), seven Asian countries

Country	Chicken	Beef	Pork	Mutton	Eggs	Fish
(1)	(2)	(3)	(4)	(5)	(6)	(7)
	Mean price log-changes					
1. Hong Kong	3.79	5.79	3.78		3.80	3.89
2. Japan	0.28	1.63	0.12		– 1.80	– 0.15
3. Philippines	3.90	4.41	5.47		4.42	5.60
4. Singapore	1.68	2.57	4.04	2.76	2.28	2.14
5. Sri Lanka	7.82	9.63	10.22	12.23	8.18	6.09
6. Taiwan	3.64	2.90	3.23	2.11	2.56	3.54
7. Thailand	0.82	5.34	4.46		3.71	4.99
Mean	3.13	4.61	4.47	5.70	3.31	3.73
Standard deviation	2.54	2.68	3.03	5.67	2.97	2.17
	Mean quantity log-changes					
1. Hong Kong	2.63	2.45	1.26		0.46	0.96
2. Japan	1.93	1.85	1.29		0.44	– 0.88
3. Philippines	4.83	2.51	2.04		1.29	– 0.53
4. Singapore	0.17	– 5.23	– 0.77	1.27	1.08	– 1.16
5. Sri Lanka	4.16	– 2.28	6.04	– 2.01	2.32	1.74
6. Taiwan	0.95	2.20	– 0.25	1.23	0.94	– 2.32
7. Thailand	1.79	– 3.39	1.66		0.87	0.94
Mean	2.31	– 0.72	1.67	0.16	1.16	– 0.37
Standard deviation	1.67	3.27	2.20	1.88	0.64	1.44

The last row of each section of Table 5.4 presents the mean and standard deviation for each food commodity. As can be seen, across the seven countries, on average, the price of chicken has grown have grown at a rate of 3.1%, eggs at 3.3%, fish at 3.7%, pork at 4.5%, beef at 4.6%, and mutton at 5.7%. Across the seven countries, on average, consumption of chicken has grown at a rate of 2.3% per annum, pork by 1.7% per annum, mutton by 0.2%, and eggs by 1.2%. The consumption of beef and fish have fallen at a rate of 0.7% and 0.4% per annum, respectively. The average mean price log-changes vary between 3.1% (chicken) and 5.7% (mutton), and average mean quantity log-changes vary between – 0.7% (beef) and 2.3% (chicken) across countries. In terms of variability, fish has the lowest and mutton has the highest price growth rate, while eggs have the lowest and beef has the highest variation in consumption growth rate.

The conditional budget shares (the proportion of total animal-derived food expenditure devoted to each animal-derived food item) of chicken, beef, pork, mutton, eggs, and fish are calculated as $w'_{it} = p_{it}q_{it}/M_{gt}$, where $M_{gt} = \sum_{i=1}^{n_g} p_{it}q_{it}$ and n_g (= 6) is the number of commodities in group g (see Sect. 2.8 of Chap. 2 for further details).

The conditional budget shares (w'_{it}) and group budget shares ($W_{gt} = M_{gt}/M_t$) for the selected years, as well as at the sample mean, are presented in Table 5.5. The findings related to animal-derived food budget shares in Asian countries reveal notable trends over the past four decades. Across the board, the budget shares for chicken and pork have experienced increases, with exceptions noted for chicken in Thailand and pork in Hong Kong. Particularly noteworthy is the upward trajectory of the budget share for beef in Hong Kong, Japan, the Philippines, and Taiwan. However, the fish budget allocation has witnessed a decline in all countries except Thailand. Delving into specific details presented in Table 5.5, it is evident that conditional budget allocation for chicken has nearly doubled in Japan, the Philippines, and Sri Lanka, while remaining relatively stable in Singapore. The beef budget share has seen significant shifts, doubling in Hong Kong, tripling in Japan, and halving in Singapore and Thailand. These findings underscore the dynamic nature of animal-derived food budget shares in the region, reflecting changing preferences and consumption patterns that warrant further exploration and analysis. The mean values provide insights into average consumer spending on animal-derived foods across various countries. Notably, it indicates that in most of these countries, consumers allocate nearly half of their animal-derived food expenditure to fish. Hong Kong, however, stands out as an exception, with almost 90% of its animal-derived food expenditure dedicated to meat. Furthermore, the budget share for beef in Hong Kong, has shown a notable increase from 12.27% in 1981 to 25.38% in 2013 and in Japan from 11.29% in 1981 to 30.62% in 2013. Despite meat constituting a smaller portion of the diet compared to fish in most of these countries, the upward trend in meat consumption is evident. This shift is influenced by factors such as rising income levels, urbanization, and the Westernization of tastes, signalling a dynamic evolution in dietary preferences and an increasing reliance on meat in these countries.

5.4 Empirical Regularities in the Animal-Derived Food Consumption Patterns in Asian Countries

As highlighted in Chap. 3, various consumption studies have observed a number of empirical regularities in the consumption patterns of consumers in a number of countries. In Sect. 3.4, we provided evidence of empirical regularities in the consumption patterns of consumers in 10 Asian countries using data for 8 broad commodities. Four such important empirical regularities we investigated are:

Empirical regularity 1: Quantity variance exceeds price variance.
Empirical regularity 2: Demand curve slopes downwards.
Empirical regularity 3: Income flexibility tends towards – 0.5.
Empirical regularity 4: Budget share of food declines with increasing income.

Below, we investigate whether these regularities are supported in the seven Asian countries using the animal-derived food consumption data.

Table 5.5 Conditional budget shares of animal-derived food commodities, selected years

Country	Year	Chicken	Beef	Pork	Mutton	Eggs	Fish	Group budget shares (W_{gt})
(1)	(2)	(3)	(4)	(5)	(6)	(7)	(8)	(9)
Hong Kong	1981	25.63	12.27	48.33		3.81	9.96	9.17
	1986	25.55	13.58	47.86		3.63	9.38	6.83
	1991	30.26	12.64	42.59		3.13	11.38	5.10
	1996	38.62	11.83	39.80		2.19	7.56	4.75
	2001	32.01	12.09	45.75		2.02	8.14	4.56
	2006	38.84	14.46	38.69		1.89	6.12	5.05
	2013	29.56	25.38	35.92		2.21	6.93	5.67
	Mean	32.89	13.85	42.64		2.58	8.03	5.87
Japan	1980	5.82	11.29	11.15		3.15	68.59	16.97
	1985	6.48	12.18	12.23		2.83	66.28	13.78
	1990	5.90	17.95	11.17		2.40	62.57	12.68
	1995	6.01	23.37	12.51		2.15	55.95	11.47
	2000	6.59	24.09	12.93		2.21	54.17	11.10
	2005	8.48	23.28	17.02		1.83	49.38	9.74
	2013	10.39	30.62	15.27		1.73	41.99	8.76
	Mean	7.20	21.04	13.51		2.20	56.05	12.07
Philippines	1990	7.27	6.42	19.85		4.11	62.34	20.06
	1995	9.29	5.62	23.83		3.66	57.60	19.50
	2000	9.81	8.95	25.41		3.53	52.30	16.72
	2005	9.92	8.52	25.71		3.63	52.22	16.00
	2013	13.12	7.63	27.08		3.70	48.47	12.84
	Mean	10.16	7.75	24.93		3.74	53.42	17.01
Singapore	1995	19.57	5.21	20.36	3.05	4.69	47.12	4.80
	2000	19.62	5.38	19.94	2.96	4.95	47.15	4.73
	2005	17.85	5.86	24.83	2.81	5.52	43.14	4.66
	2010	17.81	8.14	28.22	3.04	5.63	37.16	4.43
	2016	19.66	2.03	27.59	4.85	6.49	39.38	4.19
	Mean	18.58	5.79	23.85	3.15	5.59	43.04	4.56
Sri Lanka	1993	11.64	7.94	0.33	0.82	4.66	74.62	8.08
	1998	21.00	6.35	0.51	1.06	5.77	65.31	7.18

(continued)

Table 5.5 (continued)

Country	Year	Chicken	Beef	Pork	Mutton	Eggs	Fish	Group budget shares (W_{gt})
(1)	(2)	(3)	(4)	(5)	(6)	(7)	(8)	(9)
	2003	23.81	8.18	0.55	0.98	3.90	62.58	5.09
	2008	25.76	6.41	0.92	0.80	3.70	62.41	4.15
	2015	23.65	5.84	1.74	1.13	6.84	60.80	3.38
	Mean	20.94	7.43	0.80	1.02	5.15	64.65	5.58
Taiwan	1993	12.56	5.07	25.95	1.41	3.25	51.76	9.71
	1998	16.45	4.50	26.47	1.41	3.72	47.46	8.56
	2003	13.84	4.89	29.36	2.68	3.28	45.96	7.69
	2008	17.54	7.12	25.99	2.29	4.08	42.98	7.23
	2015	19.41	8.75	28.14	1.66	3.96	38.08	7.36
	Mean	16.61	5.74	27.27	2.20	3.72	44.47	8.11
Thailand	1990	25.19	14.68	17.42		8.74	33.97	11.66
	1995	23.75	13.18	14.96		6.61	41.50	10.82
	2000	21.31	7.13	18.29		6.67	46.59	9.69
	2005	17.72	5.35	23.22		6.49	47.23	7.94
	2013	15.42	7.71	23.84		8.41	44.61	6.87
	Mean	20.91	8.92	19.47		7.41	43.30	9.39

Empirical Regularity 1: Quantity Variance (K) > Price Variance (Π)

As in Chap. 3, we measure the overall growth in prices and consumption of animal-derived food in the seven countries using the Divisia price and quantity indices which are defined for the group as

$$DP_{gt} = \sum_{i=1}^{n_g} \overline{w}'_{it} Dp_{it} \quad \text{and} \quad DQ_{gt} = \sum_{i=1}^{n_g} \overline{w}'_{it} Dq_{it}$$

where $\overline{w}'_{it} = (1/2)\left(w'_{it} + w'_{it-1}\right)$ is the arithmetic average of the budget shares in periods t and $t-1$. These indices are presented in Tables 5.6 and 5.7, respectively. The last row of the tables presents the mean values for each country, averaged over the sample periods. The last row of Table 5.6, shows that, on average, overall prices of animal-derived food commodities have increased at an annual rate of approximately 4.06% in Hong Kong, 0.22% in Japan, 5.29% in the Philippines, 2.52% in Singapore, 6.75% in Sri Lanka, 3.39% in Taiwan, and 3.94% in Thailand. Accordingly, the lowest and highest annual overall price growth has been experienced in Japan and Sri Lanka, respectively. As can be seen from the last row of Table 5.7, the highest growth in animal-derived food consumption comes from Sri Lanka (2.01%) and the lowest (indeed, negative) consumption growth is in Taiwan (– 0.78%).

Table 5.8 displays the relative growth in prices ($Dp_{it} - DP_{gt}$) and relative growth in consumption ($Dq_{it} - DQ_{gt}$) of six animal-derived food items for each country. As can be seen across the countries, the average relative price growth rate is positive for beef, pork, and mutton while chicken, eggs, and fish have a negative relative price growth. An interesting observation on the consumption of animal-derived food in these Asian countries is that beef, mutton, and fish have the lowest (negative) relative consumption growth rates while chicken, pork, and eggs have a positive growth rate. This indicates that, although fish has made up a larger portion of the Asian diet, its popularity is declining. A comparison of relative price with relative consumption reveals that the pairs have opposite signs for the majority of the items.

To measure the overall variability in prices and consumption, we use the Divisia second order moments, Divisia price variance (Π_t), and Divisia quantity variance (K_t), defined as

$$\Pi_{gt} = \sum_{i=1}^{n_g} \overline{w}'_{it}\left[Dp_{it} - DP_{gt}\right]^2 \quad \text{and} \quad K_{gt} = \sum_{i=1}^{n_g} \overline{w}'_{it}\left[Dq_{it} - DQ_{gt}\right]^2$$

Tables 5.9 and 5.10 present the Divisia price and quantity variances for the animal-derived food group in the seven Asian countries. A comparison of the quantity variances (K_t) with the corresponding price variances (Π_t) reveals that, in almost all the years, quantity variance systematically exceeds that of the price variance. Figure 5.2 plots $\sqrt{K_t}$ against $\sqrt{\Pi_t}$ for $t = 1, \ldots, T$, together with the 45° line for all countries. They show that most of the points lie above the 45° line. This indicates that, on average, the quantity variance does indeed exceed the price variance for the animal-derived food group. Figure 5.3 shows the plot for the seven countries combined; again, the majority of the points lie above the 45° line for all countries except for Japan. This provides support for empirical regularity 1 even at the disaggregated level of the animal-derived food group.

Empirical Regularity 2: Demand Curve Slopes Downwards

The co-movements of price and quantity for the group are measured by the Divisia price-quantity correlation

$$\rho_{gt} = \frac{\Gamma_{gt}}{\sqrt{\Pi_{gt} K_{gt}}},$$

and Π_{gt} and K_{gt} are defined as before; where

$$\Gamma_{gt} = \sum_{i=1}^{n_g} \overline{w}'_{it}\left[Dp_{it} - DP_{gt}\right]\left[Dq_{it} - DQ_{gt}\right],$$

Table 5.6 Divisia price index for the animal-derived food group, seven Asian countries

Year	Hong Kong	Japan	Philippines	Singapore	Sri Lanka	Taiwan	Thailand
(1)	(2)	(3)	(4)	(5)	(6)	(7)	(8)
1981		– 0.37					
1982	11.59	7.87					
1983	6.51	– 1.48					
1984	7.58	– 3.83					
1985	– 7.00	– 4.25					
1986	– 2.21	– 1.24					
1987	1.15	– 0.41					
1988	7.08	– 0.72					
1989	11.48	1.55					
1990	1.86	6.89					
1991	8.04	2.35	15.44				5.27
1992	7.83	– 0.81	9.75				2.45
1993	4.13	– 0.51	2.22				– 1.92
1994	5.45	– 2.67	9.50		1.63	3.13	5.79
1995	6.64	– 1.91	8.25		2.73	7.29	4.74
1996	6.56	1.93	5.87	1.77	3.68	4.89	8.17
1997	– 1.18	1.75	3.46	2.85	5.53	4.13	6.09
1998	4.01	1.16	5.07	– 3.20	9.90	9.55	1.88
1999	– 6.41	– 0.15	5.29	4.42	– 18.57	– 1.34	3.82
2000	– 1.19	– 0.04	1.73	8.62	4.42	11.58	– 2.76
2001	– 2.38	– 1.20	6.03	– 1.04	12.42	– 3.85	3.54
2002	– 4.21	– 1.04	1.28	– 0.96	12.26	– 3.21	– 0.21
2003	– 6.21	– 0.72	1.25	0.74	3.79	– 0.17	– 3.22
2004	11.44	1.06	12.98	4.83	5.35	1.46	4.65
2005	0.70	0.77	4.88	1.77	15.90	3.23	6.94
2006	6.47	0.06	2.77	1.85	14.71	4.45	0.88
2007	14.01	6.19	3.11	2.20	20.63	4.84	– 2.91
2008	21.10	0.15	8.16	5.80	11.87	5.93	14.52
2009	1.04	3.13	4.63	2.75	14.31	0.48	5.31
2010	5.35	– 2.57	2.70	3.59	8.68	3.29	2.64
2011	– 0.62	1.20	3.10	5.69	0.33	6.70	10.02
2012	5.34	– 5.36	2.34	1.58	4.17	– 19.09	– 3.26
2013	5.91	0.54	1.80	1.99	7.89	25.26	18.15
2014				2.53	0.46	1.39	
2015				1.53	6.39	4.74	

(continued)

Table 5.6 (continued)

Year	Hong Kong	Japan	Philippines	Singapore	Sri Lanka	Taiwan	Thailand
(1)	(2)	(3)	(4)	(5)	(6)	(7)	(8)
2016				3.59			
Mean	4.06	0.22	5.29	2.52	6.75	3.39	3.94

Note All entries are to be divided by 100

is the Divisia price-quantity covariance.

Table 5.11 presents the Divisia price-quantity correlations for the animal-derived food group in the seven Asian countries. Almost 90% of the individual price-quantity correlations are negative. At the sample means, the average correlations vary between – 0.36 and – 0.08. This means that, in general, when the price rises, consumption falls; this equates to a downward-sloping demand curve.

Empirical Regularity 3: Income Flexibility Is About – 0.5

As in Chap. 3, we plot the relative consumption $(Dq_{it} - DQ_{gt})$ against the relative price $(Dp_{it} - DP_{gt})$, $t = 1, \ldots, T$, for the animal-derived food group for each country, thereby obtaining the slope estimates for all seven countries. These slope estimates are interpreted as estimates of income flexibility, ϕ, for each country. Figure 5.4 presents the corresponding plots for the pooled animal-derived food group data for each country. As can be seen, the points are scattered around a negatively sloping line, implying that, in all seven countries, consumption of animal-derived food group falls when relative price increases.

Table 5.12 presents the estimates of income flexibility, ϕ, collected from all the plots in Fig. 5.4 for each country. All the estimates are negative. The estimates range from – 0.57 to – 0.34 with an average of – 0.45.

Empirical Regularity 4: Budget Share of Animal-Derived Food Declines with Increasing Income

In Sect. 3.4 of Chap. 3, we found that consumer behaviour in the ten Asian countries supported Engel's Law, which states that the budget share of food declines with increasing income. We now re-investigate this for total animal-derived food consumption for the seven Asian countries. Figure 5.5 presents the plot of the conditional budget share of the combined consumption of animal-derived food commodities against the logarithmic of the per capita total animal food consumption expenditure for each country. The points are scattered around a negatively sloping line in all the plots; in other words, the share of expenditure on meat, eggs, and fish falls as income increases, consistent with Engel's Law.

Table 5.7 Divisia quantity index for the animal-derived food group, seven Asian countries

Year	Hong Kong	Japan	Philippines	Singapore	Sri Lanka	Taiwan	Thailand
(1)	(2)	(3)	(4)	(5)	(6)	(7)	(8)
1981		0.78					
1982	5.70	– 1.03					
1983	– 0.71	3.38					
1984	– 0.60	2.05					
1985	6.43	1.81					
1986	0.63	1.94					
1987	5.12	3.10					
1988	– 1.69	5.23					
1989	– 1.19	1.34					
1990	6.83	– 1.01					
1991	0.91	– 3.79	5.56				15.11
1992	4.47	0.51	– 2.45				5.36
1993	– 4.43	4.14	– 1.05				7.51
1994	11.73	4.09	– 0.27		5.63	– 9.17	– 1.16
1995	2.05	3.56	– 0.33		13.25	1.66	3.02
1996	– 1.04	– 2.19	1.54	0.60	0.93	0.32	– 0.17
1997	– 5.12	– 4.48	0.05	1.65	2.71	6.96	– 6.22
1998	4.43	– 1.12	– 2.75	– 6.85	4.07	– 3.21	– 0.61
1999	3.04	3.00	7.31	– 2.26	3.53	7.38	– 3.73
2000	0.21	2.07	– 1.23	– 0.22	– 1.99	– 5.53	5.56
2001	– 4.39	– 0.08	1.30	– 4.17	2.97	– 6.47	– 5.39
2002	– 0.92	– 4.10	3.36	3.06	– 1.91	2.07	4.82
2003	5.85	0.28	0.99	4.79	7.34	3.75	1.70
2004	3.92	– 5.51	– 0.19	– 4.76	– 2.08	– 11.80	1.06
2005	3.88	0.50	3.25	0.96	– 17.93	– 0.28	1.55
2006	1.77	– 3.70	2.56	1.48	6.28	– 0.98	– 2.81
2007	1.37	– 0.19	6.39	1.03	10.11	8.61	1.14
2008	0.28	– 0.51	0.10	– 2.43	– 2.93	– 6.27	– 12.20
2009	3.16	0.22	1.70	– 1.93	2.52	– 7.68	1.71
2010	8.73	– 0.32	– 1.61	– 1.33	8.72	9.26	0.68
2011	– 1.49	– 0.80	– 2.95	0.95	8.04	2.59	0.69
2012	6.19	1.19	– 0.46	– 2.40	– 0.95	– 0.01	0.72
2013	– 3.75	– 2.56	– 0.55	– 6.92	– 8.05	– 3.11	0.53
2014				– 0.11	4.03	2.32	
2015				– 0.44	– 0.06	– 7.52	

(continued)

Table 5.7 (continued)

Year	Hong Kong	Japan	Philippines	Singapore	Sri Lanka	Taiwan	Thailand
(1)	(2)	(3)	(4)	(5)	(6)	(7)	(8)
2016				4.63			
Mean	1.92	0.24	0.88	– 0.70	2.01	– 0.78	0.82

Note All entries are to be divided by 100

Table 5.8 Relative price and quantity log-changes of animal-derived food items (at sample means), seven Asian countries

Country	Chicken	Beef	Pork	Mutton	Eggs	Fish
(1)	(2)	(3)	(4)	(5)	(6)	(7)
	Mean relative price log-changes					
1. Hong Kong	– 0.27	1.74	– 0.28		– 0.25	– 0.17
2. Japan	0.06	1.41	– 0.10		– 2.02	– 0.37
3. Philippines	– 1.39	– 0.88	0.19		– 0.86	0.31
4. Singapore	– 0.84	0.05	1.52	0.24	– 0.24	– 0.38
5. Sri Lanka	1.07	2.88	3.47	5.49	1.43	– 0.66
6. Taiwan	0.25	– 0.50	– 0.16	– 1.28	– 0.83	0.14
7. Thailand	– 3.11	1.40	0.52		– 0.23	1.05
Mean	– 0.60	0.87	0.73	1.48	– 0.43	– 0.01
Standard deviation	1.36	1.35	1.35	3.55	1.04	0.57
	Mean relative quantity log-changes					
1. Hong Kong	0.71	0.53	– 0.65		– 1.45	– 0.96
2. Japan	1.70	1.61	1.06		0.21	– 1.12
3. Philippines	3.95	1.63	1.16		0.41	– 1.41
4. Singapore	0.86	– 4.53	– 0.07	1.96	1.78	– 0.46
5. Sri Lanka	2.15	– 4.29	4.03	– 4.02	0.31	– 0.28
6. Taiwan	1.73	2.97	0.53	2.01	1.71	– 1.54
7. Thailand	0.97	– 4.21	0.84		0.05	0.13
Mean	1.72	– 0.90	0.98	– 0.02	0.43	– 0.81
Standard deviation	1.12	3.30	1.49	3.47	1.10	0.62

Note All entries are to be divided by 100

5.5 Estimation of the Demand Model

A number of demand systems such as the Rotterdam Demand System (Barten, 1964; Theil, 1965), the Translog Demand System (Christensen et al., 1975), the Almost Ideal Demand System (AIDS) (Deaton & Muellbauer, 1980), and the Miniflex Laurent Demand System (Barnett, 1983), have been used in applied demand

Table 5.9 Divisia price variance for the animal-derived food group, seven Asian countries

Year	Hong Kong	Japan	Philippines	Singapore	Sri Lanka	Taiwan	Thailand
(1)	(2)	(3)	(4)	(5)	(6)	(7)	(8)
1981		11.80					
1982	8.39	41.73					
1983	12.44	8.02					
1984	23.64	10.02					
1985	17.28	10.06					
1986	8.92	1.98					
1987	12.02	37.86					
1988	16.15	0.62					
1989	13.15	2.91					
1990	3.49	9.92					
1991	6.29	3.74	8.52				6.31
1992	4.05	24.80	13.04				3.23
1993	8.24	1.40	13.53				18.60
1994	5.16	3.28	9.01		14.14	12.77	2.43
1995	24.64	2.52	10.86		28.75	26.02	39.66
1996	5.46	2.52	10.85	28.85	60.56	15.12	0.50
1997	28.42	2.36	1.77	3.56	68.81	18.21	69.80
1998	43.43	6.01	7.44	5.31	192.97	17.92	10.45
1999	13.14	2.27	0.75	39.41	952.35	11.14	11.27
2000	11.36	0.42	5.51	65.26	225.15	97.85	18.46
2001	17.71	15.99	1.15	1.20	46.32	241.84	1.95
2002	13.21	39.53	1.69	4.38	11.96	20.64	1.01
2003	9.47	15.00	1.21	13.34	6.87	32.08	27.61
2004	202.32	2.86	19.00	65.20	7.64	26.49	36.06
2005	5.12	4.62	2.09	24.10	58.19	27.09	4.99
2006	23.99	2.91	4.14	4.20	68.64	23.50	6.75
2007	10.45	33.30	6.83	0.53	11.95	2.66	77.06
2008	51.59	5.96	10.93	59.65	17.45	24.61	4.70
2009	99.72	16.54	0.45	13.04	22.56	8.38	8.56
2010	32.13	10.37	7.70	4.64	106.91	34.74	19.34
2011	342.55	20.34	7.01	10.07	19.51	32.71	2.64
2012	22.68	13.96	5.53	3.25	25.19	757.61	87.27
2013	30.75	0.73	3.63	2.82	7.36	657.44	15.80
2014				4.63	19.99	21.70	
2015				1.22	8.59	41.88	

(continued)

Table 5.9 (continued)

Year	Hong Kong	Japan	Philippines	Singapore	Sri Lanka	Taiwan	Thailand
(1)	(2)	(3)	(4)	(5)	(6)	(7)	(8)
2016				3.17			
Mean	35.23	11.10	6.64	17.04	90.08	97.84	20.63

Note All entries are to be divided by 10,000

analysis over the last five decades. In this chapter, we have selected the Rotterdam demand system (Barten, 1964; Theil, 1965) on the basis that: it is also consistent with demand theory (Theil, 1980); has excellent aggregate properties (Barnett, 1983; Selvanathan, 1991); can be interpreted as approximations to the true, unknown ones (Mountain, 1988), and; due to its simplicity, it is easy to estimate and easy to interpret the parameter estimates. Further this model has continued to be well utilized for over five decades since its development (see Clements & Gao, 2015; Kinnucan et al., 2001). In this section, we first re-introduce the Rotterdam demand equations from Chap. 2 in three forms,[2] namely, (1) Group demand equations, (2) Conditional demand equations, and (3) Unconditional demand equations. Unconditional demand equations involve all n prices and total real expenditure (DQ). We then block the n goods such that they form G groups that are separable in the consumer's utility function (also known as block-independence preference). This leads to a composite demand equation for each group g (= 1, 2, …, G) that depends on group prices (DP_{gt}) and group expenditure (DQ_{gt}) and conditional demand equations, one for each commodity within the group. Conditional demand equations relate to the allocation of total expenditure on the group (DQ_{gt}) to the goods within that group, assuming that the total consumption of the group is held constant. The variables of the conditional demand equation are exclusively concerned within the group to which the good belongs, allowing us to focus our attention on the demand within the group. The detailed derivations for these equations can be found in Theil (1975/76), Clements and Johnson (1983), Duffy (1987), Selvanathan and Clements (1995), and Nelson (1997).

Composite Demand Equations

The *composite demand equation* in relative prices for group S_g is (Theil & Clements, 1987)

$$\overline{W}_{gt} DQ_{gt} = \alpha_g + \Theta_g DQ_t + \phi\Theta_g(1 - \Theta_g)(DP'_{gt} - DP_{0t}) + E_{gt}, \qquad (5.5.1)$$

[2] In this chapter we assumed (1) non-separability within the animal-derived food group as there is some level of substitutability/complementarity expected between the meat types, (2) product aggregation as Barnett (1983) and Selvanathan (1991) theoretically showed that the Rotterdam Demand System satisfies the aggregation properties, (3) block separability as a number of studies in the applied demand analysis literature have tested block separability for broadly aggregated goods such as food, clothing, housing etc., and found the data support block separability (for example see Theil, 1975/76), (4) expenditure endogeneity since we estimated the group and conditional demand equations simultaneously (for example see, Kinnucan et al., 2001; LaFrance, 1991).

Table 5.10 Divisia quantity variance for the animal-derived food group, seven Asian countries

Year	Hong Kong	Japan	Philippines	Singapore	Sri Lanka	Taiwan	Thailand
(1)	(2)	(3)	(4)	(5)	(6)	(7)	(8)
1981		6.32					
1982	3.99	4.77					
1983	23.69	16.72					
1984	2.68	8.71					
1985	14.36	5.00					
1986	9.87	3.80					
1987	19.35	0.75					
1988	41.57	78.76					
1989	78.89	13.16					
1990	13.88	3.40					
1991	59.93	9.61	34.37				89.67
1992	159.31	15.93	6.33				143.41
1993	17.98	11.10	84.61				48.19
1994	47.72	4.60	10.37		65.36	164.42	75.99
1995	74.34	13.75	32.65		118.02	17.25	32.35
1996	1.48	10.76	191.05	5.98	188.60	33.08	26.41
1997	52.89	8.25	21.66	5.64	104.85	41.99	31.03
1998	41.34	11.57	29.43	14.11	67.78	55.29	37.45
1999	5.57	7.31	32.71	427.13	160.01	27.96	66.81
2000	15.43	2.02	5.03	68.32	33.43	22.56	134.48
2001	94.86	27.48	3.87	2.66	344.37	38.94	151.89
2002	6.04	38.61	2.50	12.97	40.40	7.83	14.25
2003	6.29	17.61	1.58	54.31	19.71	58.78	23.49
2004	8.41	42.32	7.11	57.80	95.70	164.13	67.92
2005	58.46	15.70	15.78	62.89	250.69	19.67	5.68
2006	34.29	8.50	11.55	27.21	247.81	46.72	54.87
2007	22.95	3.18	12.81	19.46	130.87	257.15	87.44
2008	18.20	0.94	5.24	8.94	21.37	43.48	137.24
2009	5.99	4.16	5.93	4.92	74.26	53.09	65.28
2010	55.53	12.58	13.55	36.37	78.52	19.47	15.33
2011	34.23	4.57	15.09	15.52	41.08	29.30	9.90
2012	247.65	0.45	4.48	67.87	60.20	38.82	8.17
2013	40.49	9.84	3.88	110.07	103.05	23.50	6.65
2014				19.25	24.19	16.51	
2015				197.14	63.43	153.89	

(continued)

Table 5.10 (continued)

Year	Hong Kong	Japan	Philippines	Singapore	Sri Lanka	Taiwan	Thailand
(1)	(2)	(3)	(4)	(5)	(6)	(7)	(8)
2016				102.54			
Mean	41.18	12.79	23.98	62.91	106.08	60.63	58.00

Note All entries are to be divided by 10,000

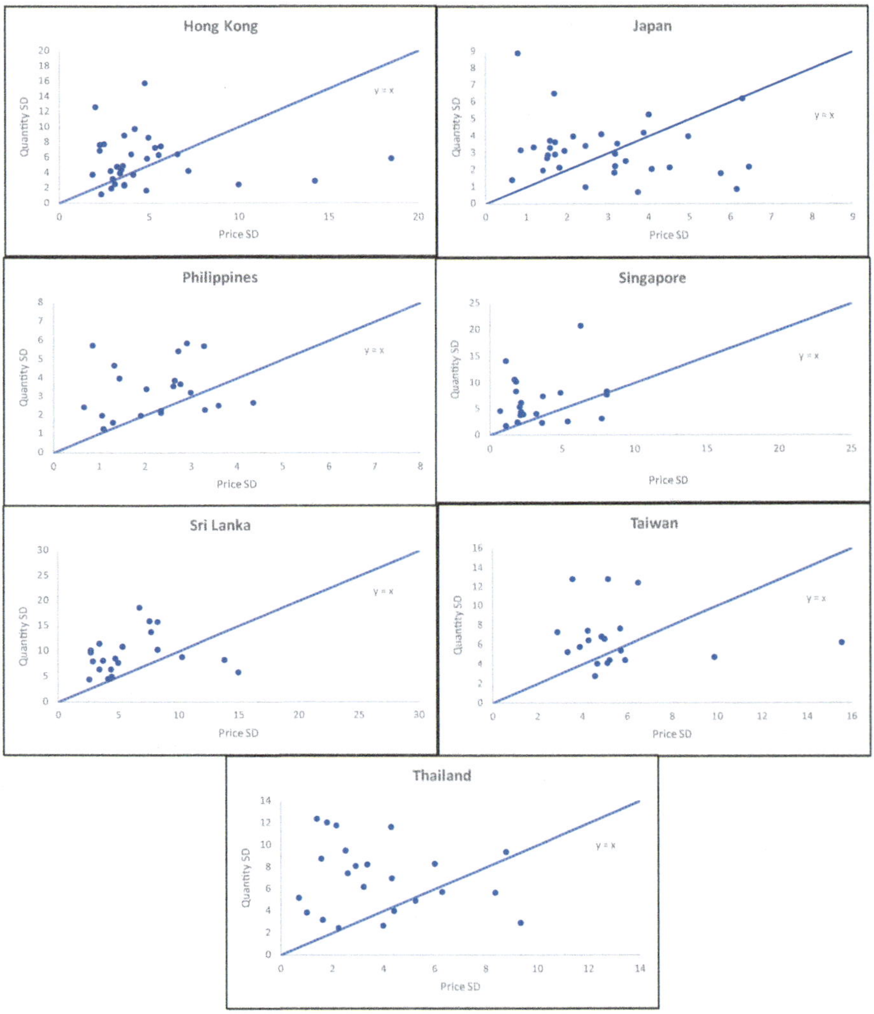

Fig. 5.2 Divisia quantity versus price variance for the animal-derived food group, seven Asian countries

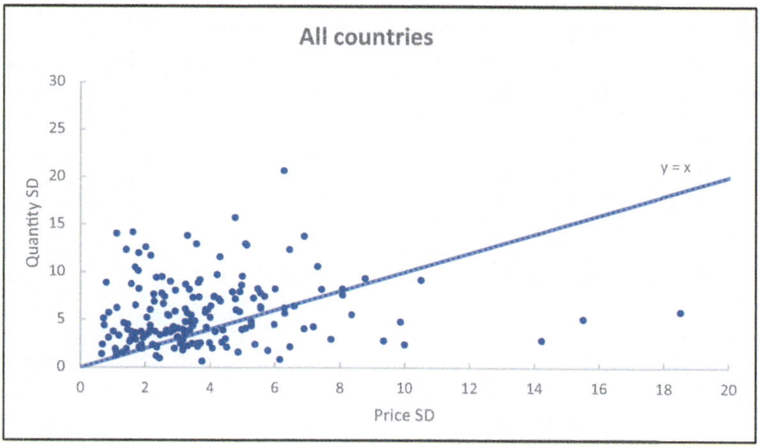

Fig. 5.3 Divisia quantity SD versus price SD for the animal-derived food group, seven Asian countries combined

where $\overline{W}_{gt} = \sum_{i \in S_g} \overline{w}_{it}$, $\Theta_g = \sum_{i \in S_g} \theta_i$ are the budget and marginal shares of group S_g, and $DQ_{gt} = \sum_{i \in S_g} \overline{w}'_{it} Dq_{it}$ and, $DP'_{gt} = \sum_{i \in S_g} \theta'_{it} Dp_{it}$ are the Divisia group volume and price indexes, α_g is a constant term and E_{gt} is a serially independent, normally distributed error term with a zero mean and constant variance. The index DP_{0t} is the log-change in implicit price deflator excluding animal-derived food.[3]

We can rewrite Eq. (5.5.1) as

$$\overline{W}_{gt} DQ_{gt} = \alpha_g + \Theta_g DQ_t + \phi \Theta_g (1 - \Theta_g) \left(\sum_{i \in s_g} \theta'_i Dp_{it} - DP_{0t} \right) + E_{gt}. \tag{5.5.2}$$

The income and own-price elasticities for the group S_g based on Eq. (5.5.1) are,

$$\eta_g = \frac{\Theta_g}{W_g} \quad \text{and} \quad \eta_{gg} = \frac{\phi \Theta_g}{W_g} (1 - \Theta_g), \quad g = 1, \ldots, G. \tag{5.5.3}$$

Conditional Demand Equations in Absolute Prices

The finite-change version of the conditional demand equation in absolute prices presented in Eq. (2.9.10) of Chap. 2 can be written in the form,

$$\overline{w}_{it} Dq_{it} = \alpha'_i + \theta'_i \overline{W}_{gt} DQ_{gt} + \sum_{j \in S_g} \pi^g_{ij} Dp_{jt} + \varepsilon_{it}, \tag{5.5.4}$$

[3] Following Clements and Johnson (1983), $DP_{0t} = (DP^*_t - \overline{W}_{gt} DP_{gt})/(1 - \overline{W}_{gt})$, where DP^*_t is the log-change in the price index of all n goods (or the CPI log-change).

Table 5.11 Divisia price-quantity correlations for the seven Asian countries

Year	Hong Kong	Japan	Philippines	Singapore	Sri Lanka	Taiwan	Thailand
(1)	(2)	(3)	(4)	(5)	(6)	(7)	(8)
1981		– 0.17					
1982	0.52	– 0.13					
1983	0.06	– 0.31					
1984	– 0.63	– 0.12					
1985	– 0.54	– 0.51					
1986	– 0.61	0.11					
1987	– 0.17	– 0.71					
1988	0.25	0.72					
1989	0.67	0.40					
1990	– 0.29	– 0.44					
1991	– 0.79	0.30	0.19				– 0.21
1992	0.44	0.03	– 0.18				– 0.74
1993	– 0.60	0.60	– 0.94				– 0.16
1994	0.30	– 0.25	– 0.82		0.27	– 0.08	– 0.71
1995	– 0.86	0.56	– 0.57		0.53	– 0.56	– 0.37
1996	– 0.05	– 0.20	– 0.73	– 0.62	– 0.44	– 0.24	– 0.71
1997	– 0.17	– 0.69	0.02	– 0.33	– 0.97	– 0.60	– 0.26
1998	– 0.81	– 0.36	– 0.70	– 0.51	0.12	0.41	– 0.69
1999	– 0.21	– 0.29	0.10	– 0.88	– 0.82	0.14	– 0.17
2000	– 0.42	– 0.68	– 0.57	– 0.08	– 0.70	– 0.80	– 0.61
2001	– 0.91	– 0.93	– 0.26	– 0.77	0.50	0.77	0.47
2002	– 0.93	– 0.26	– 0.57	0.03	0.19	0.36	– 0.32
2003	0.38	0.93	– 0.87	0.88	– 0.22	– 0.11	– 0.10
2004	– 0.44	0.31	– 0.80	– 0.34	– 0.91	– 0.10	– 0.67
2005	– 0.94	– 0.17	– 0.64	– 0.42	0.23	– 0.49	– 0.30
2006	– 0.72	0.52	– 0.85	0.50	0.31	0.02	– 0.84
2007	0.19	0.58	– 0.19	– 0.30	– 0.30	0.56	– 0.70
2008	– 0.09	– 0.41	– 0.02	0.35	– 0.15	– 0.37	0.11
2009	0.34	0.73	– 0.50	– 0.99	– 0.31	– 0.83	0.52
2010	0.69	– 0.50	0.72	– 0.25	– 0.70	– 0.42	– 0.31
2011	– 0.72	– 0.32	– 0.81	0.77	– 0.07	0.38	– 0.48
2012	0.54	– 0.18	– 0.58	– 0.19	– 0.97	– 0.57	– 0.62
2013	– 0.85	– 0.67	0.17	0.89	– 0.05	– 0.14	– 0.50
2014				0.31	– 0.35	0.51	
2015				– 0.29	– 0.24	0.14	
2016				– 0.45			
Mean	– 0.23	– 0.08	– 0.41	– 0.13	– 0.23	– 0.09	– 0.36

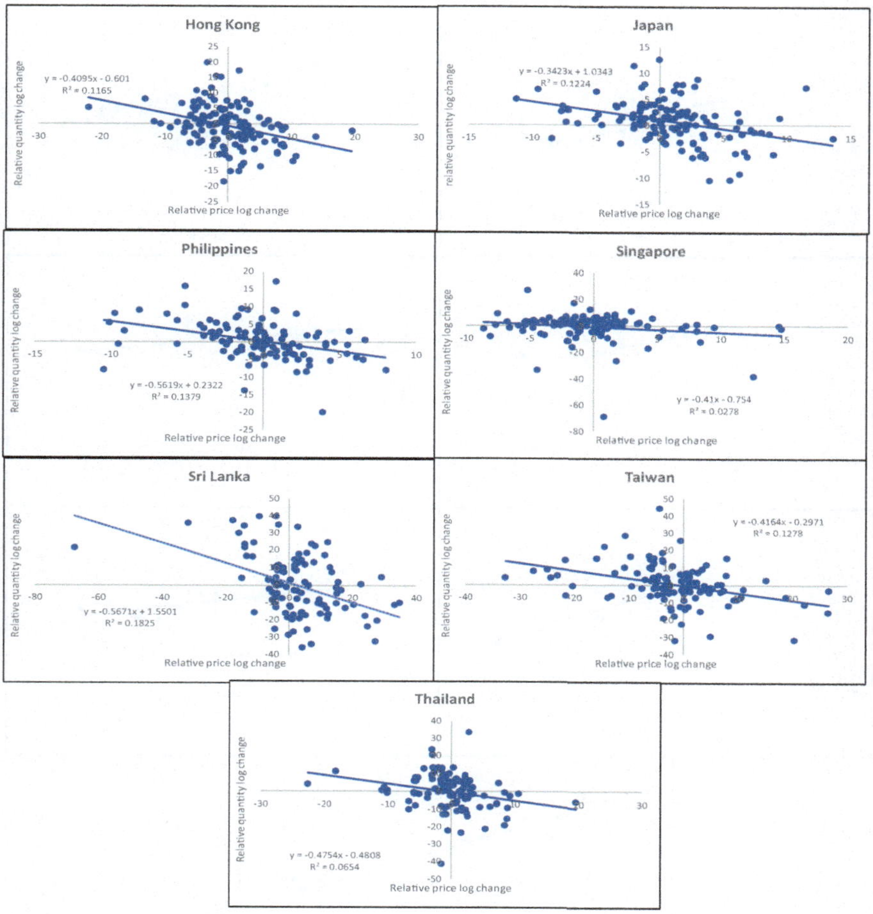

Fig. 5.4 Relative quantity against relative prices of animal-derived food group in the seven Asian countries

Table 5.12 Slope estimates of the demand curve, income flexibility (ϕ), seven Asian countries

Country	Income flexibility
Hong Kong	– 0.41
Japan	– 0.34
Philippines	– 0.56
Singapore	– 0.41
Sri Lanka	– 0.57
Taiwan	– 0.42
Thailand	– 0.48
Mean	– 0.45

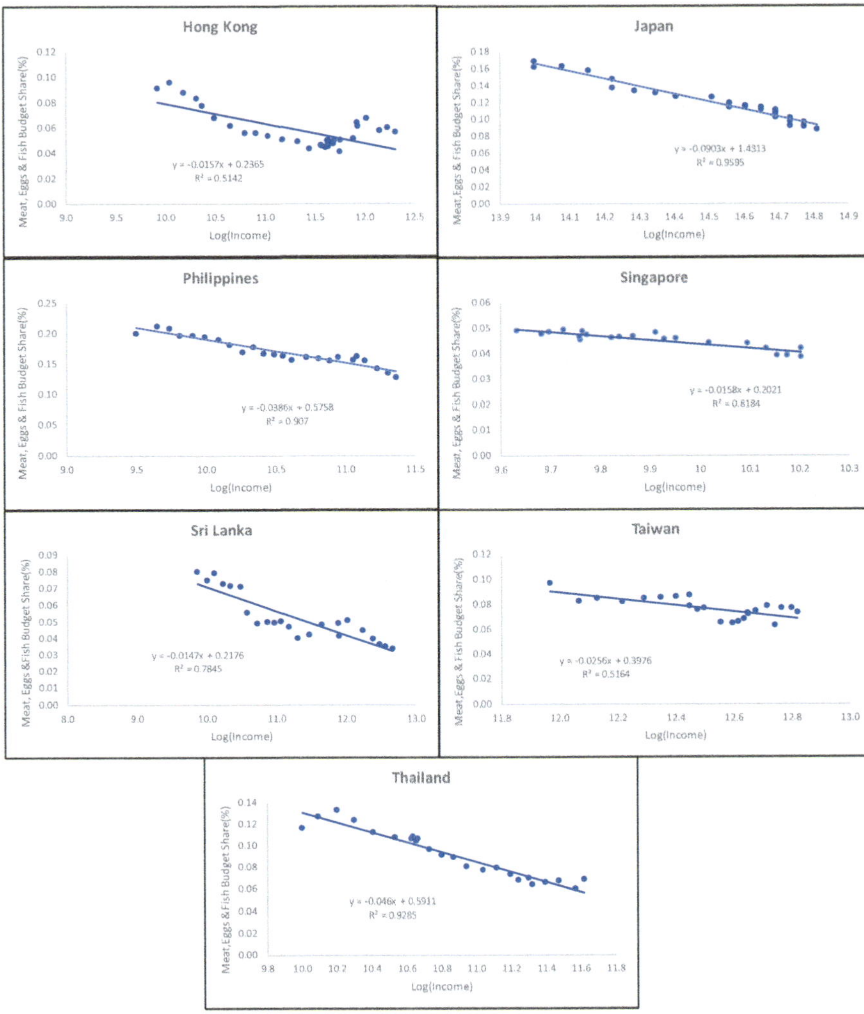

Fig. 5.5 Animal-derived food budget share against logarithm of per capita total animal-derived food consumption expenditures

where π_{ij}^{g} is the conditional Slutsky coefficient and $\theta_i' = \theta_i/\Theta_g$ is the ith conditional marginal share. The conditional marginal share θ_i' answers the question, "if the expenditure on the group increased by \$1, what proportion of this additional expenditure on the group is spent on good i?" The conditional marginal shares add up to 1. The conditional Slutsky coefficients satisfy demand homogeneity and Slutsky symmetry given by Eq. (5.5.5).

$$\sum_{j \in S_g} \pi_{ij}^{g} = 0, \qquad \pi_{ij}^{g} = \pi_{ji}^{g}, \qquad i, j \in S_g. \tag{5.5.5}$$

The constant term α_i' is included to account for autonomous trends in consumption due to variables such as the demographic structure of the population, social, and religious factors, as well as nutritional and health factors which affect animal-derived food consumption. The ε_{it} variables are serially independent, normally distributed error terms with zero means and a constant contemporaneous covariance matrix. The conditional income and price elasticities for commodity i implied by Eq. (5.5.4) are

$$\eta_i' = \frac{\theta_i'}{\overline{w}_{it}'}, \qquad \eta_{ij}' = \frac{\pi_{ij}^g}{\overline{w}_{it}} \tag{5.5.6}$$

Unconditional Demand Responses

The conditional demand equation (5.5.4) considers the demand for an animal-derived food commodity in terms of total expenditure on animal-derived food and the prices of the six animal-derived food commodities. Now we give the unconditional demand equations which explain the demand for an animal-derived food commodity in terms of total consumption expenditure of the consumer ("income" for short) and the prices of the six animal-derived food commodities (see Selvanathan & Clements, 1995)

$$\overline{w}_{it} Dq_{it} = \alpha_i + \theta_i DQ_t + \sum_{j \in S_g} \pi_{ij} Dp_{jt} + \pi_{i0} DP_{0t} \tag{5.5.7}$$

where

$$\theta_i = \Theta_g \theta_i' \tag{5.5.8}$$

is the unconditional marginal share of i;

$$\pi_{ij} = \pi_{ij}^g + \phi\Theta_g(1 - \Theta_g)\theta_i'\theta_j' \quad \text{and} \quad \pi_{i0} = -\phi\Theta_g(1 - \Theta_g)\theta_i', \tag{5.5.9}$$

are the unconditional Slutsky coefficients; and they satisfy $\sum_{j \in S_g} \pi_{ij} + \pi_{i0} = 0$ and $\pi_{ij} = \pi_{ji}$.

The unconditional income and price elasticities implied by Eq. (5.5.7) are given by

$$\eta_i = \frac{\theta_i}{\overline{w}_{it}} \quad \eta_{ij} = \frac{\pi_{ij}}{\overline{w}_{it}} \quad \eta_{i0} = \frac{\pi_{i0}}{\overline{w}_{it}}. \tag{5.5.10}$$

5.6 Estimation Procedures and Results

Before the estimation of the demand equations, we investigated the stationarity of all the variables in the demand systems, Eqs. (5.5.2) and (5.5.4), to avoid spurious results. According to the test results of the Augmented Dickey–Fuller unit root test (Dickey & Fuller, 1979), we found all the variables to be used in the demand systems are stationary.[4]

We estimate the demand equation (5.5.4) and test the demand theory hypotheses homogeneity and symmetry to determine whether they are compatible with the animal-derived food group data. We follow the same estimation and testing procedures described in Sect. 4.2 of Chap. 4, with unconditional versions of the equations for broad commodity groups in Sect. 4.2 replaced by their conditional counterparts for the animal-derived food commodities. The test results are reported in Table 5.13. Comparing the observed values of the test statistic with the corresponding critical values, we can conclude that for all countries, homogeneity, symmetry and the joint test for homogeneity and symmetry at the 5% level of significance are compatible with the animal-derived food group data.

Following Clements and Johnson (1983), Kinnucan et al. (2001), group demand equation (5.5.2) and conditional demand equation (5.5.4) are estimated jointly in Stata 16 using the non-Linear version of the Seemingly Unrelated Regression (NL-SUR) using the iterated Feasible Generalized Non-linear Least Squares (FGNLS) estimation method. By estimating Eqs. (5.5.2) and (5.5.4) simultaneously, we have resolved the endogeneity problem with respect to group expenditure (see, Kinnucan et al., 2001; LaFrance, 1991). However, elasticity estimates obtained from models that ignore food price endogeneity are also likely to be biased, resulting in erroneous policy advice and unreliable forecasts of future food demand (Dhar et al., 2003; Henneberry & Hwang, 2007; Hovhannisyan & Bozic, 2017). Therefore, we investigate the issue of price endogeneity using the Wu–Hausman endogeneity test as described in Johnston and DiNardo (1997, p. 342) and applied by Henneberry and Hwang (2007, p. 54). We performed this test by regressing prices on lagged prices as instruments and found no evidence for price endogeneity.

Estimated parameters of group demand equation (5.5.2) and group demand elasticities using Eq. (5.5.3) are presented in Table 5.14. As can be seen, all group marginal shares (θ_g) presented in column (3) are positive and statistically significant, as they should be. Group marginal share for Hong Kong is 1.4%, Japan 11.2%, Philippines 10.3%, Singapore 1.5%, Sri Lanka 1.9%, Taiwan 8.9%, and Thailand 2.4%. These estimates mean that if income increases by \$100, for example, Hong Kong consumers will allocate an extra \$1.40 on animal-derived food while the Japanese will allocate an extra \$11.20. The estimated income flexibilities (ϕ) are negative for all seven countries, as they should be. The group income elasticities are all less than 1 (except for Taiwan), indicating that the animal-derived food group is generally a necessity.

---

[4] We also checked the normality and autocorrelation based on the residuals and found no violation. Further, we found the correlation between the independent variables are reasonably small to conclude that the degree of multicollinearity is very low.

Table 5.13 Testing demand homogeneity and Slutsky symmetry for the animal-derived food group, seven Asian countries

Country	Homogeneity			Symmetry			Homogeneity and symmetry		
	Test statistic	$F_{Critical}$	Conclusion	Test statistic	$F_{Critical}$	Conclusion	Test statistic	$F_{Critical}$	Conclusion
(1)	(2)	(3)	(4)	(5)	(6)	(7)	(8)	(9)	(10)
Hong Kong	0.89	2.76	Accept	1.08	2.49	Accept	1.10	2.23	Accept
Japan	1.05	2.74	Accept	0.86	2.47	Accept	0.90	2.22	Accept
Philippines	0.39	3.01	Accept	0.55	2.74	Accept	0.52	2.49	Accept
Singapore	1.02	2.90	Accept	0.78	2.54	Accept	0.95	2.40	Accept
Sri Lanka	1.41	2.96	Accept	0.78	2.60	Accept	0.71	2.46	Accept
Taiwan	1.42	2.90	Accept	0.85	2.54	Accept	0.96	2.40	Accept
Thailand	1.27	3.06	Accept	0.37	2.79	Accept	0.71	2.54	Accept

The estimated own-price elasticities for the group are negative and less than 1 in absolute value for all the countries (except Sri Lanka and Taiwan) indicating that the demand for the animal-derived food group is generally price inelastic.

Table 5.15 presents the estimated conditional marginal shares of Eq. (5.5.4) under the homogeneity and symmetry restrictions. As can be seen, all the estimated marginal shares are positive and the majority of them are statistically significant. For example, for Hong Kong consumers, the estimates of the conditional marginal shares of chicken, beef, pork, eggs, and fish are 0.45, 0.15, 0.36, 0.01, and 0.03, respectively. These values indicate that when Hong Kong consumers' expenditure on animal-derived food increases by $1, 45¢ of that one dollar will be spent on chicken, 15¢ on beef, 36¢ on pork, 1¢ on eggs, and the remaining 3¢ on fish.

Table 5.16 presents the conditional and unconditional income elasticities calculated at sample means as in Eqs. (5.5.6) and (5.5.10). We classify a commodity as a necessity if its conditional (unconditional) income elasticity is less than one, and as a luxury if the conditional (unconditional) income elasticity is greater than one. This means that, when group expenditure (income) increases by 10% while consumption increases by less than 10%, the item is classified as a necessity. In contrast, if consumption increases by more than 10% the item is determined to be a luxury. The unconditional income elasticity results reveal that chicken is considered a necessity in all 7 countries, with an elasticity less than 1 in all countries. This implies that as income rises by 10%, chicken consumption increases, but by less than 10%,

Table 5.14 Parameter estimates and demand elasticities of group demand equations

Country	α	Θ_g	ϕ	Group income elasticity (η_g)	Own-price elasticity (η_{gg})
(1)	(2)	(3)	(4)	(5)	(6)
Hong Kong	0.002*	0.014*	– 0.811*	0.244*	– 0.202*
	(0.000)	(0.005)	(0.294)	(0.079)	(0.076)
Japan	– 0.009*	0.112*	– 0.659*	0.953*	– 0.696*
	(0.002)	(0.027)	(0.221)	(0.230)	(0.233)
Philippines	0.021*	0.103*	– 0.230	0.632*	– 0.157
	(0.001)	(0.031)	(0.145)	(0.189)	(0.099)
Singapore	– 0.014*	0.015*	– 0.447*	0.330*	– 0.150*
	(0.001)	(0.001)	(0.039)	(0.174)	(0.013)
Sri Lanka	0.002*	0.019*	– 2.770	0.374*	– 1.090
	(0.001)	(0.009)	(1.646)	(0.171)	(0.646)
Taiwan	– 0.002*	0.089*	– 0.828	1.155*	– 1.066
	(0.001)	(0.022)	(0.751)	(0.289)	(0.967)
Thailand	– 0.001	0.024*	– 0.960	0.268*	– 0.265*
	(0.001)	(0.010)	(0.532)	(0.108)	(0.086)

Standard errors are in parentheses
* Significant at the 5% level

Table 5.15 Estimates of conditional marginal shares for six animal-derived food items, seven Asian countries

Country	Conditional marginal shares					
	Chicken	Beef	Pork	Mutton	Eggs	Fish
(1)	(2)	(3)	(4)	(5)	(6)	(7)
Hong Kong	0.451*	0.154*	0.357*		0.008*	0.030*
	(0.104)	(0.053)	(0.083)		(0.003)	(0.012)
Japan	0.058*	0.425*	0.035		0.003*	0.485*
	(0.018)	(0.066)	(0.041)		(0.001)	(0.160)
Philippines	0.029*	0.091*	0.165*		0.011*	0.704*
	(0.008)	(0.038)	(0.045)		(0.005)	(0.305)
Singapore	0.153	0.173*	0.419*	0.047*	0.035*	0.173*
	(0.072)	(0.051)	(0.143)	(0.023)	(0.010)	(0.080)
Sri Lanka	0.220*	0.035*	0.008*	0.001	0.027*	0.709*
	(0.073)	(0.016)	(0.002)	(0.005)	(0.012)	(0.340)
Taiwan	0.089	0.069*	0.039*	0.002*	0.009*	0.874*
	(0.037)	(0.025)	(0.012)	(0.001)	(0.004)	(0.412)
Thailand	0.330*	0.080*	0.126*		0.025*	0.364*
	(0.061)	(0.034)	(0.062)		(0.005)	(0.165)

Standard errors are in parentheses
* Significant at the 5% level

underscoring its status as a staple food item in most Asian nations. Intriguingly, beef emerges as a unconditional luxury in Japan and Taiwan, given its unconditional income elasticity exceeding 1, while in all other countries, it remains a necessity. The unconditional income elasticities further reveal that chicken, pork, mutton, and eggs are unconditional necessities in all countries, implying that their consumption is relatively less responsive to changes in income. Additionally, fish and beef are identified as necessities in all countries except in Taiwan. These economic insights provide a nuanced understanding of the varying roles and significance of different animal-derived food items in the dietary patterns of Asian countries, highlighting the interplay between income levels and consumption preferences.

Table 5.17 presents the conditional price elasticities given by Eq. (5.5.6) for the six animal-derived food items in the seven countries. All the conditional own-price elasticities (see columns CC, BB, PP, MM, EE, and FF) are negative, as they should be. They are also less than 1 in absolute value (except chicken and pork in Singapore and fish in the Philippines), indicating that the demand for all the animal-derived food items is price inelastic. Furthermore, we can identify the substitutes and complementarities for each food item, considering the positive and negative signs of cross-price elasticities. For instance, for consumers in Hong Kong, all food items are found to be substitutes (cross-price elasticities are positive) for each other except chicken-fish and beef-pork. The complementarity of chicken-fish and beef-pork is likely due to

Table 5.16 Conditional and unconditional income elasticities for six animal-derived food items, seven Asian countries

Country	Chicken	Beef	Pork	Mutton	Eggs	Fish
	Conditional					
Hong Kong	1.364*	1.124*	0.837*		0.300*	0.378*
	(0.314)	(0.387)	(0.195)		(0.116)	(0.149)
Japan	0.813*	2.020*	0.260		0.151	0.865*
	(0.251)	(0.313)	(0.306)		(0.112)	(0.285)
Philippines	0.288	1.173	0.660*		0.287	1.319*
	(0.282)	(0.869)	(0.180)		(0.410)	(0.571)
Singapore	0.826*	2.934*	1.757*	1.517*	0.621*	0.403*
	(0.389)	(0.873)	(0.597)	(0.752)	(0.179)	(0.186)
Sri Lanka	1.043*	0.464	0.993*	0.102	0.533*	1.099*
	(0.349)	(0.489)	(0.225)	(0.511)	(0.234)	(0.527)
Taiwan	0.537*	1.117*	0.143	0.096	0.249*	1.965*
	(0.224)	(0.440)	(0.120)	(0.565)	(0.107)	(0.926)
Thailand	1.577*	0.907*	0.649*		0.338	0.838*
	(0.293)	(0.385)	(0.319)		(0.206)	(0.379)
	Unconditional					
Hong Kong	0.340*	0.271*	0.201*		0.070*	0.091*
	(0.078)	(0.092)	(0.046)		(0.027)	(0.036)
Japan	0.797*	2.028*	0.255		0.140*	0.808
	(0.246)	(0.903)	(0.561)		(0.014)	(2.189)
Philippines	0.176*	0.714*	0.399		0.172*	0.788
	(0.048)	(0.229)	(0.271)		(0.030)	(1.838)
Singapore	0.273*	0.960*	0.582*	0.502*	0.206*	0.133*
	(0.015)	(0.011)	(0.030)	(0.005)	(0.002)	(0.017)
Sri Lanka	0.387*	0.166*	0.390*	0.037*	0.196*	0.389
	(0.128)	(0.028)	(0.004)	(0.009)	(0.021)	(0.598)
Taiwan	0.626*	1.378*	0.167*	0.113*	0.289*	2.261
	(0.259)	(0.175)	(0.084)	(0.007)	(0.028)	(2.887)
Thailand	0.391*	0.223*	0.179*		0.090*	0.223
	(0.072)	(0.040)	(0.073)		(0.006)	(0.195)

the common practise in Hong Kong where most households simultaneously consume chicken soup and fish curry or meals containing beef and pork.

Table 5.18 presents the unconditional price elasticities (η_{ij}) for the six animal-derived food commodities in the seven selected Asian countries. The unconditional own-price elasticities are larger than their corresponding conditional demand elasticities. The majority of the cross-price elasticity estimates are positive, meaning

Table 5.17 Conditional price elasticities for six animal-derived food items, seven Asian countries

Country	**CC**	CB	CP	CM	CE	CF	BC	**BB**	BP
Hong Kong	**– 0.200***	0.136*	0.107*		0.002*	– 0.045*	0.327*	**– 0.331***	– 0.231*
	(0.006)	(0.004)	(0.004)		(0.000)	(0.002)	(0.010)	**(0.016)**	(0.013)
Japan	**– 0.028***	– 0.068	– 0.170*		– 0.044*	0.310*	– 0.068	**– 0.861***	0.461*
	(0.010)	(0.016)	(0.021)		(0.002)	(0.015)	(0.005)	**(0.021)**	(0.013)
Philippines	**– 0.531***	– 0.161*	0.278*		0.037*	0.376*	– 0.161*	**– 0.430***	– 0.269*
	(0.042)	(0.031)	(0.037)		(0.013)	(0.036)	(0.041)	**(0.096)**	(0.070)
Singapore	**– 1.511***	0.198*	0.923*	0.357*	0.023*	0.009	0.198*	**– 0.028***	0.294*
	(0.019)	(0.007)	(0.017)	(0.004)	(0.002)	(0.012)	(0.023)	**(0.010)**	(0.023)
Sri Lanka	**– 0.162***	0.039*	0.004*	0.001*	0.102*	– 0.015*	0.030*	**– 0.232***	0.121*
	(0.006)	(0.002)	(0.000)	(0.000)	(0.002)	(0.007)	(0.006)	**(0.016)**	(0.001)
Taiwan	**– 0.272**	0.084*	0.161*	– 0.004	0.092*	– 0.060*	0.248*	**– 0.243***	– 0.238*
	(0.152)	(0.005)	(0.009)	(0.004)	(0.002)	(0.006)	(0.015)	**(0.010)**	(0.012)
Thailand	**– 0.227***	0.039*	0.020		0.049*	0.118*	0.092*	**– 0.227***	– 0.079
	(0.024)	(0.018)	(0.021)		(0.006)	(0.019)	(0.043)	**(0.062)**	(0.053)
	MC	MB	MP	**MM**	ME	MF	EC	EB	EP
Hong Kong							0.031	0.030*	0.006
							(0.024)	(0.009)	(0.007)
Japan							– 0.044*	0.092*	– 0.048
							(0.009)	(0.009)	(0.012)
Philippines							0.037*	0.038*	– 0.061*
							(0.064)	(0.047)	(0.054)
Singapore	0.357*	– 0.042*	– 0.225*	**– 0.151***	0.003	0.057*	0.023*	0.010*	0.017*

(continued)

Table 5.17 (continued)

Country	**CC**	CB	CP	CM	CE	CF	BC	**BB**	BP
	(0.028)	(0.011)	(0.021)	**(0.017)**	(0.006)	(0.020)	(0.007)	(0.003)	(0.005)
Sri Lanka	0.758*	– 0.004	0.003	**– 0.053***	– 0.025*	0.837*	0.303*	0.191*	0.011*
	(0.007)	(0.026)	(0.008)	**(0.025)**	(0.011)	(0.017)	(0.007)	(0.012)	(0.001)
Taiwan	– 0.025	0.312*	0.195*	**– 0.655***	0.065*	0.272*	0.405*	– 0.078*	0.168*
	(0.032)	(0.018)	(0.037)	**(0.029)**	(0.010)	(0.016)	(0.009)	(0.005)	(0.009)
Thailand							0.265	– 0.625*	0.092*
							(0.017)	(0.025)	(0.038)

Country	BM	BE	BF	PC	PB	**PP**	PM	PE	PF
Hong Kong		0.006*	0.229*	0.083*	– 0.074*	**– 0.007***		0.000	0.002*
		(0.001)	(0.008)	(0.003)	(0.004)	**(0.002)**		(0.000)	(0.001)
Japan		0.092*	0.376*	– 0.170*	0.461*	**– 0.117***		– 0.048*	– 0.127*
		(0.000)	(0.015)	(0.011)	(0.021)	**(0.026)**		(0.001)	(0.018)
Philippines		0.038*	0.822*	0.278*	– 0.269*	**– 0.406**		– 0.061*	0.457*
		(0.012)	(0.088)	(0.015)	(0.022)	**(0.030)**		(0.008)	(0.022)
Singapore	– 0.042*	0.010*	– 0.433*	0.923*	0.294*	**– 1.430***	– 0.225*	0.017*	0.421*
	(0.006)	(0.002)	(0.019)	(0.013)	(0.005)	**(0.019)**	(0.002)	(0.001)	(0.012)
Sri Lanka	0.022	0.085*	0.094	0.758*	– 0.004	**0.203***	– 0.053*	– 0.025*	0.837*
	(0.014)	(0.029)	(0.014)	(0.004)	(0.012)	**(0.006)**	(0.010)	(0.006)	(0.009)
Taiwan	0.090*	– 0.040*	0.183*	0.098*	– 0.049*	**– 0.074***	0.016*	0.024*	– 0.015*
	(0.007)	(0.003)	(0.007)	(0.005)	(0.003)	**(0.006)**	(0.003)	(0.001)	(0.003)
Thailand		– 0.437*	0.650*	0.024	– 0.040	**– 0.449***		0.034*	0.431
		(0.021)	(0.053)	(0.021)	(0.024)	**(0.037)**		(0.015)	(0.023)

(continued)

Table 5.17 (continued)

Country	BM	BE	BF	PC	PB	**PP**	PM	PE	PF
	EM	**EE**	EF	FC	FB	FP	FM	FE	**FF**
Hong Kong		**– 0.204***	0.137*	– 0.805*	1.572*	0.662*		0.041*	**– 0.145***
		(0.006)	(0.008)	(0.008)	(0.014)	(0.013)		(0.002)	**(0.014)**
Japan		**– 0.029***	0.029*	0.309*	0.376*	– 0.127*		0.029*	**– 0.588***
		(0.002)	(0.008)	(0.002)	(0.005)	(0.004)		(0.000)	**(0.006)**
Philippines		**– 0.105***	0.090*	0.376*	0.822*	0.457*		0.090*	**– 1.744***
		(0.055)	**(0.051)**	(0.006)	(0.013)	(0.011)		(0.003)	**(0.018)**
Singapore	0.003	**– 0.065***	0.013*	0.008	– 0.433*	0.422*	0.058*	0.013*	**– 0.068***
	(0.003)	**(0.002)**	(0.004)	(0.005)	(0.002)	(0.006)	(0.001)	(0.001)	**(0.007)**
Sri Lanka	0.101*	**– 0.384***	– 0.122*	– 0.483*	0.041*	0.016*	– 0.006*	– 0.044*	**– 0.491***
	(0.003)	**(0.010)**	(0.013)	(0.002)	(0.002)	(0.000)	(0.000)	(0.001)	**(0.003)**
Taiwan	0.042*	**– 0.522***	– 0.133*	– 0.022*	0.035*	– 0.006*	0.019*	– 0.025*	**– 0.010***
	(0.006)	**(0.005)**	(0.004)	(0.002)	(0.001)	(0.002)	(0.001)	(0.000)	**(0.003)**
Thailand		**– 0.650***	0.765*	0.061*	0.138*	0.265*		0.268*	**– 0.837***
		(0.022)	(0.021)	(0.009)	(0.011)	(0.010)		(0.004)	**(0.015)**

Bold values are own price elasticities of commodities. Others are cross price elasticities
* Significant at the 5% level

that there is a higher degree of substitutability between chicken, beef, pork, mutton, eggs, and fish. However, in cross-price elasticities, we can see some sign switches from conditional price elasticities to unconditional price elasticities. For instance, chicken and pork switch from net substitutes (conditional responses) to net complements (unconditional response). These sign switches and numerical differences in demand elasticities, tend to confirm that conditional elasticities may be inappropriate for policy analysis (Edgerton, 1997; Kinnucan et al., 2001). Summary findings of substitutes and complements among the six food items (based on the unconditional price elasticities) for each country are presented in Table 5.19.

5.7 A Decomposition Analysis of the Growth in Animal-Derived Food Consumption

While elasticity estimates can be used to measure the change in consumer demand related to changes in income and prices, it is also desirable to know the level of contribution of income and prices on consumption related to changes in income or commodity prices. Several studies highlight the importance of considering the distributional effects of various policies alongside changes in demand (Dong, 2006; Heien & Wessells, 1988; Karagiannis & Velentzas, 2004; Rathnayaka et al., 2019; Selvanathan et al., 2016). Therefore, in this section, we use the estimation results presented in Sect. 5.5 to decompose the growth in chicken, beef, pork, mutton, eggs, and fish consumption in terms of autonomous trend, income, own-price, and cross-prices.

Now we divide both sides of the demand system in Eq. (5.5.4) by the budget share $\overline{w}_{it}$ to give

$$Dq_{it} = \alpha^*_{it} + \eta'_i DQ_{gt} + \eta'_{ii} Dp_{it} + \sum_{j(\neq i)=1}^{6} \eta'_{ij} Dp_{jt} + \varepsilon^*_{it} \quad i = 1, \ldots, 6; \; t = 1, \ldots, T, \quad (5.7.1)$$

where $\alpha^*_{it} = \alpha'_i/\overline{w}_{it}$ is the autonomous trend in consumption of item i, which measures the proportionate change in consumption of food item i in year t in the absence of changes in prices and income. This is generally interpreted as a trend effect, due to the effect of changes in tastes and preferences. The coefficients η'_i and η'_{ij} are conditional income and price elasticities. Therefore, growth in consumption of item i (Dq_{it}) in each year can be decomposed into the following five components: (1) Autonomous trend component (α^*_{it}), (2) Income component ($\eta'_i DQ_{gt}$), (3) Own-price component ($\eta'_{ii} Dp_{it}$), (4) Cross-price component ($\sum_{j(\neq i)=1}^{6} \eta'_{ij} Dp_{jt}$), and (5) Residual component (ε^*_{it}).

Table 5.20 presents the components in the above equation at sample means for each food commodity and for each of the seven countries using the conditional elasticity estimates corresponding to Eq. (5.5.4), presented in Tables 5.16 and 5.17. Looking at row 1 of the section for chicken in the table, it can be seen that, on average, the total

Table 5.18 Unconditional price elasticities for six animal-derived food items, seven Asian countries

	CC	CB	CP	CM	CE	CF	BC	BB	BP
Hong Kong	**– 0.253**	0.078	0.010		0.021	– 0.270*	0.033	**– 0.410**	– 0.054
	(0.115)	(0.076)	(0.083)		(0.038)	(0.076)	(0.174)	**(0.284)**	(0.229)
Japan	**– 0.269***	– 0.276	– 0.798*		– 1.208*	0.303*	– 0.791*	**– 3.137***	2.077*
	(0.067)	(0.147)	(0.191)		(0.137)	(0.147)	(0.051)	**(0.192)**	(0.125)
Philippines	**– 0.315**	– 1.250*	0.662*		0.595*	0.411*	– 0.960*	**– 1.054***	– 0.649
	(0.254)	(0.188)	(0.225)		(0.216)	(0.188)	(0.245)	**(0.575)**	(0.421)
Singapore	**– 1.538***	0.483*	0.710*	2.073*	0.107*	– 0.007	0.155	**– 0.162**	0.198
	(0.420)	(0.164)	(0.381)	(0.105)	(0.050)	(0.266)	(0.512)	**(0.348)**	(0.518)
Sri Lanka	**– 0.364***	– 0.020	– 0.136*	0.055*	0.373*	– 0.240	– 0.007	**– 0.411**	0.004
	(0.134)	(0.044)	(0.003)	(0.007)	(0.033)	(0.142)	(0.121)	**(0.305)**	(0.023)
Taiwan	**– 0.315***	0.155*	0.086*	– 0.038	0.390*	– 0.174*	0.053	**– 0.312***	– 0.058
	(0.152)	(0.067)	(0.033)	(0.056)	(0.027)	(0.075)	(0.199)	**(0.134)**	(0.167)
Thailand	**– 0.292***	0.055*	0.065*		0.148*	– 0.088*	0.024	**– 0.138***	– 0.075
	(0.024)	(0.018)	(0.021)		(0.006)	(0.019)	(0.043)	**(0.062)**	(0.053)
Country	MC	MB	MP	**MM**	ME	MF	EC	EB	EP
Hong Kong							– 0.002	– 0.002	– 0.001
							(0.082)	(0.163)	(0.125)
Japan							– 0.389*	0.277	– 0.222
							(0.051)	(0.192)	(0.125)
Philippines							0.223	0.295	– 0.145
							(0.245)	(0.575)	(0.422)
Singapore	0.346	– 0.143	– 0.182	**– 0.900***	– 0.001	0.020	0.032	0.013	0.004

(continued)

Table 5.18 (continued)

	CC	CB	CP	CM	CE	CF	BC	**BB**	BP
	(0.420)	(0.164)	(0.381)	**(0.105)**	(0.050)	(0.266)	(0.512)	(0.348)	(0.518)
Sri Lanka	0.003	0.001	– 0.263*	**– 0.482***	0.026	0.006	0.092	0.289	0.256*
	(0.134)	(0.044)	(0.002)	**(0.007)**	(0.033)	(0.142)	(0.121)	(0.305)	(0.023)
Taiwan	– 0.005	0.088	0.016	**– 0.711***	0.030	0.009	0.088	– 0.050	0.023
	(0.152)	(0.068)	(0.033)	**(0.056)**	(0.027)	(0.075)	(0.200)	(0.134)	(0.167)
Thailand							0.049	– 0.025	0.026
							(0.043)	(0.062)	(0.053)
	BM	BE	BF	PC	PB	**PP**	PM	PE	PF
Hong Kong		0.035	0.473*	0.014	– 0.168*	**– 0.119**		– 0.022	0.017*
		(0.190)	(0.230)	(0.061)	(0.074)	**(0.090)**		(0.043)	(0.000)
Japan		2.458*	0.200*	– 1.506*	1.368*	**– 0.546***		– 1.296*	– 0.152*
		(0.140)	(0.073)	(0.101)	(0.190)	**(0.229)**		(0.158)	(0.027)
Philippines		0.604	0.892*	0.153*	1.644*	**– 2.097***		– 0.754*	– 0.964*
		(0.527)	(0.293)	(0.090)	(0.130)	**(0.180)**		(0.133)	(0.006)
Singapore	– 0.275*	0.014	– 0.193	0.898*	0.792*	**– 1.284***	– 1.395*	0.015	0.168*
	(0.137)	(0.064)	(0.434)	(0.297)	(0.130)	**(0.435)**	(0.062)	(0.031)	(0.007)
Sri Lanka	0.007	0.430*	– 0.036	– 0.005	0.000	**– 0.798***	– 0.185	0.037	– 0.001
	(0.068)	(0.161)	(0.275)	(0.077)	(0.239)	**(0.127)**	(0.207)	(0.134)	(0.091)
Taiwan	0.226*	– 0.076	– 0.091	0.142*	– 0.279*	**– 0.078**	0.197*	0.170*	– 0.076*
	(0.093)	(0.043)	(0.184)	(0.070)	(0.034)	**(0.082)**	(0.040)	(0.015)	(0.016)
Thailand		– 0.033	0.003	0.055*	– 0.146*	**– 0.113***		0.066*	– 0.034*
		(0.021)	(0.054)	(0.022)	(0.024)	**(0.037)**		(0.015)	(0.013)

(continued)

Table 5.18 (continued)

	BM	BE	BF	PC	PB	**PP**	PM	PE	PF
Country	EM	**EE**	EF	FC	FB	FP	FM	FE	**FF**
Hong Kong		**– 0.223***	0.044	– 0.068	0.277	0.003		0.134	**– 0.337***
		(0.141)	(0.447)	(0.148)	(0.247)	(0.227)		(0.241)	**(0.000)**
Japan		**– 0.787***	0.030	2.485*	0.574*	– 0.659*		0.747*	**– 0.857***
		(0.140)	(0.073)	(0.101)	(0.190)	(0.229)		(0.158)	**(0.027)**
Philippines		**– 0.790**	0.097	2.201*	2.238*	1.032*		1.392*	**– 0.410***
	(0.135)	**(0.527)**	(0.293)	(0.090)	(0.130)	(0.179)		(0.133)	**(0.006)**
Singapore	– 0.001	**– 0.234***	0.001	– 0.013	– 1.406*	0.306	0.276*	0.008	**– 0.047***
	(0.137)	**(0.064)**	(0.434)	(0.297)	(0.129)	(0.436)	(0.062)	(0.031)	**(0.007)**
Sri Lanka	0.128*	**– 1.575***	0.013	– 0.770*	– 0.312	– 0.124	0.376	0.177	**– 0.798***
	(0.068)	**(0.161)**	(0.275)	(0.077)	(0.239)	(0.127)	(0.207)	(0.134)	**(0.092)**
Taiwan	0.051	**– 0.521***	– 0.019	– 0.473*	– 0.724*	– 0.125*	0.183*	– 0.230*	**– 1.491***
	(0.093)	**(0.044)**	(0.184)	(0.070)	(0.034)	(0.082)	(0.040)	(0.015)	**(0.016)**
Thailand		**– 0.225***	– 0.008	– 0.171*	0.016	– 0.080*		– 0.048*	**– 0.077***
		(0.021)	(0.055)	(0.021)	(0.024)	(0.037)		(0.015)	**(0.013)**

Bold values are own price elasticities of commodities. Others are cross price elasticities
* Significant at the 5% level

Table 5.19 Substitutes and complements based on unconditional elasticities, seven Asian countries

Commodity	Chicken		Beef		Pork	
Chicken			SUB	Hong Kong, Singapore, Taiwan, Thailand	SUB	Hong Kong, Philippines, Singapore, Taiwan, Thailand
			COMP	Japan, Philippines, Sri Lanka	COMP	Japan, Sri Lanka
Beef	SUB	Hong Kong, Singapore, Taiwan, Thailand			SUB	Japan, Singapore, Sri Lanka
	COMP	Japan, Philippines, Sri Lanka			COMP	Hong Kong, Philippines, Taiwan, Thailand
Pork	SUB	Hong Kong, Philippines, Singapore, Taiwan, Thailand	SUB	Japan, Philippines, Singapore, Sri Lanka		
	COMP	Japan, Sri Lanka	COMP	Hong Kong, Taiwan, Thailand		
Mutton	SUB	Singapore, Sri Lanka	SUB	Sri Lanka, Taiwan	SUB	Taiwan
	COMP	Taiwan	COMP	Singapore	COMP	Singapore, Sri Lanka
Eggs	SUB	Philippines, Singapore, Sri Lanka, Taiwan, Thailand	SUB	Japan, Philippines, Singapore, Sri Lanka	SUB	Singapore, Sri Lanka, Taiwan, Thailand
	COMP	Hong Kong, Japan	COMP	Hong Kong, Taiwan, Thailand	COMP	Hong Kong, Japan, Philippines
Fish	SUB	Japan, Philippines	SUB	Hong Kong, Japan, Philippines, Thailand	SUB	Hong Kong, Philippines, Singapore, Sri Lanka, Thailand
	COMP	Hong Kong, Singapore, Sri Lanka, Taiwan, Thailand	COMP	Singapore, Sri Lanka, Taiwan	COMP	Japan, Sri Lanka, Taiwan, Thailand
Commodity	Mutton		Eggs		Fish	

(continued)

Table 5.19 (continued)

Commodity	Chicken		Beef		Pork	
Chicken	SUB	Singapore, Sri Lanka	SUB	Hong Kong, Philippines, Singapore, Sri Lanka, Taiwan, Thailand	SUB	Japan, Philippines
	COMP	Taiwan	COMP	Japan	COMP	Hong Kong, Singapore, Sri Lanka, Taiwan, Thailand
Beef	SUB	Sri Lanka, Taiwan	SUB	Hong Kong, Philippines, Singapore, Sri Lanka, Japan	SUB	Hong Kong, Japan, Philippines, Thailand
	COMP	Singapore	COMP	Taiwan, Thailand	COMP	Singapore, Sri Lanka, Taiwan
Pork	SUB	Taiwan	SUB	Singapore, Sri Lanka, Taiwan, Thailand	SUB	Hong Kong, Singapore
	COMP	Singapore, Sri Lanka	COMP	Hong Kong, Japan, Philippines	COMP	Japan, Philippines, Sri Lanka, Taiwan, Thailand
Mutton			SUB	Sri Lanka, Taiwan	SUB	Singapore, Sri Lanka, Taiwan
			COMP	Singapore		
Eggs	SUB	Sri Lanka, Taiwan			SUB	Hong Kong, Japan, Philippines, Singapore, Sri Lanka, Thailand
	COMP	Singapore			COMP	Taiwan, Thailand
Fish	SUB	Singapore, Sri Lanka, Taiwan	SUB	Hong Kong, Philippines, Singapore, Japan		
			COMP	Taiwan, Thailand		

growth in consumption of chicken in Hong Kong is 2.63% per annum. This growth comprises: autonomous trend (– 0.09), income (2.62), own-price component (– 0.76), cross-price component (0.75), and residual component (0.000). The two terms involving the own- and cross-prices almost cancel and the autonomous trend is negative and small, leaving income as the dominant component in the growth in chicken consumption. The results for the remaining six countries and other commodities can also be interpreted in a similar way. On average, across the seven countries, chicken consumption grew at a rate of 2.35% per annum. The components of this growth are autonomous trend (0.79), income (0.72), own-price component (− 1.12), cross-price component (1.47), and residual component (− 0.026). Overall mean values for the six commodities in column (3) show that the autonomous trend component is positive for chicken, pork, mutton, and eggs, while it is negative for beef and fish. For all commodities, among the five determinants, income and prices are the most important factors that affect consumption. However, autonomous trend (changes in consumer taste) plays a comparatively dominant role in the consumption growth of pork and mutton.

5.8 Discussion and Policy Implications

This chapter explored the consumer demand for animal-derived food products in seven economically diverse Asian countries. In contrast to many prior studies in the literature on food demand, our approach involved estimating group demand elasticities, both conditional and unconditional, for six specific animal-derived food items. This was achieved using the system-wide approach and the latest consumption and price data available. Examination of the data through descriptive analysis unveiled notable trends, such as the observation that consumers in most countries allocate approximately half of their animal-derived food budget to fish. In contrast, Hong Kong residents diverge significantly, dedicating nearly 90% of their animal-derived food expenditure to meat (chicken, beef, pork, and mutton). Intriguingly, most countries exhibited a faster rate of increase in chicken consumption compared to the other five animal-derived food items.

We estimated the group demand equation and conditional demand equations simultaneously. The group income elasticities are less than one for all countries (except for Taiwan), indicating that the animal-derived food group is a necessity for almost all of the countries. The group own-price elasticity for all 7 countries are negative and are less than one in absolute value for the majority of the countries indicating that the demand for the group is mostly price inelastic. The unconditional income elasticities reveal that chicken, beef, pork, mutton, eggs, and fish are all necessities (income elasticity less than one, except beef in Japan and Taiwan and fish in Taiwan). The unconditional own-price elasticities are all negative and mostly less than one in absolute value which indicates that the demand for the six animal-derived food items is price inelastic and the majority of the cross-price elasticities are positive implying high-level substitutability among the six items. The estimated unconditional demand elasticities of meat, fish and eggs deviate substantially from the corresponding conditional demand elasticities. This deviation shows the need for the use of unconditional elasticities in policy and welfare analyses. For example, from a multistage budgeting perspective, a change in the price of chicken will not have a direct effect on the demands for each food item within the animal-derived food group. However, it will change the price index for meats and hence expenditure

Table 5.20 Growth in the consumption of animal-derived food and its components (average annual log-changes × 100)

Country	Components of growth					
	Total growth	Autonomous trend	Income	Own-price	Cross-price	Residual
(1)	(2)	(3)	(4)	(5)	(6)	(7)
Chicken						
1. Hong Kong	2.63	− 0.09	2.62	− 0.76	0.75	0.0000
2. Japan	1.93	2.37	0.20	− 0.01	0.26	− 0.1838
3. Philippines	4.83	3.66	0.25	− 2.07	2.67	− 0.0001
4. Singapore	0.17	− 1.81	− 0.58	− 2.54	3.79	0.0000
5. Sri Lanka	4.16	0.44	2.10	− 1.27	0.97	− 0.0001
6. Taiwan	0.95	1.34	− 1.10	− 0.99	0.79	− 0.0001
7. Thailand	1.79	− 0.36	1.57	− 0.19	1.09	0.0000
Mean	2.35	0.79	0.72	− 1.12	1.47	− 0.0263
Beef						
1. Hong Kong	2.45	1.11	2.16	− 1.91	1.93	0.0001
2. Japan	1.85	1.37	0.48	− 1.41	− 1.01	0.3365
3. Philippines	2.51	1.15	1.03	− 1.90	2.92	0.0000
4. Singapore	− 5.23	− 2.24	− 2.05	− 0.07	0.18	0.0001
5. Sri Lanka	− 2.28	− 2.58	0.93	− 2.23	2.55	0.0000
6. Taiwan	2.20	2.82	− 0.86	− 0.70	0.84	0.0000
7. Thailand	− 3.39	− 5.83	1.64	− 1.21	1.26	0.0001
Mean	− 0.27	− 0.60	0.48	− 1.35	1.24	0.0481
Pork						
1. Hong Kong	1.26	− 0.12	1.61	− 0.03	0.19	0.0000
2. Japan	1.29	0.98	0.06	− 0.01	− 0.20	− 0.0829
3. Philippines	2.04	1.62	0.58	− 2.22	1.98	0.0000
4. Singapore	− 0.77	3.59	− 1.23	− 5.78	3.99	0.0000
5. Sri Lanka	6.04	8.40	2.00	− 2.07	11.77	0.0000
6. Taiwan	− 0.25	− 0.11	− 0.08	− 0.24	0.20	− 0.0004
7. Thailand	1.66	1.04	0.33	− 2.00	2.27	0.0000
Mean	1.61	2.20	0.47	− 1.77	2.89	− 0.0119
Mutton						
1. Hong Kong						
2. Japan						
3. Philippines						
4. Singapore	1.27	5.61	− 1.06	− 0.42	0.37	0.0000
5. Sri Lanka	− 2.01	0.27	0.21	− 0.65	12.23	0.0021

(continued)

Table 5.20 (continued)

Country	Components of growth					
	Total growth	Autonomous trend	Income	Own-price	Cross-price	Residual
(1)	(2)	(3)	(4)	(5)	(6)	(7)
6. Taiwan	1.23	0.95	− 0.21	− 1.50	2.28	0.0000
7. Thailand						
Mean	0.16	2.28	− 0.36	− 0.86	4.96	0.0007
Eggs						
1. Hong Kong	0.46	0.00	0.58	− 0.78	0.85	0.0000
2. Japan	0.44	0.23	0.04	0.05	0.02	0.1105
3. Philippines	1.29	0.97	0.25	− 0.47	0.61	0.0000
4. Singapore	1.08	1.57	− 0.43	− 0.15	0.17	− 0.0002
5. Sri Lanka	2.32	1.50	1.07	− 3.14	5.04	− 0.0001
6. Taiwan	0.94	0.89	− 0.20	− 1.33	1.40	− 0.0004
7. Thailand	0.87	0.68	0.10	− 2.00	2.93	− 0.0001
Mean	1.06	0.83	0.20	− 1.12	1.57	0.0157
Fish						
1. Hong Kong	0.96	− 0.94	0.73	− 0.57	− 1.08	− 0.0001
2. Japan	− 0.88	− 1.00	0.21	0.09	0.77	0.0042
3. Philippines	− 0.53	− 1.65	1.16	− 9.76	8.67	0.0000
4. Singapore	− 1.16	− 1.50	− 0.28	− 0.15	− 0.61	0.0000
5. Sri Lanka	1.74	− 0.06	2.21	− 2.99	− 4.42	− 0.0001
6. Taiwan	− 2.32	− 0.90	− 1.53	0.00	0.01	0.0000
7. Thailand	0.94	0.91	0.63	− 2.68	2.39	0.0000
Mean	− 0.18	− 0.73	0.45	− 2.29	0.82	0.0006

allocations to the meat and other expenditure groups in the previous budgeting stage and cause further indirect changes within the animal-derived food group. Therefore, our estimated unconditional demand elasticities will be most relevant in welfare analyses and policy review and development. Next, we decomposed the growth in chicken, beef, pork, mutton, eggs, and fish consumption into the effect of changes in consumer taste, income effect, own-price effect, and cross-price effect for each of the seven countries. The results of the decomposition analysis, which show the effect of simultaneous changes in prices, income, and tastes, can be applied to policy considerations.

The derived demand elasticities from our study can be used as valuable input parameters in both partial equilibrium and general equilibrium models, enabling projections on various fronts such as tariff adjustments and the repercussions of changes in imports, exports, and domestic prices. These findings hold particular significance in the context of evolving discussions on utilizing food price policies to enhance public health. For instance, policymakers interested in gauging the potential impact of implementing a tax on meat consumption can leverage the information gleaned from the demand elasticities of meat. The escalating intricacies within both domestic and international food markets in the Asian region emphasize the critical need for reliable market parameter estimates concerning different meat types, eggs, and fish products. These estimates are indispensable for major stakeholders in the food industry, guiding their strategic planning, marketing initiatives, promotional campaigns, forecasting efforts, and the formulation of prices. The integration of our study's insights into policy formulations and business strategies stands to enhance the effectiveness and informed decision-making in the realms of both public governance and the food business sector.

Appendix

Stationarity Test Results of the Demand System Variables for the Seven Asian Countries

Stationarity Test Results of the Demand System Variables: ***Hong Kong***

Commodity i	$\overline{w}_{it} Dq_{it}$		Dp_{it}	
	Test statistics	p-value	Test statistics	p-value
Chicken	− 5.000	0.000	− 6.874	0.000
Beef	− 9.004	0.000	− 3.329	0.014
Pork	− 7.249	0.000	− 4.450	0.000
Eggs	− 6.206	0.000	− 5.496	0.000
Fish	− 5.755	0.000	− 3.810	0.003
DQ_t	− 4.358	0.000		
$\overline{W}_{gt} DQ_{gt}$	− 7.697	0.000		
DP_{0t}	− 6.046	0.000		

Stationarity Test Results of the Demand System Variables: ***Japan***

Commodity i	$\overline{w}_{it} Dq_{it}$		Dp_{it}	
	Test statistics	p-value	Test statistics	p-value
Chicken	− 6.486	0.000	− 6.012	0.000
Beef	− 4.810	0.000	− 5.685	0.000
Pork	− 5.834	0.000	− 4.280	0.001
Eggs	− 4.683	0.000	− 6.157	0.000

(continued)

(continued)

Commodity i	$\overline{w}_{it} Dq_{it}$		Dp_{it}	
	Test statistics	p-value	Test statistics	p-value
Fish	– 3.375	0.012	– 5.447	0.000
DQ_t	– 4.342	0.000		
$\overline{W}_{gt} DQ_{gt}$	– 3.725	0.004		
DP_{0t}	– 3.554	0.007		

Stationarity Test Results of the Demand System Variables: ***Philippines***

Commodity i	$\overline{w}_{it} Dq_{it}$		Dp_{it}	
	Test statistics	p-value	Test statistics	p-value
Chicken	– 4.462	0.000	– 4.770	0.000
Beef	– 7.030	0.000	– 5.422	0.000
Pork	– 7.519	0.000	– 4.956	0.000
Eggs	– 6.538	0.000	– 7.911	0.000
Fish	– 4.176	0.001	– 4.267	0.001
DQ_t	– 3.482	0.013		
$\overline{W}_{gt} DQ_{gt}$	– 5.920	0.000		
DP_{0t}	– 5.564	0.000		

Stationarity Test Results of the Demand System Variables: ***Singapore***

Commodity i	$\overline{w}_{it} Dq_{it}$		Dp_{it}	
	Test statistics	p-value	Test statistics	p-value
Chicken	– 5.821	0.000	– 3.928	0.002
Beef	– 4.122	0.001	– 4.856	0.000
Pork	– 4.978	0.000	– 4.745	0.000
Mutton	– 1.967	0.049	– 3.276	0.016
Eggs	– 7.884	0.000	– 5.998	0.000
Fish	– 4.984	0.000	– 4.444	0.000
DQ_t	– 5.069	0.000		
$\overline{W}_{gt} DQ_{gt}$	– 4.394	0.000		
DP_{0t}	– 4.445	0.000		

Stationarity Test Results of the Demand System Variables: ***Sri Lanka***

Commodity i	$\overline{w}_{it} Dq_{it}$		Dp_{it}	
	Test statistics	p-value	Test statistics	p-value
Chicken	– 5.051	0.000	– 6.949	0.000
Beef	– 5.168	0.000	– 4.749	0.000
Pork	– 3.806	0.003	– 4.652	0.000
Mutton	– 6.942	0.000	– 3.764	0.003
Eggs	– 8.617	0.000	– 6.609	0.000
Fish	– 3.431	0.010	– 2.306	0.170
DQ_t	– 5.052	0.000		
$\overline{W}_{gt} DQ_{gt}$	– 4.001	0.001		
DP_{0t}	– 3.441	0.010		

Stationarity Test Results of the Demand System Variables: ***Taiwan***

Commodity i	$\overline{w}_{it} Dq_{it}$		Dp_{it}	
	Test statistics	p-value	Test statistics	p-value
Chicken	– 5.003	0.000	– 3.452	0.009
Beef	– 7.567	0.000	– 3.371	0.012
Pork	– 3.592	0.006	– 4.457	0.000
Mutton	– 5.236	0.000	– 3.577	0.006
Eggs	– 5.730	0.000	– 5.125	0.000
Fish	– 5.783	0.000	– 8.438	0.000
DQ_t	– 3.293	0.015		
$\overline{W}_{gt} DQ_{gt}$	– 6.091	0.000		
DP_{0t}	– 4.183	0.001		

Stationarity Test Results of the Demand System Variables: ***Thailand***

Commodity i	$\overline{w}_{it} Dq_{it}$		Dp_{it}	
	Test statistics	p-value	Test statistics	p-value
Chicken	– 4.868	0.000	– 6.975	0.000
Beef	– 8.763	0.000	– 3.409	0.011
Pork	– 4.805	0.000	– 5.680	0.000
Eggs	– 5.850	0.000	– 7.445	0.000
Fish	– 3.606	0.006	– 3.700	0.004
DQ_t	– 4.762	0.000		
$\overline{W}_{gt} DQ_{gt}$	– 5.353	0.000		
DP_{0t}	– 4.354	0.000		

Results of the Price Endogeneity Test for the Seven Asian Countries

Country	Commodity					
	Chicken		Beef		Pork	
	Test statistic	*p*-value	Test statistic	*p*-value	Test statistic	*p*-value
Hong Kong	F(5, 19) = 1.28	0.314	F(5, 19) = 1.14	0.374	F(5, 19) = 1.22	0.340
Japan	F(5, 20) = 0.85	0.531	F(5, 20) = 0.78	0.575	F(5, 20) = 0.34	0.885
Philippines	F(5, 9) = 2.10	0.157	F(5, 9) = 2.39	0.122	F(5, 9) = 0.72	0.623
Singapore	F(6, 6) = 3.79	0.066**	F(6, 6) = 2.07	0.198	F(6, 6) = 1.54	0.306
Sri Lanka	F(6, 7) = 1.28	0.372	F(6, 7) = 0.15	0.983	F(6, 7) = 0.54	0.765
Taiwan	F(6, 7) = 0.93	0.525	F(6, 7) = 1.30	0.365	F(6, 7) = 0.99	0.496
Thailand	F(4, 11) = 0.92	0.487	F(4, 11) = 0.11	0.976	F(4, 11) = 3.44	0.047*
Country	Commodity					
	Mutton		Eggs		Fish	
	Test statistic	*p*-value	Test statistic	*p*-value	Test statistic	*p*-value
Hong Kong			F(5, 19) = 0.84	0.537	F(5, 19) = 0.76	0.592
Japan			F(5, 20) = 2.45	0.069	F(5, 20) = 1.17	0.358
Philippines			F(5, 9) = 1.51	0.279	F(5, 9) = 1.71	0.229
Singapore	F(6, 6) = 0.31	0.907	F(6, 6) = 1.18	0.422	F(6, 6) = 1.65	0.278
Sri Lanka	F(6, 7) = 1.43	0.323	F(6, 7) = 0.85	0.568	F(6, 7) = 0.89	0.549
Taiwan	F(6, 7) = 1.93	0.205	F(6, 7) = 1.99	0.194	F(6, 7) = 1.52	0.296
Thailand			F(4, 11) = 3.30	0.062**	F(4, 11) = 0.25	0.903

The null hypothesis of no endogeneity is supported by the data at the 5% level of significance for all countries and commodities and at the 1% level for Thailand/pork

References

Baharumshah, A. Z., & Mohamed, Z. A. (1993). Demand for meat in Malaysia: An application of the almost ideal demand system analysis. *Pertanika Social Science and Humanities, 1*(1), 91–95.

Baker, P., & Friel, S. (2016). Food systems transformations, ultra-processed food markets and the nutrition transition in Asia. *Globalization and Health, 12*, 1–15.

Barnett, W. A. (1983). New indices of money supply and the flexible Laurent demand system. *Journal of Business and Economic Statistics, 1*(1), 7–23.

Barten, A. P. (1964). Consumer demand functions under conditions of almost additive preferences. *Econometrica, 32*, 1–38.

Capps, O., Jr., Tsai, R., Kirby, R., & Williams, G. W. (1994). A comparison of demands for meat products in the Pacific Rim Region. *Journal of Agricultural and Resource Economics*, 210–224.

Carpentier, A., & Guyomard, H. (2001). Unconditional elasticities in two-stage demand systems: An approximate solution. *American Journal of Agricultural Economics, 83*(1), 222–229.

Christensen, L. R., Jorgenson, D. W., & Lau, L. J. (1975). Transcendental logarithmic utility functions. *American Economic Review, 65*, 367–383.

Clements, K. W., & Gao, G. (2015). The Rotterdam demand model half a century on. *Economic Modelling, 49*, 91–103.

Clements, K. W., & Johnson, L. W. (1983). The demand for beer, wine, and spirits: A systemwide analysis. *Journal of Business, 56*(3), 273–304.

De Roos, B., Roos, N., Ara, G., Ahmed, T., Mamun, A. A., Sneddon, A. A., Murray, F., Grieve, E., & Little, D. C. (2020). Linkages of agroecosystems producing farmed seafood on food security, nutritional status and adolescent health in Bangladesh. *Maternal and Child Nutrition, 16*, 1–8.

Deaton, A. S., & Muellbauer, J. (1980). An almost ideal demand system. *American Economic Review, 70*, 312–326.

Dey, M. M. (2000). Analysis of demand for fish in Bangladesh. *Aquaculture Economics and Management, 4*(1–2), 63–81.

Dey, M. M., Garcia, Y. T., Praduman, K., Piumsombun, S., Haque, M. S., Li, L., & Koeshendrajana, S. (2008). Demand for fish in Asia: A cross-country analysis. *Australian Journal of Agricultural and Resource Economics, 52*(3), 321–338.

Dhar, T., Chavas, J., & Gould, B. W. (2003). An empirical assessment of endogeneity issues in demand analysis for differentiated products. *American Journal of Agricultural Economics, 85*(3), 605–617.

Dharmasena, K. H., Abeygunawardena, P., Zuhair, S. M. M., & Pinnaduwage, S. (1990). Demand elasticities of selected proteinous food in Sri Lanka. *Tropical Agricultural Research, 2*, 169–182.

Dickey, D. A., & Fuller, W. A. (1979). Distribution of the estimators for autoregressive time series with a unit root. *Journal of the American Statistical Association, 74*(366), 427–431.

Dong, F. (2006). The outlook for Asian dairy markets: The role of demographics, income, and prices. *Food Policy, 31*(3), 260–271.

Duffy, M. H. (1987). Advertising and the inter-product distribution of demand: A Rotterdam model approach. *European Economic Review, 31*(5), 1051–1070.

Durning, A. B., & Brough, H. B. (1991). *Taking stock: Animal farming and the environment* (Worldwatch Paper No. 103). Worldwatch Institute, Washington, DC.

Dutilh, C. E., & Kramer, K. J. (2000). Energy consumption in the food chain. *AMBIO: A Journal of the Human Environment, 29*(2), 98–101.

Eales, J., Durham, C., & Wessells, C. R. (1997). Generalized models of Japanese demand for fish. *American Journal of Agricultural Economics, 79*(4), 1153–1163.

Eales, J., & Wessells, C. R. (1999). Testing separability of Japanese demand for meat and fish within differential demand systems. *Journal of Agricultural and Resource Economics, 24*(1), 114–126.

Edgerton, D. L. (1997). Weak separability and the estimation of elasticities in multistage demand systems. *American Journal of Agricultural Economics, 79*(1), 62–79.

Ellis, C. (2003). Participatory environmental research in tourism: A global view. *Tourism Recreation Research, 28*(3), 45–55.

FAO. (2013). *Food balance sheets*. Food and Agriculture Organization of the United Nations. http://www.fao.org/faostat/en/#data/FBS. Retrieved June 1, 2023.

Forgenie, D., Khoiriyah, N., & Elbaar, E. F. (2023). Estimating household price and income elasticities for animal-derived sources of food using the QUAIDS model: The case of Jakarta, Indonesia. *Tropical Agriculture, 100*(4), 317–328.

Gale, H. F., & Huang, K. (2007). *Demand for food quantity and quality in China* (Economic Research Report Number 32). United Sates Department of Agriculture, Washington, DC.

Gallet, C. A. (2010a). Meat meets meta: A quantitative review of the price elasticity of meat. *American Journal of Agricultural Economics, 92*(1), 258–272.

Gallet, C. A. (2010b). The income elasticity of meat: A meta-analysis. *Australian Journal of Agricultural and Resource Economics, 54*(4), 477–490.

Gerbens-Leenes, P. W., & Nonhebel, S. (2002). Consumption patterns and their effects on land required for food. *Ecological Economics, 42*(1–2), 185–199.

Goodland, R. (1997). Environmental sustainability in agriculture: Diet matters. *Ecological Economics, 23*(3), 189–200.

Harrison, P., & Pearce, F. (2000). *AAAS atlas of population and environment*. University of California Press.

Hayes, D. J., Ahn, H., & Baumel, C. P. (1991). Meat demand in South Korea: A systems estimate and policy projections. *Agribusiness, 7*(5), 433–446.

Hayes, D. J., Wahl, T. I., & Williams, G. W. (1990). Testing restrictions on a model of Japanese meat demand. *American Journal of Agricultural Economics, 72*(3), 556–566.

Heien, D. M., & Wessells, C. R. (1988). The demand for dairy products: Structure, prediction, and decomposition. *American Journal of Agricultural Economics, 70*(2), 219–228.

Henneberry, S. R., & Hwang, S. H. (2007). Meat demand in South Korea: An application of the restricted source-differentiated almost ideal demand system model. *Journal of Agricultural and Applied Economics, 39*(1), 47–60.

Hovhannisyan, V., & Bozic, M. (2017). Price endogeneity and food demand in urban China. *Journal of Agricultural Economics, 68*(2), 386–406.

Hovhannisyan, V., & Gould, B. W. (2014). Structural change in urban Chinese food preferences. *Agricultural Economics, 45*(2), 159–166.

Huang, J., & Bouis, H. E. (1996). *Structural changes in the demand for food in Asia* (Vol. 2020). Washington, DC: International Food Policy Research Institute

Huang, J., & Bouis, H. E. (2001). Structural changes in the demand for food in Asia: Empirical evidence from Taiwan. *Agricultural Economics, 26*(1), 57–69.

Huang, J., & David, C. C. (1993). Demand for cereal grains in Asia: The effect of urbanization. *Agricultural Economics, 8*(2), 107–124.

Hubacek, K., Guan, D., & Barua, A. (2007). Changing lifestyles and consumption patterns in developing countries: A scenario analysis for China and India. *Futures, 39*(9), 1084–1096.

Ishida, T., Ishikawa, N., & Fukushige, M. (2010). Impact of BSE and bird flu on consumers' meat demand in Japan. *Applied Economics, 42*(1), 49–56.

Jackson, J. B., Kirby, M. X., Berger, W. H., Bjorndal, K. A., Botsford, L. W., Bourque, B. J., … Hughes, T. P. (2001). Historical overfishing and the recent collapse of coastal ecosystems. *Science, 293*(5530), 629–637.

Johnston, J., & DiNardo, J. (1997). *Econometric methods*. McGraw-Hill.

Jung, J., & Koo, W. W. (2000). *An econometric analysis of demand for meat and fish products in Korea* (Agricultural Economics Report No. 468). Department of Agricultural Economics, Northern Plain Trade Research Center, North Dakota State University, Fargo, ND.

Karagiannis, G., Katranidis, S., & Velentzas, K. (2000). An error correction almost ideal demand system for meat in Greece. *Agricultural Economics, 22*(1), 29–35.

Karagiannis, G., & Velentzas, K. (2004). Decomposition analysis of consumers' demand changes: An application to Greek consumption data. *Applied Economics, 36*(5), 497–504.

Kinnucan, H. W., Miao, Y., Xiao, H., & Kaiser, H. M. (2001). Effects of advertising on US non-alcoholic beverage demand: Evidence from a two-stage Rotterdam model. *Advances in Applied Microeconomics, 10*, 1–29.

Klonaris, S., & Hallam, D. (2003). Conditional and unconditional food demand elasticities in a dynamic multistage demand system. *Applied Economics, 35*(5), 503–514.

LaFrance, J. T. (1991). When is expenditure 'exogenous' in separable demand models? *Western Journal of Agricultural Economics, 16*, 49–62.

Lucas, S., Soler, L. G., & Revoredo-Giha, C. (2021). Trend analysis of sustainability claims: The European fisheries and aquaculture markets case. *Food Policy, 104*, 102141.

Mazzocchi, M., Monache, D. D., & Lobb, A. E. (2006). A structural time series approach to modelling multiple and resurgent meat scares in Italy. *Applied Economics, 38*(14), 1677–1688.

Mountain, D. C. (1988). The Rotterdam model: An approximation in variable space. *Econometrica, 56*(2), 477–484.

Myers, R. A., & Worm, B. (2003). Rapid worldwide depletion of predatory fish communities. *Nature, 423*, 280–283.

Nelson, J. P. (1997). Economic and demographic factors in US alcohol demand: A growth-accounting analysis. *Empirical Economics, 22*(1), 83–102.

Pingali, P. (2007). Westernization of Asian diets and the transformation of food systems: Implications for research and policy. *Food Policy, 32*(3), 281–298.

Rae, A. N. (1997). Changing food consumption patterns in East Asia: Implications of the trend towards livestock products. *Agribusiness: An International Journal, 13*(1), 33–44.

Rae, A. N. (1998). The effects of expenditure growth and urbanisation on food consumption in East Asia: A note on animal products. *Agricultural Economics, 18*(3), 291–299.

Rathnayaka, S. D., Revoredo-Giha, C. L., & de Roos, B. (2023, August 29–September 1). An analysis of household demand for fish in Scotland. In *17th Congress of European Association of Agricultural Economists*. European Association of Agricultural Economists.

Rathnayaka, S. D., Selvanathan, E. A., & Selvanathan, S. (2019). Consumption patterns in Sri Lanka: A decomposition analysis. *Applied Economics, 51*(37), 4056–4072.

Rathnayaka, S. D., Selvanathan, S., & Selvanathan, E. A. (2021). Demand for animal-derived food in selected Asian countries: A system-wide analysis. *Agricultural Economics, 52*(1), 97–122.

Selvanathan, E. A. (1991). Further results on aggregation of differential demand equations. *Review of Economic Studies, 58*, 799–805.

Selvanathan, E. A., & Clements, K. W. (1995). *Recent developments in applied demand analysis: Alcohol*. Springer-Verlag.

Selvanathan, S., Selvanathan, E. A., Albalawi, S., & Hossain, M. (2016). Meat and fish consumption patterns in Saudi Arabia. *Applied Economics, 48*(5), 446–460.

Shue, W. F. (1987). *Research on demand for Taiwanese main agricultural products-livestock section*. Agricultural Economics, National Taiwan University.

Speedy, A. W. (2003). Global production and consumption of animal source foods. *The Journal of Nutrition, 133*(11), 4048S–4053S.

Theil, H. (1965). The information approach to demand analysis. *Econometrica, 33*, 67–87.

Theil, H. (1975/76). *Theory and measurement of consumer demand*. North-Holland Publishing Company.

Theil, H. (1980). *The system-wide approach to microeconomics*. The University of Chicago Press.

Theil, H., & Clements, K. W. (1987). *Applied demand analysis: Results from system-wide approaches*. Ballinger Publishing Company.

Tonsor, G. T., & Marsh, T. L. (2007). Comparing heterogeneous consumption in US and Japanese meat and fish demand. *Agricultural Economics, 37*(1), 81–91.

Tonsor, G. T., Mintert, J. R., & Schroeder, T. C. (2010). US meat demand: Household dynamics and media information impacts. *Journal of Agricultural and Resource Economics, 35*(1), 1–17.

Wadud, M. A. (2006). An analysis of meat demand in Bangladesh using the almost ideal demand system. *The Empirical Economics Letters, 5*(1), 29–35.

White, T. (2000). Diet and the distribution of environmental impact. *Ecological Economics, 34*, 145–153.

Wong, L., Selvanathan, E. A., & Selvanathan, S. (2015). Modelling the meat consumption patterns in Australia. *Economic Modelling, 49*, 1–10.

Wu, Y., Wang, L., Zhu, J., Gao, L., & Wang, Y. (2021). Growing fast food consumption and obesity in Asia: Challenges and implications. *Social Science and Medicine, 269*, 113601.

Zheng, Z., & Henneberry, S. R. (2010). The impact of changes in income distribution on current and future food demand in urban China. *Journal of Agricultural and Resource Economics, 35*, 51–71.

Zheng, Z., & Henneberry, S. R. (2011). Household food demand by income category: Evidence from household survey data in an urban Chinese province. *Agribusiness, 27*(1), 99–113.

Zheng, Z., & Henneberry, S. R. (2012). Estimating the impacts of rising food prices on nutrient intake in urban China. *China Economic Review, 23*(4), 1090–1103.

Zheng, Z., Henneberry, S. R., Zhao, Y., & Gao, Y. (2018). Predicting the changes in the structure of food demand in China. *Agribusiness, 35*(3), 301–328.

Chapter 6
Dynamic Consumption Patterns in Asian Countries

6.1 Introduction

For over a century, economists have been examining the intricate relationship between consumption of commodities, consumer income, and market prices of commodities and persistently refining their understanding of these relationships. The evolution of theories on consumer behaviour has led to sophisticated mathematical models capturing equilibrium relationships between demand/supply and its determinants. Traditionally, these models focus on changes in steady-state equilibrium triggered by shifts in demand determinants, as extensively reviewed in De Mello (2001). Such studies reveal that most empirical studies commonly employ static demand systems in modelling the consumption-income-price relationship and model estimation.

However, the reliance on static demand systems overlooks the myriad adjustments that transpire in the short run, as highlighted by Hassan et al. (1977). In reality, consumers do not necessarily reach equilibrium in each time period, challenging the assumption of instantaneous adjustments. Short-run behaviour is influenced by additional factors such as habit persistence, adjustment costs, inaccurate expectations, and misinterpretation of real price changes. Hence, during the transitional phases before full adjustments occur, consumers are potentially operating 'out of equilibrium'. Recognizing the significance of these short-run dynamics unveils a more realistic portrayal of consumer behaviour in economic models.

Static models are unlikely to provide reasonably maintained explanations of time-series data. Application of static models to time-series data can potentially lead to misspecification and relatively low explanatory power. This is due to the specification of the error term of each equation, which partially depends on its own past value and the past values of the errors of the demand equations of all other goods (Edgerton et al., 1996; Tridimas, 2000). Hence, a more general structure for demand systems

S. D. Rathnayaka et al., *Economic Development and Consumption Patterns in Asian Countries*, https://doi.org/10.1007/978-981-97-2628-8_6

is required, one that allows for a test of the static model itself as well as the theoretical restrictions and simplifications from demand theory (Anderson & Blundell, 1983). Therefore, appropriate modelling of the dynamic adjustment of consumers' expenditure is essential before testing these restrictions.

The dynamic modelling approach offers a lens into the intertemporal rationality inherent in consumer behaviour, intricately capturing the mechanisms governing short-run adjustments. In contrast, static demand model specifications overlook potentially significant short-run elasticity measures, which may diverge from long-run estimates. This distinction is particularly crucial in the realm of tax policies and business strategies, where decision-makers are predominantly concerned with short-run elasticity estimates and the pace at which these estimates converge to their long-run counterparts, as underscored by Eakins and Gallagher (2003).

The differentiation between short- and long-run demand elasticities underscores the distinct impacts of policies affecting product prices and consumer income across both time periods, in the short- and long run. This nuanced understanding becomes particularly pertinent for businesses and producers navigating the landscape of promotional pricing strategies. An acute awareness of the dynamics of consumer behaviour and precise estimations of short-run price elasticities are indispensable for assessing the implications of strategies like short-term reductions in product pricing, providing invaluable insights for strategic decision-making in the dynamic market environment.

In this context, a number of recent studies in the area of consumption economics have recognized the importance of including dynamic adjustments within demand systems and have done so by adopting several approaches. The conventional approach has been to include lagged values of selected variables that exert significant influence on current consumption. This approach assumes that consumers' reactions to changes in incomes and prices occur in a gradual fashion, as opposed to switching immediately. The origins of these lags are elucidated by Brown (1952), Houthakker and Taylor (1970), and Philips (1983). Firstly, consumers adjust slowly to changes in income and prices due to inertia caused by memories of prior levels of income and prices. Secondly, the lag effect in consumer demand is produced by consumption habits informed by past consumption. The habits, customs, and levels associated with past consumption remain ingrained in the memory of consumers, affecting current consumption. Although appropriate dynamic structure can be incorporated by expressing the dependent consumption variable as a function of the contemporaneous and lagged values of the independent variables, as well as the lagged values of the dependent variables, choosing a suitable demand system to add to the dynamic specifications is more complicated.

Of the many flexible demand systems available to describe long-run behaviour (given the complications of estimating demand models in a dynamic setting), the AIDS proposed by Deaton and Muellbauer (1980) is a particularly convenient choice. This is because it is essentially linear in its variables and does not assume homogeneity or symmetry; it does neatly allow the testing of these, as well as the homotheticity and homothetic separability restrictions (Anderson & Blundell, 1983). The simplest way to introduce dynamics into the AIDS is to include the lagged budget share $w_{i,t-1}$ on the right-hand side of the AIDS equation. This is performed by modifying the intercept term of the share equation, α_i (for example, Blanciforti & Green, 1983; Blanciforti et al., 1986; Karagiannis & Velentzas, 1993; Mergos & Donatos, 1989; Molina, 1994). These models incorporate both the effect of inventories and the influence of habits arising from past consumption on current demand. Unfortunately, such models do not satisfy the adding-up constraint, unless we impose the additional restriction that the parameter of the lagged budget share is the same in all equations (Edgerton et al., 1996; Klonaris & Hallam, 2003). A more general dynamic AIDS model that avoids over-parameterisation was introduced by Alessie and Kapteyn (1991), Assarson (1991) and Kesavan et al. (1993). In this new model, the α_i parameter is related not only to its own past consumption level but also to those of other items. Hence, the model has become *de rigueur* among empirical consumer demand researchers (see Edgerton, 1997; Klonaris & Hallam, 2003; Mazzocchi, 2003; Shukur, 2002).

Recent developments in time-series analytic techniques have opened an alternate route for introducing dynamics into demand systems. Anderson and Blundell (1983), Balcombe and Davis (1996), Edgerton et al. (1996), and Karagiannis and Velentzas (1997) have incorporated dynamic elements into AIDS by relying on the statistical properties of the data. Anderson and Blundell (1983) developed a vector time-series model of expenditure shares in the context of a singular dynamic demand system. Balcombe and Davis (1996) suggested a canonical cointegrating regression procedure for estimating AIDS when commodity prices follow a distributed lag process or if a seasonal pattern exists. Edgerton et al. (1996) and Karagiannis and Velentzas (1997) demonstrated the potential use of an error correction model (ECM) for AIDS. They clearly show that as long as cointegration between the dependent and a linear combination of independent variables is guaranteed, an ECM for AIDS can be established and econometrically estimated with an Iterative Seemingly Unrelated Regression (ISUR) procedure.

This has led to the application of the Error Corrected (EC) Linear Approximated (LA) AIDS (EC LA-AIDS) in a number of recent studies on demand for nondurable goods, such as food and meat products. Using EC LA-AIDS, Karagiannis et al. (2000) analysed the demand for meat in Greece. Eakins and Gallagher (2003) analysed the dynamics of alcohol expenditure in Ireland, while Fanelli and Mazzocchi (2002) estimated demand for meat in Italy and Nzuma and Sarker (2010) estimated demand for major cereals consumed in Kenya. Singh et al. (2011) employed an EC LA-AIDS to estimate demand for major crustaceans at a disaggregated level in the United States. Also, a few studies have applied this method to analyse tourism demand (for example, Durbarry & Sinclair, 2003; Li et al., 2004; Wu et al., 2011, 2012). More recently, Rathnayaka et al. (2019) modelled the dynamic behaviour of Sri Lankan consumers in consuming eight broad commodity groups employing EC LA-AIDS. Selvanathan et al. (2024) model the consumption patterns of consumers in developed and developing countries estimating the Dynamic LA-AIDS and the error-corrected LA-AIDS.

While various types of dynamic demand models have been utilized in previous studies, it is crucial to specify the suitable dynamic structure for representing the data. This is essential because the use of inappropriate dynamic structures can result in misspecifications, leading to potentially unreliable estimates, invalid inferences, and inaccurate forecasts. Ultimately, such inaccuracies may provide incorrect information to policymakers (Anderson & Blundell, 1983; De Mello & Fortuna, 2005; Shukur, 2002).

In a departure from the bulk of the literature, this study considers, in addition to the static LA-AIDS, two dynamic versions of AIDS to model the dynamic behaviour of consumers in ten Asian countries in consuming all consumer goods. These are grouped into eight broad commodity groups: food, clothing, housing, durables, medical care, transport, recreation and miscellaneous as in Chap. 3. We have then selected the most preferred demand model using the goodness-of-fit measure, known as the information inaccuracy, before calculating both the short- and long-run demand elasticities implied by the preferred demand system. To the best of our knowledge, there are no other published comprehensive econometric studies available that analyse the dynamic behaviour in Asian consumption patterns. All previous studies which analyse consumer demand in Asia have utilized static demand models that assume that the consumers adjust instantly to the new equilibrium when incomes or prices change. This investigation, therefore, adds to the literature by bridging this gap.

The remainder of this chapter is organized as follows. Section 6.2 discusses three versions of AIDS, followed by Sect. 6.3, which presents the data, tests for stationarity and cointegration, estimates the three demand models, and tests demand theory hypotheses. In Sect. 6.4, we select the preferred demand model using the goodness-of-fit measure to establish any information inaccuracy, while Sect. 6.5 reports the estimated short- and long-run demand elasticities implied by the preferred demand systems. Section 6.6 presents the concluding comments.

6.2 Demand Models for Estimation

In this section, we discuss the three different versions of AIDS, which will be estimated in Sect. 6.3.

Static LA-AIDS

The AIDS developed by Deaton and Muellbauer (1980) has been the model of choice for many applied demand analysts for almost three decades. The reason for the popularity of this particular demand system is its strong theoretical underpinning, well-structured analytical framework, ability to accommodate certain types of aggregation, and ease of estimation, which also permits testing of the standard classical demand theory hypotheses (Buse, 1994; Wu et al., 2012).

The standard static AIDS in budget share has been presented in Eqs. (4.2.7)–(4.2.8) of Sect. 4.2, which we reproduce here

$$w_i = \alpha_i + \beta_i \log \frac{M}{P} + \sum_{j=1}^{n} \gamma_{ij} \log p_j, \quad i = 1, 2, \ldots, n, \tag{6.2.1}$$

where w_i is the budget share of the ith commodity, p_j is the price of the jth commodity, $M = \sum_{i=1}^{n} p_i q_i$ is the total expenditure on all commodities and P is an aggregate price index defined as follows:

$$\log P = \sum_{k=1}^{n} \alpha_k \log p_k + \frac{1}{2} \sum_{k=1}^{n} \sum_{j=1}^{n} \gamma_{kj} \log p_k \log p_j.$$

The adding-up condition requires that

$$\sum_{i=1}^{n} \alpha_i = 1, \quad \sum_{i=1}^{n} \beta_i = 0, \quad \sum_{i=1}^{n} \gamma_{ij} = 0,$$

and homogeneity holds if

$$\sum_{j=1}^{n} \gamma_{ij} = 0,$$

and the symmetry conditions require that

$$\gamma_{ij} = \gamma_{ji}, \qquad i, j = 1, 2, \ldots, n.$$

One drawback in estimating AIDS is that the price index is nonlinear in its parameters, resulting in some empirical difficulties in estimation, particularly when aggregate annual time-series data are utilized. To overcome these issues, Deaton and Muellbauer (1980) proposed an appropriately specified price index that can be defined outside of the AIDS system to replace the above nonlinear price index. This price index is the well-known Stone's (1954) share-weighted geometric mean price index:

$$\log P = \sum_{k=1}^{n} w_k \log p_k.$$

Equation (6.2.1) with log P replaced by Stone's price index is known as the Static LA-AIDS, which has been extensively used in the literature. As shown by Asche and Wessells (1997), the Static AIDS and the LA-AIDS representations are identical at the point of approximation as long as the prices in the system are normalized to one.

Income and price elasticities implied by the Static LA-AIDS are as follows:

$$\eta_i = 1 + \frac{\beta_i}{w_i}, \qquad i = 1, \ldots, n, \tag{6.2.2}$$

and

$$\eta_{ij} = -\delta_{ij} + \frac{\gamma_{ij}}{w_i} - \frac{\beta_i w_j}{w_i} \quad i, j = 1, \ldots, n. \tag{6.2.3}$$

Dynamic LA-AIDS

Several researchers have considered the problem of developing a dynamic version of AIDS. Two crucial problems concerning consistency with economic theory have been put forward for consideration. Firstly, the dynamic system should be derived from a proper expenditure function and, secondly, the adding-up property should be satisfied (Edgerton et al., 1996).

Blanciforti and Green (1983) operationalised a dynamic AIDS by incorporating habit effects following Pollak and Wales (1969), given by the following specification:

$$\alpha_i = \alpha_i^* + \alpha_i^{**} q_{it-1}, \quad i = 1, 2, \ldots, n. \tag{6.2.4}$$

However, this does not meet the adding-up requirement. Ray (1984) suggested a method to simply add the term $\sum_j \alpha_j^{**} q_{jt-1}$ to the expenditure function. However, this will only change the form of the price index. Alessie and Kapteyn (1991), Assarson (1991) and Kesavan et al. (1993) proposed the following specification to derive a more general Dynamic AIDS model, which does not involve excessive over-parameterisation.

$$\alpha_i = \alpha_i^* + \sum_j \theta_{ij} w_{jt-1}, \quad i = 1, 2, \ldots, n. \tag{6.2.5}$$

Substituting Eq. (6.2.5) into Eq. (6.2.1) results in the following dynamic version of AIDS:

$$w_{it} = \alpha_i^* + \sum_{j=1}^{n} \theta_{ij} w_{jt-1} + \beta_i \log \frac{M}{P} + \sum_{j=1}^{n} \gamma_{ij} \log p_j, \tag{6.2.6}$$

where, in addition, we impose $\sum_i \alpha_i^* = 1$ and $\sum_j \theta_{ij} = 0$ for identification and $\sum_i \theta_{ij} = 0$ for adding up.

Error-Corrected LA-AIDS

Because time-series data are used to estimate the demand system, it is appropriate to first investigate whether the time-series variables used for estimation are non-stationary. Moreover, before specifying the appropriate dynamic version of AIDS, it is necessary, *ex ante*, to investigate the time-series properties of the data to formally assess whether the long-run demand relationships are economically meaningful or spurious (Karagiannis et al., 2000; Nzuma & Sarker, 2010). Initially, all relevant variables are tested for unit root (or order of integration). A number of empirical tests available in the literature can be employed for this purpose; the most frequently used tests are the augmented Dickey and Fuller (ADF) (1979) test and the Phillips and Perron (PP) (1988) test.

Once the order of integration of the variables has been identified, the system is tested for cointegration. This can be implemented using either the ADF and PP tests or Johansen's maximum likelihood cointegration analysis (Johansen, 1969). However, a major limitation of Johansen's approach in the case of applied demand analysis is that there is no a priori information to exclude some vectors as theoretically inconsistent whenever more than one cointegrated vector is found (Karagiannis et al., 2000; Nzuma & Sarker, 2010).

When the variables in Eq. (6.2.1) are $I(1)$ and cointegrated, an EC LA-AIDS can be specified as follows:

$$\Delta w_{it} = \alpha_i + \theta_i \Delta w_{it-1} + \beta_i \Delta \ln\left(\frac{M_t}{P_t}\right) + \sum_{j=1}^{n} \gamma_{ij} \Delta \ln p_{jt} + \lambda_i \mu_{it-1} + \varepsilon_{it}, \tag{6.2.7}$$

where Δ is the difference operator and μ_{it-1} is the error correction term that measures the adjustment of the decision errors made in the previous period, which is estimated using the residual term from the long-run static AIDS model in Eq. (6.2.1). We incorporate habit effects into Eq. (6.2.7) by including the lagged dependent variable. This is to indicate that last year's consumption pattern would affect current budget allocation decisions. This formulation is similar to that used by Karagiannis et al. (2000), Li et al. (2004) and Nzuma and Sarker (2010). The coefficient λ_i is expected to be negative; it represents the adjustment of Eq. (6.2.1) in response to the disequilibrium of the budget allocation related to commodity i at time $t-1$. However, the adding-up condition requires θ_i and λ_i to be constants with respect to i and equal in each equation in the system, as suggested by Edgerton et al. (1996, p. 197).

6.3 Estimation of the Demand Models

Below we present details of the data sources, estimate the model, discuss the estimation results and present the results of testing demand theory hypotheses.

The Data

The annual consumption expenditures (in current and constant prices) of goods and services and population data for each country were drawn from various country-level publications of statistics departments, national economic and social development boards and central banks. In addition, some earlier years' data were extracted from Selvanathan and Selvanathan (2003). Goods and services are classified into ($n = 8$) broad commodity groups and details about the cross-country data set are given in Tables 3.3 and 3.4.

Testing for Stationarity and Cointegration

As previously noted, the estimation of relevant econometric models is initiated by investigating the time-series properties of the data. This research utilized the ADF unit root test to determine the presence of unit root; the test results are presented in the Appendix. According to the unit root test results of all ten countries, the hypothesis that all the variables in Eq. (6.2.1) contain a unit root cannot be rejected at the 5% level of significance. However, when each series is first differenced, the unit root (non-stationarity) hypothesis is rejected at the same level of significance. This suggests that all the variables in all the ten countries used in this study (in level form) are non-stationary, integrated of order one, $I(1)$.

Next, a cointegration test is carried out to investigate whether the variables in Eq. (6.2.1) are cointegrated. The concept of cointegration (CI), first proposed by Engle and Granger (1987), states that a linear combination of non-stationary variables may be stationary. This means that two variables will be cointegrated if they have a long-term or equilibrium relationship. We used two residual-based tests, the Dickey–Fuller cointegration test and Phillips–Perron cointegration test, to examine the possibility of cointegration (see the Appendix). Both tests reject the hypothesis of no cointegration for budget shares for all the commodities in all ten countries. Cointegration ensures that shocks affecting commodity prices or real expenditure will be reflected similarly in different budget shares. This indicates that these variables used for all the ten countries are moving together in the long run and obey an equilibrium constraint.

Testing for Demand Theory Hypotheses

We now estimate the static LA-AIDS given in Eq. (6.2.1), the dynamic form of LA-AIDS given in Eq. (6.2.6) and the error-corrected LA-AIDS given in Eq. (6.2.7) by utilizing the seemingly unrelated regression (SUR) procedure available in STATA 16. As the sum of all expenditure shares in both Eqs. (6.2.1) and (6.2.6) equals unity, the residuals variance–covariance matrix is singular. The orthodox solution is to delete one of the equations from the system and estimate the remaining $(n - 1)$ equations. We thus exclude the 'miscellaneous' equation and proceed to calculate the parameters in the deleted equation in accordance with the adding-up restrictions. Since SUR is sensitive to the dropped equation, the procedure should be iterated, consistent with the majority of empirical demand studies. According to Judge et al. (1980), the process of iteration ensures that the obtained estimates asymptotically approach those of the maximum likelihood method.

Due to a long-run cointegrating relationship among the variables, we estimate the EC LA-AIDS specified in Eq. (6.2.7) using the two-step method of Engle and Granger (1987), where the estimated residuals of Eq. (6.2.1) are used as a regressor that represents the EC term in Eq. (6.2.7).

Initially, we estimated the three demand systems in their unrestricted form for all the ten countries and tested the demand theory hypotheses of homogeneity and symmetry. As in Chaps. 4 and 5, we use the sample size-corrected F-statistic to test the homogeneity and Slutsky symmetry hypotheses. The test results for demand theory hypotheses under the three demand systems for the ten countries are presented in Table 6.1. The values of the test statistic for testing homogeneity and the critical values for the test of homogeneity, based on finite-sample distributions at the 5% significance level for the 10 countries, are presented in columns (3) and (4) of the table. Comparing the observed values of the test statistic with the corresponding critical values, we can conclude that homogeneity is acceptable across the board, except Static LA-AIDS for Hong Kong and Japan, Dynamic LA-AIDS for India and EC LA-AIDS for South Korea. The value of the test statistic for testing Slutsky symmetry and the critical values are presented in columns (6) and (7). As can be seen, Slutsky symmetry is acceptable for almost all the countries, except Static LA-AIDS for Japan, Dynamic LA-AIDS for Singapore, South Korea, and Thailand and EC LA-AIDS for Hong Kong, India, Singapore and Taiwan.

6.4 The Preferred Demand Model

In Chap. 4 (Sect. 4.3), we used the goodness-of-fit measure, information inaccuracy, to select the preferred demand system by calculating information inaccuracy for each commodity and for the complete model. Likewise, in this section, we use the same goodness-of-fit measures to select the preferred demand system for each country.

The information inaccuracies measure the extent to which the predicted budget shares $\hat{w}_{it}$ differ from the corresponding observed budget shares w_{it}. The information inaccuracies for the predictions for commodity i is given by (see Sect. 4.3),

$$I_{it} = w_{it} \ln\left(\frac{w_{it}}{\hat{w}_{it}}\right) + (1 - w_{it}) \ln\left(\frac{1 - w_{it}}{1 - \hat{w}_{it}}\right), \tag{6.4.1}$$

and the overall information inaccuracy for the complete model predictions is given by

$$I_t = \sum_{i=1}^{n} w_{it} \ln\left(\frac{w_{it}}{\hat{w}_{it}}\right). \tag{6.4.2}$$

Both I_{it} and I_t are non-negative; the larger their observed value, the poorer the quality of the predicted budget shares $\hat{w}_{1t}, \ldots, \hat{w}_{nt}$.

Table 6.2 presents these mean information inaccuracies ($\overline{I}$), averaged over the sample period, for each of the ten countries under the three demand systems. We make use of the information inaccuracies displayed in columns (2)–(4) to select the preferred demand model for each country as we did in Chap. 4. For instance, if we consider the calculated information inaccuracies presented for Hong Kong for the three models, we note that the lowest value among the three information inaccuracies is 531, which corresponds to the EC LA-AIDS.

Table 6.1 Testing demand homogeneity and Slutsky symmetry results, ten Asian countries

Country	Model	Homogeneity			Symmetry		
		Test statistic	F_{Critical}	Conclusion	Test statistic	F_{Critical}	Conclusion
(1)	(2)	(3)	(4)	(5)	(6)	(7)	(8)
1. Hong Kong	Static LA-AIDS	2.97	2.42	Reject	1.64	1.87	Accept
	Dynamic LA-AIDS	1.58	1.77	Accept	1.37	1.48	Accept
	EC LA-AIDS	1.43	1.72	Accept	2.02	1.42	Reject
2. India	Static LA-AIDS	1.14	2.25	Accept	1.93	1.85	Accept**
	Dynamic LA-AIDS	3.61	2.01	Reject	1.17	1.57	Accept
	EC LA-AIDS	1.57	2.01	Accept	2.48	1.57	Reject
3. Japan	Static LA-AIDS	4.11	2.25	Reject	2.16	1.85	Reject
	Dynamic LA-AIDS	1.42	2.01	Accept	1.46	1.57	Accept
	EC LA-AIDS	1.31	2.01	Accept	1.34	1.57	Accept
4. Malaysia*	Static LA-AIDS	0.85	3.20	Accept	1.02	2.44	Accept
	Dynamic LA-AIDS						
	EC LA-AIDS	0.98	2.33	Accept	0.71	1.84	Accept
5. Philippines	Static LA-AIDS	1.16	2.94	Accept	0.93	2.16	Accept
	Dynamic LA-AIDS						
	EC LA-AIDS	1.42	2.17	Accept	1.18	1.75	Accept
6. Singapore	Static LA-AIDS	1.16	2.25	Accept	1.56	1.82	Accept
	Dynamic LA-AIDS	1.33	2.01	Accept	2.12	1.57	Reject
	EC LA-AIDS	2.11	2.01	Accept**	1.95	1.57	Reject
7. South Korea	Static LA-AIDS	1.91	2.71	Accept	1.45	1.93	Accept**

(continued)

Table 6.1 (continued)

Country	Model	Homogeneity			Symmetry		
		Test statistic	F_{Critical}	Conclusion	Test statistic	F_{Critical}	Conclusion
(1)	(2)	(3)	(4)	(5)	(6)	(7)	(8)
	Dynamic LA-AIDS	1.53	2.01	Accept	2.44	1.57	Reject
	EC LA-AIDS	2.25	2.01	Reject	1.38	1.57	Accept
8. Sri Lanka	Static LA-AIDS	1.19	2.72	Accept	0.94	1.94	Accept
	Dynamic LA-AIDS	1.38	2.01	Accept	1.23	1.57	Accept
	EC LA-AIDS	1.59	2.01	Accept	1.31	1.57	Accept
9. Taiwan	Static LA-AIDS	1.75	2.70	Accept	1.10	1.91	Accept
	Dynamic LA-AIDS	1.38	2.01	Accept	1.10	1.57	Accept
	EC LA-AIDS	1.83	2.01	Accept	1.75	1.57	Reject
10. Thailand	Static LA-AIDS	1.84	2.70	Accept	1.36	1.84	Accept
	Dynamic LA-AIDS	2.19	2.01	Accept**	2.51	1.57	Reject
	EC LA-AIDS	1.89	2.01	Accept	1.29	1.57	Accept

* $n = 7$; ** Denotes critical value and conclusion at $\alpha = 0.01$

Therefore, for Hong Kong, the preferred demand system is the EC LA-AIDS. A similar comparison leads to the conclusions presented in column (5), which lists the preferred demand system for each country based on the minimum information inaccuracy. The EC LA-AIDS is the preferred demand system for Hong Kong, Malaysia, the Philippines, Sri Lanka, and Taiwan. However, the preferred demand system for India, Japan, Singapore, South Korea, and Thailand is the Dynamic LA-AIDS. For none of the ten countries, has the static LA-AIDS been selected as the preferred demand system.

Table 6.2 Mean information inaccuracies and the preferred demand models, ten Asian countries

Country	Mean information inaccuracy			Preferred demand model
	Static LA-AIDS	Dynamic LA-AIDS	EC LA-AIDS	
(1)	(2)	(3)	(4)	(5)
1. Hong Kong	740	747	531	EC LA-AIDS
2. India	813	655	778	Dynamic LA-AIDS
3. Japan	229	215	283	Dynamic LA-AIDS
4. Malaysia	347		325	EC LA-AIDS
5. Philippines	176		157	EC LA-AIDS
6. Singapore	749	488	590	Dynamic LA-AIDS
7. South Korea	327	322	717	Dynamic LA-AIDS
8. Sri Lanka	3255	2178	1647	EC LA-AIDS
9. Taiwan	555	388	378	EC LA-AIDS
10. Thailand	1628	760	834	Dynamic LA-AIDS

6.5 Estimation Results and Demand Elasticities

The preferred demand model outlined in Table 6.2 was utilized to calculate short-run elasticities for each country. Additionally, the static LA-AIDS model was estimated to obtain the long-run demand elasticities across all ten countries. The implied short- and long-run income elasticity estimates and own-price elasticities are provided in Tables 6.3 and 6.4, respectively.

The estimated income elasticities in both the short- and long run reported in Table 6.3, are uniformly positive. Food elasticities given in column (2) reveal that both in the short run and long run, it is a necessity, and the demand is income inelastic. The income elasticity for food is generally higher in the short run compared to the long run across several Asian countries, including Hong Kong, India, Singapore, South Korea, Sri Lanka, Taiwan and Thailand. This phenomenon suggests that consumers exhibit greater responsiveness to income changes in the immediate term when it comes to essential needs such as food. Possible explanations for this trend include immediate consumption adjustments driven by factors like sudden income fluctuations, responses to temporary income shocks, and rapid adjustments during crisis situations or transitional periods.

As can be seen in columns (3) and (4) of the table, the income elasticities for housing and durable goods, in the long run, are higher compared to the short run in most Asian countries. This phenomenon can be attributed to several factors. Firstly, housing and durable goods are often perceived as long-term investments, and consumers may exhibit a more elastic response to changes in income over an

Table 6.3 Short-run and long-run income elasticities

Country		Food	Clothing	Housing	Durables	Medical	Transport	Recreation	Miscellaneous
(1)	(2)	(3)	(4)	(5)	(6)	(7)	(8)	(9)	(10)
1. Hong Kong	SR	0.456	1.105	0.885	0.710	0.890	1.278	0.673	1.042
	LR	0.352	1.613	1.001	1.841	1.674	0.978	0.712	1.140
2. India	SR	0.774	1.264	0.542	1.631	0.872	0.980	1.568	2.381
	LR	0.479	1.385	0.610	1.779	1.446	1.677	1.579	2.617
3. Japan	SR	0.408	0.789	0.738	1.153	1.343	1.306	1.596	1.241
	LR	0.573	1.157	0.831	1.355	1.593	1.458	1.433	0.536
4. Malaysia*	SR	0.040	3.898	0.137	1.577	1.088	1.285		1.899
	LR	0.411	2.694	0.881	1.681	1.014	1.337		1.468
5. Philippines	SR	0.843	0.094	0.972	1.039	1.191	1.241	0.862	1.319
	LR	0.906	0.288	0.920	0.791	1.282	1.303	0.929	1.158
6. Singapore	SR	0.571	0.994	0.412	0.781	0.686	0.987	1.597	1.256
	LR	0.373	1.020	0.913	0.945	1.084	1.277	1.308	1.108
7. South Korea	SR	0.811	1.290	0.789	1.019	0.806	1.311	1.052	1.094
	LR	0.417	1.552	0.925	1.242	1.366	1.246	1.424	1.077
8. Sri Lanka	SR	0.776	1.092	1.741	0.843	1.005	1.276	1.258	0.983
	LR	0.665	0.560	1.794	1.081	0.863	1.797	0.984	0.969
9. Taiwan	SR	0.675	1.069	0.886	1.161	0.888	1.483	1.161	1.000
	LR	0.515	1.030	1.025	1.393	0.855	1.501	1.254	0.918
10. Thailand	SR	0.792	1.009	0.397	0.772	1.014	1.135	1.199	1.859
	LR	0.734	0.997	0.666	1.142	1.245	1.344	0.995	1.722

* Recreation is included in miscellaneous. *SR* short run, *LR* long run

Table 6.4 Short-run and long-run own-price elasticities

Country		Food	Clothing	Housing	Durables	Medical	Transport	Recreation	Miscellaneous
(1)	(2)	(3)	(4)	(5)	(6)	(7)	(8)	(9)	(10)
1. Hong Kong	SR	– 0.297	– 0.759	– 0.391	– 0.239	– 0.529	– 0.538	– 0.335	– 0.504
	LR	– 0.202	– 0.590	– 0.686	– 0.279	– 0.697	– 0.726	– 0.130	– 0.075
2. India	SR	– 0.542	– 0.260	– 0.091	– 0.152	– 0.320	– 0.760	– 0.900	– 0.384
	LR	– 0.206	– 0.916	– 0.167	– 0.484	– 0.894	– 0.400	– 0.893	– 0.449
3. Japan	SR	– 0.746	– 0.690	– 0.389	– 0.930	– 0.512	– 0.836	– 0.985	– 0.605
	LR	– 0.775	– 0.856	– 0.723	– 0.945	– 0.056	– 0.938	– 0.910	– 0.683
4. Malaysia*	SR	– 0.627	– 0.947	– 0.541	– 0.735	– 0.739	– 0.852		– 0.951
	LR	– 0.947	– 0.627	– 0.756	– 0.843	– 0.802	– 0.573		– 0.771
5. Philippines	SR	– 0.541	– 0.810	– 0.335	– 0.130	– 0.204	– 0.981	– 0.218	– 0.286
	LR	– 0.735	– 0.645	– 0.359	– 0.102	– 0.572	– 0.059	– 0.160	– 0.034
6. Singapore	SR	– 0.419	– 0.619	– 0.274	– 0.257	– 0.378	– 0.536	– 0.375	– 0.543
	LR	– 0.216	– 0.481	– 0.373	– 0.339	– 0.011	– 0.465	– 0.329	– 0.679
7. South Korea	SR	– 0.274	– 0.218	– 0.521	– 0.271	– 0.505	– 0.711	– 0.572	– 0.434
	LR	– 0.257	– 0.591	– 0.660	– 0.631	– 0.982	– 0.580	– 0.438	– 0.455
8. Sri Lanka	SR	– 0.378	– 0.878	– 0.162	– 0.562	– 0.273	– 0.617	– 0.604	– 0.990
	LR	– 0.536	– 0.929	– 0.832	– 0.929	– 0.167	– 0.697	– 0.732	– 0.961
9. Taiwan	SR	– 0.375	– 0.422	– 0.271	– 0.352	– 0.112	– 0.416	– 0.528	– 0.457
	LR	– 0.543	– 0.296	– 0.520	– 0.483	– 0.420	– 0.625	– 0.452	– 0.531
10. Thailand	SR	– 0.482	– 0.453	– 0.079	– 0.036	– 0.475	– 0.664	– 0.621	– 0.324
	LR	– 0.391	– 0.292	– 0.242	– 0.160	– 0.415	– 0.225	– 0.417	– 0.252

* Recreation is included in miscellaneous. *SR* short run, *LR* long run

extended period. In the short run, immediate needs may take precedence, leading to a relatively inelastic demand. However, as incomes rise and individuals accumulate wealth, the demand for these significant investments becomes more elastic in the long run. This shift could be influenced by considerations such as delayed gratification, where consumers, over time, become more willing to allocate a larger portion of their income to substantial purchases. Additionally, increased access to long-term financing options, especially for housing, as individuals establish a more stable financial profile, may contribute to the higher income elasticity observed in the long run. Overall, these findings underscore the importance of understanding consumer behaviour and the evolving dynamics of expenditure patterns over extended time frames.

Moreover, the income elasticity of transport is generally larger than one or closer to unity in the long run and in the short run across most Asian countries, meaning that it is a luxury. In Hong Kong, India, Japan, the Philippines, and South Korea the long-run income elasticity for clothing surpasses that of the short run. This suggests a more sustained and gradual adjustment of clothing expenses to changes in income. This may reflect a tendency for consumers in these countries to plan and make enduring adjustments to their wardrobe based on overall income changes. On the contrary, in Malaysia and Sri Lanka, where short-run income elasticity for clothing exceeds the long-run counterpart, it could signify a more immediate and responsive adjustment to income fluctuations, perhaps driven by fashion trends, seasonal variations, or short-term economic shifts. The minimal difference between short-run and long-run income elasticity for clothing in Singapore, Taiwan, and Thailand indicates a relatively consistent and stable responsiveness of consumers in these countries to changes in income when it comes to clothing expenses. This stability might be attributed to factors like consistent fashion preferences, a well-established and predictable clothing market, or a cultural context where clothing purchases are less influenced by short-term income changes. Overall, the findings highlight the multifaceted nature of consumer behaviour in the context of clothing expenditures, shaped by diverse economic, cultural, and market-specific factors.

The disparities in income elasticity for recreation across various Asian countries shed light on the nuanced dynamics of consumer behaviour concerning leisure and recreational activities. In Japan, Singapore, Sri Lanka, and Thailand, where short-run income elasticity for recreation exceeds the long-run counterpart, it suggests a more immediate and pronounced response to changes in income regarding leisure activities. This could indicate that consumers in these countries are more inclined to allocate additional resources to recreation during periods of increased disposable income, possibly reflecting a desire for immediate gratification or discretionary spending. Contrastingly, in South Korea, the finding of higher income elasticity for recreation in the long run implies a more sustained and enduring adjustment of recreational spending to changes in income. This might be indicative of a culture where individuals plan and make more stable adjustments to their leisure activities over time. In Hong Kong, India, the Philippines, and Taiwan where the difference between short-run and long-run income elasticity for recreation is minimal, it suggests a relatively consistent and stable responsiveness of consumers to changes in income when it comes to recreational expenditures. This stability could be influenced by factors such as cultural norms, well-established recreational markets, or the availability of diverse leisure options that remain consistent over time. Overall, the findings underscore the multifaceted nature of consumer behaviour in the realm of recreation, shaped by a complex interplay of cultural, economic, and individual factors.

As can be seen in Table 6.4, all own-price elasticities are negative and less than one for all eight broad commodity groups across all ten countries in both the short run and long run. This implies that these commodities are generally inelastic with respect to their own prices. Inelastic demand suggests that changes in the prices of these commodities have a relatively smaller impact on the quantity demanded. Notably, the own-price elasticities of housing and durables are higher in the long run compared to the short run across all ten Asian countries (except for the Philippines for durables). This suggests that consumers tend to be more responsive to changes in the prices of housing and durable goods over an extended period. This pattern indicates that, given time, consumers are more likely to adjust their behaviour in response to changes in the prices of these commodities. Several factors could contribute to this phenomenon. Firstly, housing and durable goods often involve more substantial financial commitments, and consumers may require more time to make adjustments or decisions regarding these long-term purchases. Additionally, consumers may be more sensitive to changes in economic conditions, interest rates, or overall market trends in the long run, influencing their responsiveness to price changes. The longer-term elasticity might also be influenced by factors such as changing preferences, income adjustments, or the availability of alternative housing and durable options over time. In the short run, consumers might be constrained by existing commitments, while in the long run, they have more flexibility to adapt to price changes.

As can be seen in column (5), there is a divergence in the own-price elasticity of medical care between the short run and long run across various Asian countries. In Japan, Singapore, and Sri Lanka, the short-run elasticity is higher, indicating that consumers in these countries may be more sensitive to immediate changes in medical prices. This could be due to the urgency or necessity of medical services, where individuals are more reactive to short-term price fluctuations. Conversely, in India, Malaysia, the Philippines, South Korea, and Taiwan, the long-run own-price elasticity for medical goods is higher, implying that consumers in these countries may exhibit a more substantial response to price changes over an extended period. This could be influenced by factors such as long-term health planning, insurance coverage, or the availability of alternative health-care options. For Hong Kong and Thailand, where the difference between short-run and long-run elasticities is marginal, it suggests a relatively consistent consumer response to changes in medical prices across different time horizons. This could be attributed to the stability of health-care systems or consistent consumer behaviours in these countries.

The variation in own-price elasticity of food commodities between the short run and long run across different Asian countries suggests diverse consumer responses to changes in food prices. In Hong Kong, India, Singapore, and Thailand, the higher short-run elasticity compared to that of the long run indicates that consumers in these countries may be more reactive to immediate shifts in food prices. This could be influenced by factors such as the urgency of satisfying basic nutritional needs, market dynamics, or the prevalence of short-term budget constraints. On the contrary, in Malaysia, the Philippines, Sri Lanka, and Taiwan, the higher long-run own-price elasticity implies that consumers in these nations may exhibit a more substantial response to sustained changes in food prices over time. This might be influenced by factors like long-term dietary adjustments, lifestyle changes, or evolving preferences that take longer to manifest. The marginal difference in Japan and South Korea suggests a relatively consistent consumer response to changes in food prices across both short- and long-term horizons. This could be due to stable dietary patterns, well-established food markets, or cultural factors that result in a relatively steady consumer response over different time frames.

In Hong Kong, Malaysia, the Philippines, Singapore, Taiwan, and Thailand, higher short-run own-price elasticity of clothing compared to the long run implies that consumers in these nations are more responsive to immediate fluctuations in clothing prices. This may be influenced by factors such as fashion trends, promotional activities, or short-term budget considerations that lead to more immediate adjustments in clothing consumption. Conversely, in India, Japan, South Korea, and Sri Lanka, the higher long-run own-price elasticity suggests that consumers in these countries exhibit a more significant response to sustained changes in clothing prices over an extended period. This could be influenced by factors like evolving fashion preferences, shifts in lifestyle, or changes in income that take longer to influence overall clothing consumption patterns.

The observed trend of higher own-price elasticity for transport in the short run compared to the long run across many Asian countries suggests that consumers tend to be more responsive to immediate changes in transportation costs. This heightened sensitivity in the short-term may be influenced by factors such as short-term fluctuations in fuel prices, changes in public transportation fares, or adjustments in commuting patterns based on immediate budget considerations. In the long run, consumers may exhibit more stable travel behaviour, adapting gradually to structural changes in transportation costs or adopting more permanent adjustments, such as changes in residence or employment that influence commuting distances. Additionally, consumers may be more inclined to make long-term decisions, such as purchasing more fuel-efficient vehicles or opting for alternative modes of transportation, in response to sustained changes in prices.

As shown in column (7) of Table 6.4, the pattern of higher own-price elasticity for recreation in the short run compared to the long run across many Asian countries implies that consumers are more responsive to immediate changes in the costs associated with recreational activities. Short-term fluctuations in prices for entertainment, leisure services, or recreational facilities may have a more pronounced impact on consumer behaviour in the short run. Consumers might be more inclined to adjust their spending on recreation based on temporary changes in pricing or promotional offers.

6.6 Conclusion

In this chapter, we modelled the dynamic behaviour of consumption patterns in ten Asian countries using annual time-series data for eight broad commodity groups, using one static and two dynamic versions of the AIDS: static LA-AIDS, dynamic LA-AIDS, and EC LA-AIDS. The study estimated the three demand models and tested the demand theory hypotheses, homogeneity and symmetry. Based on the goodness-of-fit measure, information inaccuracy, we selected the preferred demand model for each country and calculated the demand (income and price) elasticities of the eight commodity groups.

In conclusion, our comprehensive analysis of consumption patterns across ten diverse Asian countries has revealed nuanced insights into the dynamics of consumer behaviour. The study encompassed income elasticities, own-price elasticities, and the short-run versus long-run responsiveness for various commodity groups, shedding light on how consumers in these countries react to changes in income and prices in the short run and the long run. Notably, we observed variations in elasticities across commodities, countries, and different time horizons, emphasizing the need for a tailored understanding of consumer preferences and market dynamics.

The findings underscore the significance of recognizing short-run and long-run distinctions in consumer behaviour. The differing responses to income changes and price fluctuations indicate that consumer decisions are influenced by both immediate circumstances and long-term considerations. Policymakers, businesses, and market participants should take these temporal dynamics into account when devising strategies related to pricing, taxation, and promotional activities. Furthermore, the study highlights the importance of acknowledging regional disparities, as each country exhibits unique patterns influenced by cultural, economic, and social factors.

Appendix

ADF Test Results for Budget Shares and Commodity Prices, Ten Asian Countries

ADF Test Results: ***Hong Kong***

Series	Level series		First differences		$I(d)$
	Test statistics	p-value	Test statistics	p-value	
(1)	(2)	(3)	(4)	(5)	(6)
Budget shares (w)					
w Food	– 2.085	0.277	– 4.821	0.000	$I(1)$

(continued)

(continued)

Series	Level series		First differences		$I(d)$
	Test statistics	p-value	Test statistics	p-value	
(1)	(2)	(3)	(4)	(5)	(6)
w Clothing	− 1.294	0.632	− 4.395	0.000	$I(1)$
w Housing	− 1.576	0.496	− 5.451	0.000	$I(1)$
w Durables	− 1.078	0.724	− 6.889	0.000	$I(1)$
w Medical care	− 2.253	0.188	− 8.247	0.000	$I(1)$
w Transport	− 1.381	0.591	− 5.48	0.000	$I(1)$
w Recreation	− 1.900	0.332	− 8.027	0.000	$I(1)$
w Miscellaneous	− 0.266	0.930	− 9.711	0.000	$I(1)$
Logarithm of commodity prices (log p)					
Log p Food	− 2.064	0.621	− 3.845	0.003	$I(1)$
Log p Clothing	0.280	0.775	− 3.452	0.009	$I(1)$
Log p Housing	− 0.365	0.721	− 4.657	0.002	$I(1)$
Log p Durables	− 0.426	0.835	− 3.375	0.011	$I(1)$
Log p Medical care	− 0.479	0.896	− 6.056	0.000	$I(1)$
Log p Transport	− 0.469	0.898	− 5.573	0.000	$I(1)$
Log p Recreation	− 0.864	0.765	− 5.663	0.000	$I(1)$
Log p Miscellaneous	− 0.542	0.884	− 4.568	0.000	$I(1)$
Log of total expenditure (M)	0.544	0.964	− 3.892	0.005	$I(1)$
Log (M/P)	− 1.843	0.360	− 4.747	0.000	$I(1)$

ADF Test Results: ***India***

Series	Level series		First differences		$I(d)$
	Test statistics	p-value	Test statistics	p-value	
(1)	(2)	(3)	(4)	(5)	(6)
Budget shares (w)					
w Food	− 0.565	0.879	− 7.539	0.000	$I(1)$
w Clothing	− 1.402	0.581	− 5.493	0.000	$I(1)$
w Housing	− 1.861	0.350	− 6.562	0.000	$I(1)$
w Durables	− 1.858	0.352	− 7.022	0.000	$I(1)$
w Medical care	− 1.636	0.464	− 6.324	0.000	$I(1)$
w Transport	− 0.371	0.915	− 4.686	0.000	$I(1)$
w Recreation	− 1.439	0.563	− 7.463	0.000	$I(1)$
w Miscellaneous	1.025	0.995	− 5.864	0.000	$I(1)$
Logarithm of commodity prices (log p)					

(continued)

(continued)

Series	Level series		First differences		$I(d)$
	Test statistics	*p*-value	Test statistics	*p*-value	
(1)	(2)	(3)	(4)	(5)	(6)
Log *p* Food	– 1.230	0.661	– 5.655	0.000	$I(1)$
Log *p* Clothing	– 1.808	0.376	– 5.946	0.000	$I(1)$
Log *p* Housing	– 1.046	0.736	– 6.608	0.000	$I(1)$
Log *p* Durables	– 2.746	0.066	– 5.878	0.000	$I(1)$
Log *p* Medical care	– 1.164	0.689	– 6.624	0.000	$I(1)$
Log *p* Transport	– 1.547	0.510	– 5.812	0.000	$I(1)$
Log *p* Recreation	– 1.124	0.706	– 8.294	0.000	$I(1)$
Log *p* Miscellaneous	– 1.536	0.516	– 7.028	0.000	$I(1)$
Log of total expenditure (*M*)	0.381	0.981	– 6.279	0.000	$I(1)$
Log (*M*/*P*)	– 1.765	0.460	– 5.032	0.000	$I(1)$

ADF Test Results: ***Japan***

Series	Level series		First differences		$I(d)$
	Test statistics	*p*-value	Test statistics	*p*-value	
(1)	(2)	(3)	(4)	(5)	(6)
Budget shares (w)					
w Food	– 0.542	0.778	– 4.987	0.000	$I(1)$
w Clothing	– 0.731	0.839	– 6.097	0.000	$I(1)$
w Housing	– 1.466	0.550	– 3.662	0.004	$I(1)$
w Durables	– 1.660	0.452	– 6.486	0.000	$I(1)$
w Medical care	– 1.416	0.575	– 7.06	0.000	$I(1)$
w Transport	– 1.452	0.557	– 7.268	0.000	$I(1)$
w Recreation	– 1.143	0.697	– 7.463	0.000	$I(1)$
w Miscellaneous	– 0.650	0.859	– 6.369	0.000	$I(1)$
Logarithm of commodity prices (log p)					
Log *p* Food	– 1.830	0.361	– 3.107	0.026	$I(1)$
Log *p* Clothing	– 1.708	0.350	– 3.551	0.007	$I(1)$
Log *p* Housing	– 1.062	0.785	– 5.442	0.000	$I(1)$
Log *p* Durables	– 1.122	0.704	– 4.052	0.001	$I(1)$
Log *p* Medical care	– 1.164	0.689	– 6.678	0.000	$I(1)$
Log *p* Transport	– 1.545	0.505	– 6.120	0.000	$I(1)$
Log *p* Recreation	– 0.437	0.904	– 5.062	0.000	$I(1)$
Log *p* Miscellaneous	– 0.951	0.771	– 4.936	0.000	$I(1)$
Log of total expenditure (*M*)	– 0.485	0.581	– 4.957	0.000	$I(1)$

(continued)

(continued)

Series	Level series		First differences		$I(d)$
	Test statistics	p-value	Test statistics	p-value	
(1)	(2)	(3)	(4)	(5)	(6)
Log (M/P)	– 1.650	0.448	– 5.116	0.000	$I(1)$

ADF Test Results: ***Malaysia***

Series	Level series		First differences		$I(d)$
	Test statistics	p-value	Test statistics	p-value	
(1)	(2)	(3)	(4)	(5)	(6)
Budget shares (w)					
w Food	– 1.407	0.579	– 5.058	0.000	$I(1)$
w Clothing	– 1.246	0.686	– 5.913	0.000	$I(1)$
w Housing	– 2.463	0.125	– 5.107	0.004	$I(1)$
w Durables	– 1.827	0.367	– 6.486	0.000	$I(1)$
w Medical care	– 0.911	0.784	– 4.935	0.000	$I(1)$
w Transport	– 1.860	0.350	– 7.268	0.000	$I(1)$
w Miscellaneous	– 1.212	0.692	– 6.609	0.000	$I(1)$
Logarithm of commodity prices (log p)					
Log *p* Food	0.630	0.988	– 2.941	0.041	$I(1)$
Log *p* Clothing	– 1.720	0.365	– 3.042	0.007	$I(1)$
Log *p* Housing	– 1.048	0.790	– 5.295	0.000	$I(1)$
Log *p* Durables	2.211	0.999	– 4.167	0.001	$I(1)$
Log *p* Medical care	1.818	0.998	– 6.500	0.000	$I(1)$
Log *p* Transport	2.320	0.860	– 5.234	0.000	$I(1)$
Log *p* Miscellaneous	2.635	0.999	– 4.936	0.000	$I(1)$
Log of total expenditure (M)	0.066	0.964	– 5.239	0.000	$I(1)$
Log (M/P)	– 0.200	0.939	– 3.174	0.022	$I(1)$

ADF Test Results: ***Philippines***

Series	Level series		First differences		$I(d)$
	Test statistics	p-value	Test statistics	p-value	
(1)	(2)	(3)	(4)	(5)	(6)
Budget shares (w)					
w Food	– 0.944	0.773	– 4.621	0.000	$I(1)$

(continued)

(continued)

Series	Level series		First differences		*I*(*d*)
	Test statistics	*p*-value	Test statistics	*p*-value	
(1)	(2)	(3)	(4)	(5)	(6)
w Clothing	– 1.947	0.310	– 5.221	0.000	*I*(1)
w Housing	– 2.208	0.204	– 5.701	0.000	*I*(1)
w Durables	0.019	0.960	– 4.208	0.001	*I*(1)
w Medical care	0.123	0.968	– 5.078	0.000	*I*(1)
w Transport	– 1.570	0.460	– 6.048	0.000	*I*(1)
w Recreation	– 0.085	0.951	– 5.72	0.000	
w Miscellaneous	0.121	0.968	– 6.220	0.000	*I*(1)
Logarithm of commodity prices (log p)					
Log *p* Food	– 1.447	0.560	– 4.703	0.000	*I*(1)
Log *p* Clothing	0.285	0.977	– 3.048	0.007	*I*(1)
Log *p* Housing	– 1.225	0.684	– 5.64	0.000	*I*(1)
Log *p* Durables	– 2.310	0.169	– 4.205	0.001	*I*(1)
Log *p* Medical care	– 0.560	0.880	– 5.051	0.000	*I*(1)
Log *p* Transport	2.480	0.745	– 5.168	0.000	*I*(1)
Log *p* Recreation	– 1.032	0.741	– 5.033	0.000	*I*(1)
Log *p* Miscellaneous	– 0.526	0.887	– 5.224	0.000	*I*(1)
Log of total expenditure (*M*)	– 0.925	0.780	– 4.48	0.000	*I*(1)
Log (*M*/*P*)	1.895	0.954	– 3.335	0.013	*I*(1)

ADF Test Results: ***Singapore***

Series	Level series		First differences		*I*(*d*)
	Test statistics	*p*-value	Test statistics	*p*-value	
(1)	(2)	(3)	(4)	(5)	(6)
Budget shares (w)					
w Food	– 2.463	0.125	– 6.163	0.000	*I*(1)
w Clothing	– 1.281	0.638	– 6.781	0.000	*I*(1)
w Housing	– 1.018	0.747	– 5.911	0.000	*I*(1)
w Durables	0.377	0.981	– 5.987	0.001	*I*(1)
w Medical care	1.091	0.968	– 6.263	0.000	*I*(1)
w Transport	– 1.068	0.728	– 5.307	0.000	*I*(1)
w Recreation	– 1.540	0.514	– 6.617	0.000	*I*(1)
w Miscellaneous	0.095	0.966	– 7.669	0.000	*I*(1)
Logarithm of commodity prices (log p)					

(continued)

(continued)

Series	Level series		First differences		I(d)
	Test statistics	p-value	Test statistics	p-value	
(1)	(2)	(3)	(4)	(5)	(6)
Log p Food	– 1.336	0.613	– 4.658	0.000	I(1)
Log p Clothing	– 1.880	0.342	– 5.815	0.000	I(1)
Log p Housing	– 1.150	0.695	– 3.683	0.004	I(1)
Log p Durables	– 1.118	0.201	– 4.881	0.000	I(1)
Log p Medical care	– 1.092	0.718	– 4.711	0.000	I(1)
Log p Transport	– 1.216	0.667	– 6.227	0.000	I(1)
Log p Recreation	– 1.925	0.320	– 7.035	0.000	I(1)
Log p Miscellaneous	– 1.018	0.747	– 4.616	0.000	I(1)
Log of total expenditure (M)	– 1.428	0.580	– 4.406	0.000	I(1)
Log (M/P)	1.821	0.989	– 5.162	0.000	I(1)

ADF Test Results: ***South Korea***

Series	Level series		First differences		I(d)
	Test statistics	p-value	Test statistics	p-value	
(1)	(2)	(3)	(4)	(5)	(6)
Budget shares (w)					
w Food	– 1.877	0.343	– 4.479	0.000	I(1)
w Clothing	– 1.568	0.500	– 7.766	0.000	I(1)
w Housing	– 0.992	0.756	– 5.247	0.000	I(1)
w Durables	– 1.006	0.751	– 4.849	0.000	I(1)
w Medical care	– 0.567	0.878	– 4.076	0.001	I(1)
w Transport	– 2.042	0.268	– 5.344	0.000	I(1)
w Recreation	– 2.390	0.145	– 3.012	0.033	I(1)
w Miscellaneous	0.375	0.981	– 7.451	0.000	I(1)
Logarithm of commodity prices (log p)					
Log p Food	– 1.028	0.523	– 2.926	0.042	I(1)
Log p Clothing	– 1.962	0.320	– 3.064	0.029	I(1)
Log p Housing	– 1.669	0.495	– 3.683	0.004	I(1)
Log p Durables	– 1.038	0.245	– 8.334	0.000	I(1)
Log p Medical care	– 1.975	0.640	– 3.381	0.012	I(1)
Log p Transport	– 1.581	0.538	– 3.193	0.020	I(1)
Log p Recreation	– 1.85	0.365	– 4.235	0.000	I(1)
Log p Miscellaneous	– 1.402	0.525	– 3.427	0.010	I(1)
Log of total expenditure (M)	– 1.179	0.720	– 3.324	0.010	I(1)

(continued)

(continued)

Series	Level series		First differences		$I(d)$
	Test statistics	p-value	Test statistics	p-value	
(1)	(2)	(3)	(4)	(5)	(6)
Log (M/P)	1.766	0.995	– 5.590	0.000	$I(1)$

ADF Test Results: ***Sri Lanka***

Series	Level series		First differences		$I(d)$
	Test statistics	p-value	Test statistics	p-value	
(1)	(2)	(3)	(4)	(5)	(6)
Budget shares (w)					
w Food	– 0.852	0.803	– 5.804	0.000	$I(1)$
w Clothing	– 0.749	0.833	– 5.131	0.000	$I(1)$
w Housing	0.041	0.961	– 6.694	0.000	$I(1)$
w Durables	– 0.850	0.760	– 5.587	0.000	$I(1)$
w Medical care	– 0.660	0.780	– 7.838	0.000	$I(1)$
w Transport	– 0.624	0.866	– 6.482	0.000	$I(1)$
w Recreation	– 2.550	0.115	– 9.153	0.000	$I(1)$
w Miscellaneous	0.390	0.965	– 7.088	0.000	$I(1)$
Logarithm of commodity prices (log p)					
Log p Food	– 2.536	0.107	– 4.677	0.000	$I(1)$
Log p Clothing	– 0.468	0.898	– 6.768	0.000	$I(1)$
Log p Housing	– 1.72	0.465	– 4.022	0.001	$I(1)$
Log p Durables	– 1.478	0.544	– 6.741	0.000	$I(1)$
Log p Medical care	– 1.223	0.664	– 6.135	0.000	$I(1)$
Log p Transport	– 1.743	0.409	– 6.150	0.000	$I(1)$
Log p Recreation	– 1.960	0.330	– 4.730	0.000	$I(1)$
Log p Miscellaneous	– 1.829	0.366	– 5.975	0.000	$I(1)$
Log of total expenditure (M)	– 2.049	0.265	– 4.908	0.000	$I(1)$
Log (M/P)	0.978	0.994	– 5.523	0.000	$I(1)$

ADF Test Results: ***Taiwan***

Series	Level series		First differences		$I(d)$
	Test statistics	p-value	Test statistics	p-value	
(1)	(2)	(3)	(4)	(5)	(6)
Budget shares (w)					

(continued)

(continued)

Series	Level series		First differences		$I(d)$
	Test statistics	p-value	Test statistics	p-value	
(1)	(2)	(3)	(4)	(5)	(6)
w Food	– 0.953	0.740	– 4.548	0.000	$I(1)$
w Clothing	– 0.766	0.829	– 7.491	0.000	$I(1)$
w Housing	– 1.250	0.652	– 5.978	0.000	$I(1)$
w Durables	– 1.463	0.550	– 6.726	0.000	$I(1)$
w Medical care	– 2.408	0.139	– 7.447	0.000	$I(1)$
w Transport	– 0.540	0.920	– 4.628	0.000	$I(1)$
w Recreation	– 1.550	0.508	– 6.015	0.000	$I(1)$
w Miscellaneous	– 1.405	0.580	– 6.493	0.000	$I(1)$
Logarithm of commodity prices (log p)					
Log p Food	– 2.169	0.218	– 5.464	0.000	$I(1)$
Log p Clothing	– 1.883	0.340	– 4.538	0.000	$I(1)$
Log p Housing	– 1.894	0.322	– 4.122	0.001	$I(1)$
Log p Durables	– 1.278	0.674	– 5.547	0.000	$I(1)$
Log p Medical care	– 1.500	0.505	– 4.179	0.001	$I(1)$
Log p Transport	– 2.257	0.186	– 5.216	0.000	$I(1)$
Log p Recreation	– 1.864	0.442	– 3.200	0.070	$I(1)$
Log p Miscellaneous	– 2.473	0.122	– 3.764	0.003	$I(1)$
Log of total expenditure (M)	– 2.110	0.242	– 2.839	0.053	$I(1)$
Log (M/P)	0.995	0.990	– 2.621	0.080	$I(1)$

ADF Test Results: ***Thailand***

Series	Level series		First differences		$I(d)$
	Test statistics	p-value	Test statistics	p-value	
(1)	(2)	(3)	(4)	(5)	(6)
Budget shares (w)					
w Food	– 1.217	0.666	– 5.313	0.001	$I(1)$
w Clothing	– 0.580	0.875	– 6.089	0.001	$I(1)$
w Housing	– 1.651	0.457	– 5.713	0.000	$I(1)$
w Durables	– 1.362	0.601	– 4.448	0.000	$I(1)$
w Medical care	– 1.047	0.736	– 6.616	0.000	$I(1)$
w Transport	– 1.376	0.594	– 5.269	0.000	$I(1)$
w Recreation	– 1.951	0.308	– 6.959	0.000	$I(1)$
w Miscellaneous	– 1.583	0.492	– 6.746	0.000	$I(1)$
Logarithm of commodity prices (log p)					

(continued)

(continued)

Series	Level series		First differences		$I(d)$
	Test statistics	*p*-value	Test statistics	*p*-value	
(1)	(2)	(3)	(4)	(5)	(6)
Log *p* Food	– 1.447	0.560	– 4.168	0.001	$I(1)$
Log *p* Clothing	– 1.768	0.433	– 4.265	0.001	$I(1)$
Log *p* Housing	– 1.894	0.322	– 5.173	0.000	$I(1)$
Log *p* Durables	– 1.543	0.514	– 3.337	0.013	$I(1)$
Log *p* Medical care	– 1.661	0.505	– 4.425	0.000	$I(1)$
Log *p* Transport	– 1.257	0.686	– 4.233	0.000	$I(1)$
Log *p* Recreation	– 1.764	0.440	– 5.151	0.000	$I(1)$
Log *p* Miscellaneous	– 2.300	0.172	– 5.181	0.000	$I(1)$
Log of total expenditure (M)	– 2.023	0.220	– 3.883	0.002	$I(1)$
Log (M/P)	– 2.113	0.239	– 4.779	0.000	$I(1)$

Cointegration Test Results, Ten Asian Countries

Cointegration Test Results: ***Hong Kong***

Series	Dickey–Fuller cointegration test		Phillips–Perron cointegration test	
	Test statistics	*p*-value	Test statistics	*p*-value
(1)	(2)	(3)	(4)	(5)
Budget shares (w)				
w Food	– 6.821	0.000	– 7.131	0.000
w Clothing	– 5.645	0.000	– 5.345	0.000
w Housing	– 3.466	0.000	– 3.486	0.008
w Durables	– 5.794	0.002	– 5.707	0.001
w Medical care	– 5.152	0.000	– 5.142	0.001
w Transport	– 4.044	0.001	– 4.001	0.001
w Recreation	– 6.168	0.000	– 6.192	0.000
w Miscellaneous	– 3.294	0.010	– 3.339	0.013

Cointegration Test Results: ***India***

Series	Dickey–Fuller cointegration test		Phillips–Perron cointegration test	
	Test statistics	*p*-value	Test statistics	*p*-value
(1)	(2)	(3)	(4)	(5)
Budget shares (w)				
w Food	– 7.062	0.000	– 7.051	0.000
w Clothing	– 4.427	0.000	– 4.392	0.000
w Housing	– 4.87	0.000	– 4.716	0.000
w Durables	– 4.263	0.002	– 4.274	0.000
w Medical care	– 3.796	0.003	– 3.953	0.002
w Transport	– 3.548	0.007	– 3.679	0.004
w Recreation	– 5.166	0.000	– 5.091	0.000
w Miscellaneous	– 5.708	0.000	– 5.587	0.000

Cointegration Test Results: ***Japan***

Series	Dickey–Fuller cointegration test		Phillips–Perron cointegration test	
	Test statistics	*p*-value	Test statistics	*p*-value
(1)	(2)	(3)	(4)	(5)
Budget shares (w)				
w Food	– 5.406	0.000	– 5.294	0.000
w Clothing	– 5.675	0.000	– 5.685	0.000
w Housing	– 5.093	0.000	– 5.059	0.000
w Durables	– 6.051	0.002	– 5.995	0.000
w Medical care	– 4.251	0.003	– 4.312	0.002
w Transport	– 4.275	0.007	– 4.305	0.004
w Recreation	– 5.923	0.000	– 5.852	0.000
w Miscellaneous	– 4.717	0.000	– 4.637	0.000

Cointegration Test Results: ***Malaysia***

Series	Dickey–Fuller cointegration test		Phillips–Perron cointegration test	
	Test statistics	*p*-value	Test statistics	*p*-value
(1)	(2)	(3)	(4)	(5)
Budget shares (w)				
w Food	– 4.014	0.001	– 4.061	0.001
w Clothing	– 5.152	0.000	– 5.101	0.000
w Housing	– 3.849	0.002	– 3.863	0.002
w Durables	– 4.49	0.002	– 4.531	0.000

(continued)

(continued)

Series	Dickey–Fuller cointegration test		Phillips–Perron cointegration test	
	Test statistics	*p*-value	Test statistics	*p*-value
(1)	(2)	(3)	(4)	(5)
w Medical care	– 6.913	0.000	– 7.819	0.000
w Transport	– 4.076	0.001	– 4.168	0.001
w Miscellaneous	– 3.937	0.002	– 3.976	0.001

Cointegration Test Results: ***Philippines***

Series	Dickey–Fuller cointegration test		Phillips–Perron cointegration test	
	Test statistics	*p*-value	Test statistics	*p*-value
(1)	(2)	(3)	(4)	(5)
Budget shares (w)				
w Food	– 4.427	0.000	– 4.438	0.001
w Clothing	– 5.328	0.000	– 4.438	0.000
w Housing	– 4.717	0.002	– 4.73	0.000
w Durables	– 5.373	0.000	– 5.325	0.000
w Medical care	– 4.904	0.000	– 4.912	0.000
w Transport	– 4.575	0.000	– 4.577	0.001
w Recreation	– 3.488	0.008	– 4.453	0.001
w Miscellaneous	– 4.267	0.001	– 4.272	0.000

Cointegration Test Results: ***Singapore***

Series	Dickey–Fuller cointegration test		Phillips–Perron cointegration test	
	Test statistics	*p*-value	Test statistics	*p*-value
(1)	(2)	(3)	(4)	(5)
Budget shares (w)				
w Food	– 6.401	0.000	– 6.329	0.001
w Clothing	– 3.998	0.001	– 4.108	0.000
w Housing	– 3.736	0.003	– 3.933	0.002
w Durables	– 4.877	0.000	– 4.874	0.000
w Medical care	– 4.534	0.000	– 4.507	0.000
w Transport	– 3.202	0.020	– 3.376	0.012
w Recreation	– 3.199	0.020	– 3.334	0.013
w Miscellaneous	– 4.227	0.001	– 4.311	0.000

Cointegration Test Results: ***South Korea***

Series	Dickey–Fuller cointegration test		Phillips–Perron cointegration test	
	Test statistics	*p*-value	Test statistics	*p*-value
(1)	(2)	(3)	(4)	(5)
Budget shares (w)				
w Food	– 5.377	0.000	– 5.331	0.001
w Clothing	– 4.195	0.000	– 4.162	0.000
w Housing	– 5.04	0.000	– 5.224	0.002
w Durables	– 4.817	0.000	– 4.874	0.000
w Medical care	– 3.588	0.006	– 3.793	0.003
w Transport	– 3.017	0.033	– 3.238	0.020
w Recreation	– 2.611	0.085	– 2.838	0.053
w Miscellaneous	– 4.286	0.000	– 4.516	0.000

Cointegration Test Results: ***Sri Lanka***

Series	Dickey–Fuller cointegration test		Phillips–Perron cointegration test	
	Test statistics	*p*-value	Test statistics	*p*-value
(1)	(2)	(3)	(4)	(5)
Budget shares (w)				
w Food	– 5.131	0.000	– 4.967	0.000
w Clothing	– 4.312	0.000	– 4.179	0.000
w Housing	– 5.506	0.000	– 5.444	0.000
w Durables	– 4.315	0.000	– 4.874	0.000
w Medical care	– 4.954	0.000	– 4.243	0.001
w Transport	– 6.509	0.000	– 4.824	0.000
w Recreation	– 6.363	0.085	– 6.372	0.000
w Miscellaneous	– 4.454	0.000	– 4.298	0.000

Cointegration Test Results: ***Taiwan***

Series	Dickey–Fuller cointegration test		Phillips–Perron cointegration test	
	Test statistics	*p*-value	Test statistics	*p*-value
(1)	(2)	(3)	(4)	(5)
Budget shares (w)				
w Food	– 3.804	0.003	– 3.928	0.001
w Clothing	– 5.121	0.000	– 5.068	0.000
w Housing	– 4.535	0.000	– 4.511	0.000

(continued)

(continued)

Series	Dickey–Fuller cointegration test		Phillips–Perron cointegration test	
	Test statistics	*p*-value	Test statistics	*p*-value
(1)	(2)	(3)	(4)	(5)
w Durables	– 4.225	0.001	– 4.28	0.001
w Medical care	– 4.954	0.000	– 4.243	0.001
w Transport	– 4.064	0.001	– 4.175	0.001
w Recreation	– 4.620	0.085	– 4.624	0.000
w Miscellaneous	– 5.287	0.000	– 2.841	0.052

Cointegration Test Results: ***Thailand***

Series	Dickey–Fuller cointegration test		Phillips–Perron cointegration test	
	Test statistics	*p*-value	Test statistics	*p*-value
(1)	(2)	(3)	(4)	(5)
Budget shares (w)				
w Food	– 5.585	0.000	– 5.499	0.001
w Clothing	– 3.379	0.012	– 3.509	0.007
w Housing	– 3.195	0.020	– 3.401	0.010
w Durables	– 4.479	0.000	– 2.841	0.053
w Medical care	– 4.235	0.000	– 5.035	0.000
w Transport	– 4.064	0.001	– 4.200	0.001
w Recreation	– 3.698	0.004	– 3.724	0.004
w Miscellaneous	– 3.384	0.011	– 3.628	0.052

References

Alessie, R., & Kapteyn, A. (1991). Habit formation, interdependent preferences and demographic effects in the almost ideal demand system. *The Economic Journal, 101*(406), 404–419.

Anderson, G., & Blundell, R. (1983). Testing restrictions in a flexible dynamic demand system: An application to consumers' expenditure in Canada. *The Review of Economic Studies, 50*(3), 397–410.

Asche, F., & Wessells, C. R. (1997). On price indices in the almost ideal demand system. *American Journal of Agricultural Economics, 79*(4), 1182–1185.

Assarson, B. (1991). *Alcoholic pricing policy and the demand for alcohol in Sweden 1978–1988* (Working Paper). Department of Economics, Uppsala University, Sweden.

Balcombe, K. G., & Davis, J. R. (1996). An application of cointegration theory in the estimation of the almost ideal demand system for food consumption in Bulgaria. *Agricultural Economics, 15*(1), 47–60.

Blanciforti, L. A., & Green, R. D. (1983). An almost ideal demand system incorporating habits: An analysis of expenditures on food and aggregate commodity groups. *The Review of Economics and Statistics,* 511–515.

Blanciforti, L. A., Green, R. D., & King, G. A. (1986). *U.S. consumer behaviour over the postwar period: An almost ideal demand system analysis* (Paper Monographs Series st 40). Giannini Foundation, University of California, Davis, United States.

Brown, T. M. (1952). Habit persistence and lags in consumer behaviour. *Econometrica, 20*(3), 355–371.

Buse, A. (1994). Evaluating the linearized almost ideal demand system. *American Journal of Agricultural Economics, 76*(4), 781–793.

De Mello, M. M. (2001). *Theoretical and empirical issues in tourism demand analysis* [Ph.D. thesis]. University of Nottingham.

De Mello, M. M., & Fortuna, N. (2005). Testing alternative dynamic systems for modelling tourism demand. *Tourism Economics, 11*(4), 517–537.

Deaton, A. S., & Muellbauer, J. (1980). An almost ideal demand system. *American Economic Review, 70,* 312–326.

Dickey, D. A., & Fuller, W. A. (1979). Distribution of the estimators for autoregressive time series with a unit root. *Journal of the American Statistical Association, 74*(366), 427–431.

Durbarry, R., & Sinclair, M. T. (2003). Market shares analysis: The case of French tourism demand. *Annals of Tourism Research, 30,* 927–941.

Eakins, J. M., & Gallagher, L. A. (2003). Dynamic almost ideal demand systems: An empirical analysis of alcohol expenditure in Ireland. *Applied Economics, 35*(9), 1025–1036.

Edgerton, D. L. (1997). Weak separability and the estimation of elasticities in multistage demand systems. *American Journal of Agricultural Economics, 79*(1), 62–79.

Edgerton, D. L., Assarsson, B., Hummelmose, A., Laurila, I. P., Rickertsen, K., & Vale, P. H. (1996). *The econometrics of demand systems: With applications to food demand in the Nordic countries.* Kluwer Academic Publishers.

Engle, R. F., & Granger, C. W. (1987). Co-integration and error correction: Representation, estimation, and testing. *Econometrica, 55*(2), 251–276.

Fanelli, L., & Mazzocchi, M. (2002). A cointegrated VECM demand system for meat in Italy. *Applied Economics, 34*(13), 1593–1605.

Hassan, Z. A., Johnson, S. R., & Green, R. (1977). *Static and dynamic demand functions: An application to the Canadian data* (Publication No. 77/14). Department of Agriculture, Canada, Ottawa.

Houthakker, H. S., & Taylor, L. D. (1970). *Consumer demand in the United States* (2nd ed.). Harvard University Press.

Johansen, L. (1969). On the relationships between some systems of demand functions. *Liiketaloudellinen Aikakauskirga, 1,* 30–41. Reprint Series No. 47. University of Oslo, Institute of Economics, Oslo, Norway.

Judge, G. G., Griffiths, W. E., Hill, R. C., Lutkepohl, H., & Lee, T. C. (1980). *The theory and practice of econometrics.* Wiley.

Karagiannis, G., Katranidis, S., & Velentzas, K. (2000). An error correction almost ideal demand system for meat in Greece. *Agricultural Economics, 22*(1), 29–35.

Karagiannis, G., & Velentzas, K. (1993). Habits and empirical analysis of demand for six aggregate commodity groups in Greece. *Spoudai, 43,* 139–154.

Karagiannis, G., & Velentzas, K. (1997). Explaining food consumption patterns in Greece. *Journal of Agricultural Economics, 48*(1–3), 83–92.

Kesavan, T., Hassan, Z. A., Jensen, H. H., & Johnson, S. R. (1993). Dynamics and long-run structure in US meat demand. *Canadian Journal of Agricultural Economics, 41*(2), 139–153.

Klonaris, S., & Hallam, D. (2003). Conditional and unconditional food demand elasticities in a dynamic multistage demand system. *Applied Economics, 35*(5), 503–514.

Li, G., Song, H., & Witt, S. F. (2004). Modelling tourism demand: A dynamic linear AIDS approach. *Journal of Travel Research, 43,* 141–150.

Mazzocchi, M. (2003). Time-varying coefficients in the almost ideal demand system: An empirical appraisal. *European Review of Agricultural Economics, 30*(2), 241–270.
Mergos, G. J., & Donatos, G. S. (1989). Demand for food in Greece: An almost ideal demand system analysis. *Journal of Agricultural Economics, 40*(2), 178–184.
Molina, J. A. (1994). Food demand in Spain: An application of the almost ideal demand system. *Journal of Agricultural Economics, 45*, 252–258.
Nzuma, J. M., & Sarker, R. (2010). An error corrected almost ideal demand system for major cereals in Kenya. *Agricultural Economics, 41*(1), 43–50.
Phlips, L. (1983). *The Economics of Price Discrimination.* Cambridge University Press.
Phillips, P. C., & Perron, P. (1988). Testing for a unit root in time series regression. *Biometrika, 75*(2), 335–346.
Pollak, R. A., & Wales, T. J. (1969). Estimation of the linear expenditure system. *Econometrica, 37*(4), 611–628.
Rathnayaka, S. D., Selvanathan, S., Selvanathan, E. A., & Kler, P. (2019). Modelling Sri Lankan consumption patterns using error corrected LA-AIDS. *Economic Modelling, 80*, 185–191.
Ray, R. (1984). A dynamic generalisation of the almost ideal demand system. *Economics Letters, 14*(2–3), 235–239.
Selvanathan, E. A., & Selvanathan, S. (2003). *International consumption comparisons: OECD versus LDC*. World Scientific.
Selvanathan, S., Jayasinghe, M., Selvanathan, E. A., & Rathnayaka, S. D. (2024). Dynamic modelling of consumption patterns using LA-AIDS: A comparative study of developed versus developing countries. *Empirical Economics, 66*(1), 75–135.
Shukur, G. (2002). Dynamic specification and misspecification in systems of demand equations: A testing strategy for model selection. *Applied Economics, 34*(6), 709–725.
Singh, K., Dey, M. M., & Thapa, G. (2011). An error corrected almost ideal demand system for crustaceans in the United States. *Journal of International Food and Agribusiness Marketing, 23*(3), 271–284.
Stone, R. (1954). Linear expenditure systems and demand analysis: An application to the pattern of British demand. *The Economic Journal, 64*(255), 511–527.
Tridimas, G. (2000). The analysis of consumer demand in Greece. Model selection and dynamic specification. *Economic Modelling, 17*(4), 455–471.
Wu, D. C., Li, G., & Song, H. (2011). Analysing tourism consumption: A dynamic system of equations approach. *Journal of Travel Research, 50*, 46–56.
Wu, D. C., Li, G., & Song, H. (2012). Economic analysis of tourism consumption dynamics: A time-varying parameter demand system approach. *Annals of Tourism Research, 39*(2), 667–685.

Chapter 7
Summary of Findings and Conclusion

7.1 Introduction

Asia has emerged as a formidable force in global economic dynamics, experiencing unprecedented growth marked by industrialization, technological advancements, and strategic investments. From established economic powerhouses like Japan and South Korea to rising giants such as China and India, the region has become a hub for innovation, trade, and development. The collective resilience and adaptability of Asian economies have further solidified their prominence on the world stage. This remarkable economic growth across Asia has not only reshaped the region's landscape but has also had a profound impact on the disposable income of its consumers. As economies diversify and expand, job opportunities proliferate, resulting in increased wages and income levels for many. This surge in disposable income, coupled with evolving employment trends and the growth of a vibrant middle class, has sparked notable shifts in consumption patterns. According to Euromonitor International (2022), the region is poised for the fastest growth in disposable income compared to other global regions. Projections indicate a more than twofold increase in real terms from 2021 to 2040, surpassing growth rates in other parts of the world, even though absolute levels remain relatively modest.

Rapid economic expansion and growing disposable incomes have not only elevated living standards but has also catalysed transformative changes in consumer behaviour. Individuals now have greater purchasing power, enabling them to engage in a more diverse array of goods and services. The impact is evident in increased spending on housing, transport, education, recreation, and other discretionary items. As Asia continues to undergo rapid economic growth and transformation, understanding the intricacies of consumption patterns becomes increasingly paramount. Against this backdrop, this book analysed the demand for consumer goods in Asian countries which are at various stages of economic development. It covered and explored the similarities and disparities in consumption patterns across borders using annual time series data and employing a system-wide framework. As highlighted in

S. D. Rathnayaka et al., *Economic Development and Consumption Patterns in Asian Countries*, https://doi.org/10.1007/978-981-97-2628-8_7

Chap. 1, increasing consumer demand and changing consumption patterns in the Asian region have driven international operators to invest resources and expand their Asian operations to capture new opportunities in these growing markets. Asia is hosting an increasing number of large companies and is a lucrative proposition for global brands. Therefore, analysing the consumption patterns of Asian countries is more crucially important than ever.

Moreover, the exploration of consumption patterns stands as a pivotal area for sustained economic research, offering profound insights into economic measurements across prolonged periods. The significance of delving into consumption patterns is underscored by various compelling factors. To begin with, as total consumption constitutes more than 60% of the GDP in most countries, it stands as the largest among macroeconomic aggregates. This large share not only exerts a profound influence on the overall economic development but also exerts a substantial impact on business conditions. Also, consumption patterns serve as a rich source of information, providing valuable insights into factors that affect both economic well-being and living standards. Beyond the macroeconomic scope, a comprehensive understanding of the responsiveness of consumption to changes in prices and income is imperative for addressing a wide range of microeconomic policy concerns. These encompass crucial areas such as the pricing of public utilities, the measurement of distortions, optimal taxation strategies, the treatment of externalities, and the formulation of economy-wide models. For instance, the findings may be used as input parameters in partial equilibrium and general equilibrium models, which in turn can project such matters as tariff changes and the effect of import, export and domestic prices. Moreover, deep insights into consumption patterns in transforming Asia will be beneficial for international operators wanting to expand their new business investments in a wide range of sectors.

As households account for approximately two-thirds of the demand for raw materials and land, the magnitude and patterns of household consumption wield substantial influence on environmental outcomes. They also contribute significantly to the waste generated by production activities, thereby imposing environmental burdens on a global scale. The income elasticities estimated in this book, in conjunction with the environmental extended multiregional input–output (MRIO) models can be used to examine the impact of income changes on consumption, and how this will translate to changes in carbon footprints. This will provide insights into the environmental impact of shifts in income dynamics. Thus, examining the complex dynamics of consumption patterns can provide policymakers with a multidimensional perspective that can improve their understanding of economic trends. This can lead to well-informed decisions and efficient policy implementation.

This book presented a review of consumer demand theory and then performed four major empirical studies using the most recent consumption and price data for ten Asian countries, employing a system-wide approach. As stated in Chap. 1 of the book, due to data limitations and other reasons, we specifically considered ten representative Asian countries, namely, Hong Kong, India, Japan, South Korea, Malaysia, the Philippines, Singapore, Sri Lanka, Taiwan, and Thailand, representing the greater Asia region.

7.2 Main Empirical Findings and Policy Implications

In Chap. 3, we performed a preliminary data analysis to identify the consumption patterns of eight broad commodity groups (food, clothing, housing, durables, medical care, transport, recreation, and miscellaneous) in ten representative countries from the Asian region. In this chapter, we first attempted to answer the research questions: are consumers in the region sensitive to income and price changes? Are there any empirical regularities in the consumption patterns of consumers from the Asian countries? This chapter used the most recent consumption data (1962–2019) and employed various data analytic techniques in consumption economics. In terms of income allocation, we found that, while food absorbs a significant percentage of consumer budget, it is lower in more affluent countries (Hong Kong, Japan and Singapore) compared to less affluent countries (India, the Philippines and Sri Lanka). Significant variations in the budget shares were also evident across countries. For example, Japanese budget allocation for medical care stood out, being several times higher than most of the other Asian countries; this could be related to the older population demographic in Japan. Transport budgets varied without any discernible pattern, whereas we observed higher budget shares spent on recreation and education in higher income Asian countries.

In terms of prices, Japan, Malaysia, and Singapore have the lowest price growth rate and Sri Lanka, South Korea and India have the highest price growth rate for consumer goods in the ten Asian countries. In terms of consumption, food has the lowest annual average consumption growth (1.8%) while transport (5.7%) has the highest. Moreover, as revealed by the overall (Divisia) price index, Sri Lanka has the highest price growth rate (8.7%) and Malaysia has the lowest (2%). However, overall consumption growth in the Asian region varies between 2% (Japan) and 5.2% (Malaysia). On average, prices across countries have increased at a rate of 4.5% per annum while consumption has increased at a slightly lower rate of 3.7% per annum. Consumption expenditure data for the ten countries supported the four important empirical regularities, including the law of demand and Engel's Law.

In Chap. 4, to model the consumer behaviour of the Asian consumers under the system-wide framework, we used the three demand models introduced in Chap. 2, the Rotterdam model, the CBS model and AIDS, and tested the demand theory hypotheses. In general, the data supported the demand theory hypotheses, demand homogeneity and Slutsky symmetry. Furthermore, we used the information inaccuracies to select the preferred demand model for each country from the three demand systems and found that the Rotterdam demand model performed best for Hong Kong, Malaysia, the Philippines, Singapore, Sri Lanka, and Thailand while CBS performed best for India, Japan, South Korea, and Taiwan. In addition, we tested the hypothesis that the eight commodities are separable in the consumption basket and found that the preference independence hypothesis is generally acceptable for all the countries except Japan and Thailand. Accordingly, the preferred demand model for Hong Kong, Malaysia, Singapore, and Sri Lanka is the preference independence version of the Rotterdam model and for India and Taiwan the preferred demand model is the preference independence version of the CBS model. Nevertheless, the preferred model for Japan and South Korea is the CBS model under symmetry restriction; for the Philippines and Thailand, it is the Rotterdam model under symmetry restriction.

Estimated income elasticities revealed that for a typical 'Asian' consumer, food, medical care and housing are necessities while clothing, durables, and transport are luxuries. Demand for all goods is mostly price inelastic. The estimated own-price elasticities were uniformly negative and less than 1 in absolute value. This means that, in general, the demand for all goods for all the countries was found to be price inelastic. The Stigler and Becker (1977) hypothesis that tastes are the same across countries was also tested to answer the question of whether Asian consumers enjoy a significant degree of similarity in their consumption patterns. This was done by pooling the data across countries and estimating a common demand system for all countries. Restrictions of the pooled model against the individual country model were formally tested employing a likelihood ratio test. We found that the Asian data do not support Stigler and Becker's (1977) claim, indicating that, in the current study, there are more dissimilarities among the consumption patterns of consumers in Asian countries than similarities. This divergence can be attributed to the rich cultural diversity across Asia, economic disparities, demographic variances, geographical influences, market dynamics, historical and political contexts, the impact of globalization, and technological differences. The intricate interplay of these factors contributes to unique consumption behaviours in each Asian country. Rather than adhering to a one-size-fits-all model of consumer preferences, the study underscores the importance of recognizing and understanding the multifaceted influences that shape consumption patterns in a region as culturally and economically diverse as Asia.

The findings of this study will be important for policymakers in designing their economic plans; it is also important for their counterparts in other countries to determine the market for their exports and for business organizations to implement their expansion targets. One notable discovery from our study is the remarkable surge in consumption growth within the transport and communication commodity group across the region. This shift in spending patterns presents enticing opportunities for businesses and investors not only within Asia but globally. The Asia–Pacific region stands as a hub for technology powerhouses, boasting six of the world's ten largest mobile phone markets and a substantial, tech-savvy, and youthful population that has embraced social media platforms. This demographic landscape positions the region as a fertile ground for diverse opportunities, encompassing online marketing, advertising, e-commerce, and m-commerce in the dynamic domains of transport and communication. The convergence of a robust technological infrastructure and a growing consumer base highlights the potential for innovative ventures and strategic investments in this thriving sector. Also, we found that the recreation and education group have the highest consumption growth. From a business perspective, this trend suggests a burgeoning market for leisure and educational services, creating opportunities for entrepreneurs and investors to cater to the growing demand. This may involve the development of recreational facilities, educational institutions, and innovative services that align with changing consumer preferences.

Food consumption patterns in the Asian region have been changing, driven mainly by rising incomes, urbanization, globalization, and the modernization of marketing infrastructure. It is shifting from starchy staples and rice to livestock and dairy products, fish, fruit and vegetables, sugar, and oils. These shifts in food consumption patterns can also have both positive and negative major implications for human health. Therefore, in Chap. 5, we isolated food from other broad commodity groups and analysed the demand for the food sub-group: animal-derived food in seven Asian countries (Hong Kong, Japan, the Philippines, Singapore, Sri Lanka, Taiwan, and Thailand; there was no comparative data available for India, South Korea and Malaysia) between 1980 and 2013 using the system-wide approach. We used the most recent consumption and price data of six animal-derived food commodities: chicken, beef, pork, mutton, eggs and fish. We found that consumers in most countries spent nearly half of their animal-derived food expenditure on fish, indicating its popularity as a source of protein. In contrast, consumers in Hong Kong spend almost 90% of their animal-derived food expenditure on meat. Prices of all food commodities in all countries have increased except for eggs and fish in Japan. Per capita chicken and egg consumption rose as well. However, the average consumption growth rate of fish shows no distinct pattern. Moreover, we found that animal-derived food consumption expenditure data in the seven countries supported the four empirical regularities, including the law of demand and Engel's Law.

We simultaneously estimated group and conditional demand equations for the seven countries. Group income elasticities, except for Taiwan, were consistently less than one, indicating that animal-derived foods are a necessity for most countries. Group own-price elasticities were negative and mostly less than one in absolute value, reflecting that the demand is price inelastic. Unconditional income elasticities indicated that chicken, beef, pork, mutton, eggs, and fish are necessities, with some exceptions. Unconditional own-price elasticities were negative and mostly less than one, revealing price inelastic demand. Cross-price elasticities were mostly positive, suggesting high substitutability among the animal-derived food items. Unconditional demand elasticities significantly differed from conditional ones, emphasizing their relevance for policy and welfare analyses. Decomposing consumption growth for the six items highlighted the impact of changes in consumer taste, income, own-price, and cross-price effects, providing valuable insights for policy considerations across the seven countries.

The bulk of demand systems used in empirical studies are static demand systems which are based on the assumption that consumers adjust instantaneously to a new equilibrium when incomes or prices change. They thus ignore adjustments that occur over time due to habit formation, purchases of durable goods, adjustment costs, incorrect expectations, and misinterpreted real-price changes (see Anderson & Blundell, 1983; Hassan et al., 1977). The dynamic modelling approach instead allows for intertemporal rationality of consumer behaviour by explicitly considering the mechanism underlying the short-run adjustment process and yields both short- and long-run demand elasticities. The difference between short- and long-run demand elasticities indicates that any policy affecting product prices and consumer income has a distinct impact in both time frames. Chapter 6 utilized two dynamic versions of the AIDS to model the dynamic behaviour of consumers in the above ten countries. In this chapter, we investigated whether habit persistence plays a major role in consumption of goods and services and if there are any differences in short- and long-run demand elasticities.

Notably, we observed variations in both short-term and long-term elasticities across commodities and countries. In policy formulations, an in-depth understanding of short-run elasticities is crucial for addressing immediate economic shifts and crafting responsive measures. For instance, during economic downturns, knowledge of short-run elasticities aids in formulating timely stimulus packages that align with current consumer behaviour. Similarly, businesses can leverage short-run elasticities to adapt swiftly to market dynamics, optimizing pricing strategies and product offerings in response to immediate consumer preferences. The incorporation of both short-run and long-run elasticities ensures a holistic approach to policy and business strategy development, fostering resilience, and adaptability in an ever-changing economic landscape.

In conclusion, this study has provided robust estimates of income and price elasticities of demand for eight broad commodity groups and animal-derived food commodities across selected Asian countries. The derived elasticities offer valuable insights for policymaking, extending their applicability to areas such as taxation, the cost-of-living index, and the formulation of international trade policies involving Asian nations. These estimates serve as crucial input parameters for partial and general equilibrium models, enabling projections of tariff changes and their repercussions on imports, exports, and domestic prices. Furthermore, a nuanced understanding of consumption patterns in evolving Asian markets is essential for international operators seeking to expand their investments across diverse sectors. The examination of consumption patterns across borders, as detailed in Chap. 5, provides a framework for analysing growth in consumption expenditure, changes in budget shares, and per capita consumption expenditures under various policy scenarios. Additionally, the application of dynamic demand models in Chap. 6 of this book sheds light on short- and long-term consumer responsiveness and the role of habit in consumption. These empirical findings cater to the multifaceted needs of economic, trade, agricultural, and health policymakers, as well as businesses, offering a comprehensive toolkit for informed decision-making.

7.3 Limitations and Future Research

While this book has made significant contributions to applied demand analysis, it is also worth noting some of the main limitations associated with it. A major constraint stems from the inability to analyse the consumption patterns of all Asian countries due to data unavailability, which may have implications for the generalizability of the findings. Moreover, the lack of disaggregated data at the commodity group level has hindered the empirical investigation of consumer demand conditionally within a group, for example, within the food group to analyse individual items such as cereals, fruits and vegetables, fats and oils, dairy, and beverages. Should price data for these food subgroups become available, an in-depth empirical study may provide a more complete picture of how food consumption patterns in Asia have been evolving in tandem with income growth and changes in prices, etc. Such a study will be highly pertinent to health and trade policymakers and businesses in the food sector.

Furthermore, the current study may not have fully explored certain aspects, such as the impact of globalization and climate change on structural changes in consumption patterns in Asia. These unexplored areas, resulting from data unavailability, represent fertile ground for future research endeavours that could shed light on the broader dynamics shaping consumption behaviours in the diverse and evolving landscape of Asia.

References

Anderson, G., & Blundell, R. (1983). Testing restrictions in a flexible dynamic demand system: An application to consumers' expenditure in Canada. *The Review of Economic Studies, 50*(3), 397–410.

Euromonitor International. (2022). *Income and expenditure in Asia Pacific*. Euromonitor International.

Hassan, Z. A., Johnson, S. R., & Green, R. (1977). *Static and dynamic demand functions; An application to the Canadian data* (Publication No. 77/14). Department of Agriculture, Canada, Ottawa.

Stigler, G. J., & Becker, G. S. (1977). De gustibus non est disputandum. *American Economic Review, 67*, 76–90.

Author Index

S. D. Rathnayaka et al., *Economic Development and Consumption Patterns in Asian Countries*, https://doi.org/10.1007/978-981-97-2628-8

Subject Index

S. D. Rathnayaka et al., *Economic Development and Consumption Patterns in Asian Countries*, https://doi.org/10.1007/978-981-97-2628-8

SPRINGER NATURE

GPSR Compliance

The European Union's (EU) General Product Safety Regulation (GPSR) is a set of rules that requires consumer products to be safe and our obligations to ensure this.

If you have any concerns about our products, you can contact us on ProductSafety@springernature.com

In case Publisher is established outside the EU, the EU authorized representative is:

Springer Nature Customer Service Center GmbH
Europaplatz 3
69115 Heidelberg, Germany

The manufacturer's authorised representative in the EU is Springer Nature Customer Service Centre GmbH, Europaplatz 3, 69115 Heidelberg, Germany. If you have any concerns regarding our products, please contact ProductSafety@springernature.com

Printed and bound by CPI Group (UK) Ltd, Croydon, CR0 4YY
30/09/2026
02225297-0011